Uncharted Waters

UNCHARTED WATERS

The UK, Nuclear Weapons and The Scottish Question

Malcolm Chalmers and William Walker

TUCKWELL PRESS

First published in Great Britain by
Tuckwell Press
The Mill House
Phantassie
East Linton
East Lothian EH40 3DG
Scotland

ISBN 1 86232 245 7

British Library Cataloguing-in-Publication Data
A catalogue record for this book is available
on request from the British Library

Typeset by Carnegie Publishing Ltd, Lancaster
Printed by Bell and Bain Ltd, Glasgow

Contents

Acknowledgements

We have spoken to innumerable people in government, the political parties, the academic and NGO communities and the armed services in the course of this study. We are very grateful to them. A special debt is owed to Paddy Bort, Michael Quinlan, John Simpson, Ian Smart, Gordon Wilson and John Woodliffe who read some or all of an earlier draft and provided valuable comments.

We would also like to thank John Ainslie, George Bunn, Christina Chuen, Michael Codner, Dennis Fakley, Theo Farrell, Ken Fraser, Eric Grove, Richard Guthrie, Robert Hazell, William Hopkinson, Iain Jamieson, Rebecca Johnson, Isobel Lindsay, David McCrone, Ronald Mason, Richard Moore, Jo Murkens, Magali Perrault, Christopher Smout and Angie Zelter for their assistance. We have learned a great deal about the issues and their complexities from many off-the-record discussions with active politicians, officials and service personnel in both Scotland and England. Although they cannot be named, we thank them for all their help. Naturally, we alone bear responsibility for the study's contents and for the opinions expressed in it.

The study would not have been possible without a grant from the Joseph Rowntree Charitable Trust, and without the generous support and advice of Juliet Prager, Steve Burkeman and the Trustees.

Abbreviations, Acronyms and Conventions

ABM	Anti-ballistic missile
AGR	Advanced gas-cooled reactor
ASW	Anti-submarine warfare
AWE	Atomic Weapons Establishment
BNFL	British Nuclear Fuels plc
BUTEC	British Underwater Test and Evaluation Centre
CIS	Commonwealth of Independent States
CND	Campaign for Nuclear Disarmament
CTBT	Comprehensive Nuclear Test-Ban Treaty
EAPC	Euro-Atlantic Partnership Council
EU	European Union
Euratom	European Atomic Energy Community
FMCT	Fissile Material Cutoff Treaty
GAOR	General Assembly Oral Record
GDP	Gross domestic product
HEU	Highly enriched uranium
HMSO	Her Majesty's Stationery Office
HSE	Health and Safety Executive
IAEA	International Atomic Energy Agency
ICJ	International Court of Justice
INFCIRC	IAEA Information Circular
LWR	Light-water reactor
MoD	Ministry of Defence
MP	Member of Parliament (Westminster)
MSP	Member of the Scottish Parliament
NATO	North Atlantic Treaty Organisation
NGO	Non-governmental organisation
NII	Nuclear Installations Inspectorate
NRTE	Nuclear research and training establishment
NWS	Nuclear weapon state
NNWS	Non-nuclear weapon state
OSCE	Organisation for Security and Cooperation in Europe
PfP	Partnership for Peace

PRO	Public Record Office
RAF	Royal Air Force
RIIA	Royal Institute of International Affairs
RNAD	Royal Navy Armaments Depot
RSA93	Radioactive Substances Act, 1993
R&D	Research and development
rUK	Rest of the United Kingdom
SEPA	Scottish Environment Protection Agency
SLBM	Submarine-launched ballistic missile
SNP	Scottish National Party
SOFA	Status of Forces Agreement
SSAC	State system of accounting and control (safeguards)
SSBN	Nuclear-powered ballistic missile submarine
SSN	Conventionally armed nuclear-powered submarine
START	Strategic Arms Reduction Talks/Treaty
THORP	Thermal Oxide Reprocessing Plant
UK	United Kingdom
UN	United Nations
UNSC	United Nations Security Council
US	United States
USSR	Union of Soviet Socialist Republics
Vulcan NRTE	Vulcan Nuclear Reactor Test Establishment
WEU	Western European Union

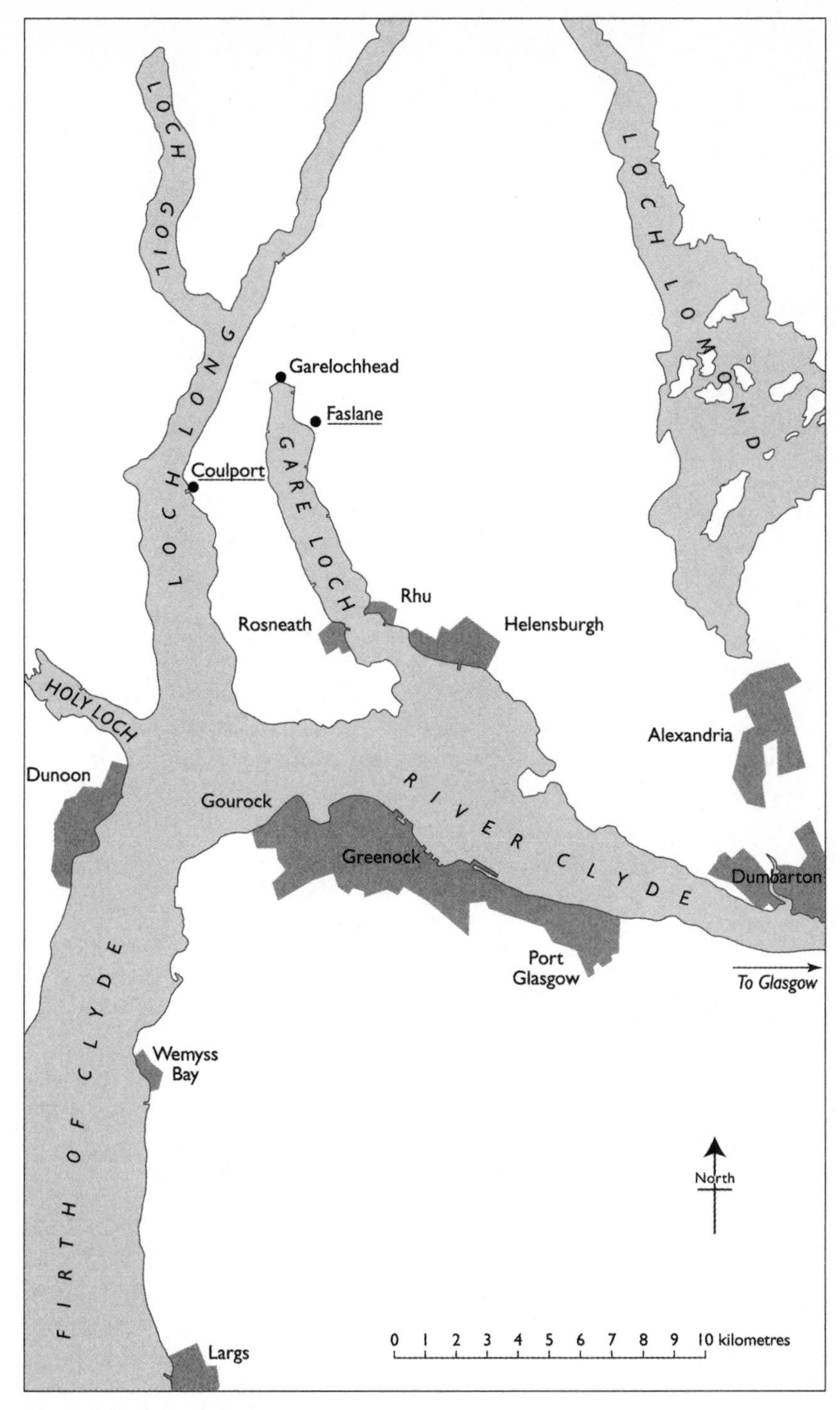

Map 1. The Firth of Clyde.

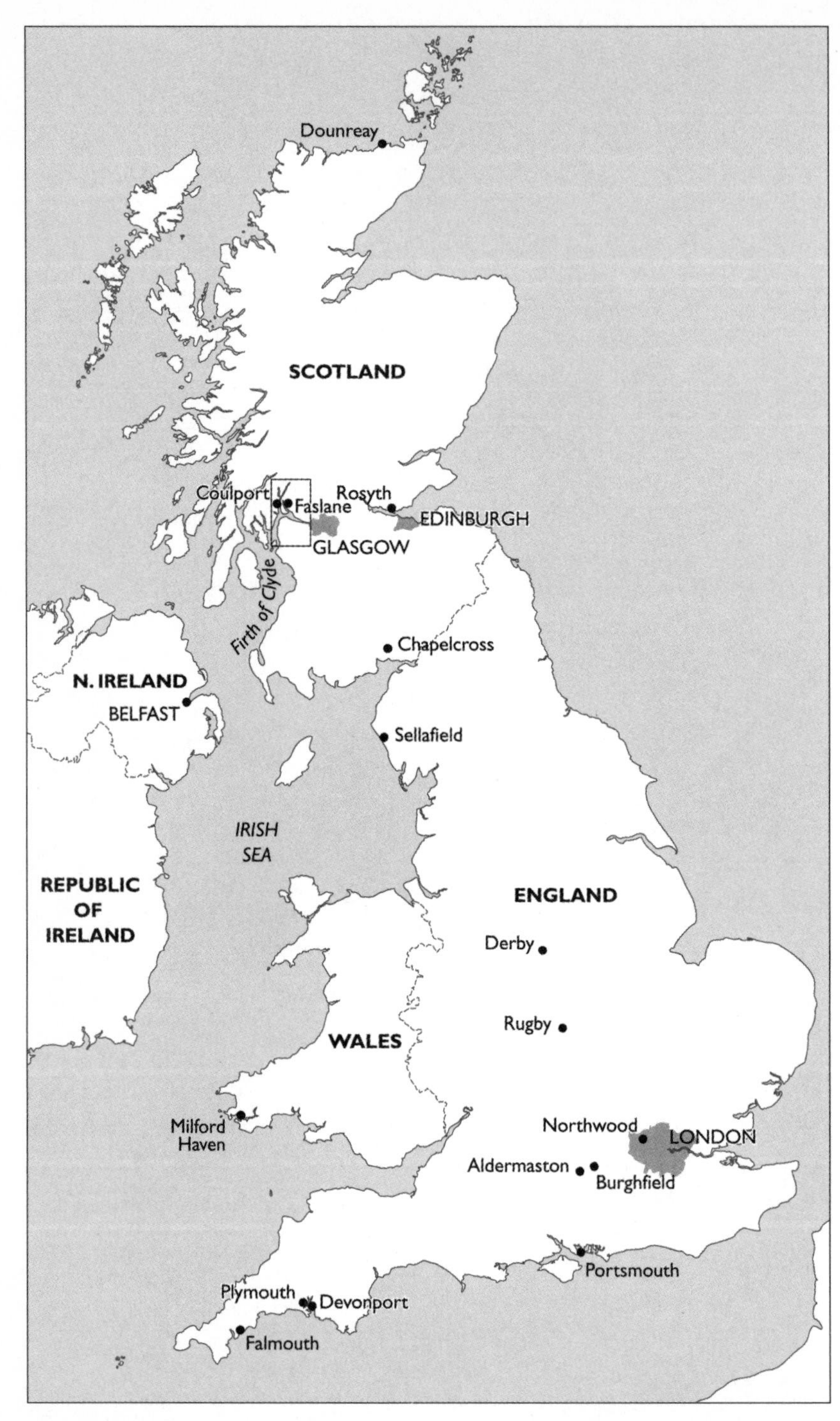
Dounreay
SCOTLAND
Coulport
Faslane
Rosyth
EDINBURGH
GLASGOW
Firth of Clyde
Chapelcross
N. IRELAND
BELFAST
Sellafield
IRISH
SEA
REPUBLIC
OF
IRELAND
ENGLAND
Derby
Rugby
WALES
Milford
Haven
Northwood
LONDON
Aldermaston
Burghfield
Portsmouth
Plymouth
Devonport
Falmouth

Map 2. The UK.

Introduction

The traveller heading north-west out of Glasgow and past Dumbarton and Helensburgh into the Highlands suddenly comes upon a heavily fortified installation tucked into a landscape of sea loch and hillside. After a couple of miles of high fences and razor wire that surround the bay, it is quickly left behind as the road returns to a typical highland scenery of moor, water, birch trees, sheep and stony villages. A glance at the map will probably give no clue to the identity of this massive facility. For this is Faslane in Gareloch, home of the UK's fleet of Trident nuclear submarines and one of Europe's most important military sites, a place that tries its best to be inconspicuous.

Out of sight, perhaps, but seldom out of mind. Together with Coulport a few miles away where Trident's warheads are stored, Faslane has long attracted political attention and protest. The protest seems to have intensified in recent years, fuelled partly by Scottish nationalist objections to the basing of UK nuclear weapons on Scottish territory and so close to Glasgow, Scotland's largest city. In nationalist eyes, Polaris and Trident have been imposed on Scotland, their presence in the Clyde a symbol of English disregard for Scottish interests.

Until recently, the fact of Faslane's location in Scotland has not much troubled the Government in London. Being part of the unitary state that is the United Kingdom, Scotland has had no more constitutional right to determine the location of nuclear weapons than any other part of the UK. The Government also drew confidence from Scotland's proud military traditions and its willingness to play a significant role in the North Atlantic's defence during the Cold War. The decision to replace Polaris with Trident at Faslane was therefore taken in the late 1970s without any thought being given, despite the upsurge in Scottish nationalism and the 1979 referendum on devolution, to political changes that might lie ahead in Scotland.

Such complacency seems out of place today. The political movement to win greater autonomy, and even to re-establish independent statehood, has gathered strength in Scotland in the meantime. Its spearhead, the Scottish National Party (SNP), has vowed to remove Trident from

Scotland after independence and to declare Scotland a non-nuclear weapon state under international law. Although the SNP is still a minority party, its views on nuclear weapons are found across the political spectrum. While nuclear deterrence certainly has its supporters in Scotland, especially in the now diminished Conservative Party, one finds greater scepticism in Scotland about the benefits of Trident and nuclear deterrence than south of the Border.

Whether the United Kingdom can hold together is becoming one of the defining questions in British politics. Various concessions to Scottish nationalism have been made over the years, culminating in the opening of a Scottish Parliament with devolved powers in Edinburgh in 1999, the last Scottish Parliament having met in 1707. Will this innovation head off, or intensify, demands for independence? No one can tell. Some maintain that devolution will protect the Union by allowing for diversity in an increasingly federal UK, and that an ingrained scepticism among Scots about the benefits of breaking up the Union, which has served Scotland well for 300 years, will always provide a check to independence. They will have drawn some comfort from the 2001 General Election, in which the SNP suffered a definite if slight drop in support. Others predict that the UK will disintegrate as the Scottish Parliament gains prestige, as England and Scotland (and Wales) react to the constitutional anomalies created by devolution, and as attitudes diverge on Europe, social and economic policy and other matters. Yet others predict an increasingly confused distribution of political authority in a loosely coordinated but still functioning 'union state'. At this stage, any of these outcomes seems plausible.

The political difficulties that are resulting from the Scottish drive for greater autonomy have been increased by the reduction and reshaping of the nuclear arsenal undertaken by the UK government in the past few years. The UK has always claimed to adhere to a doctrine of 'minimum deterrence', but until recently that doctrine still permitted several nuclear-armed weapon systems on land, sea and air operating out of various places. Since 1998, however, the scrapping of the RAF's nuclear weapons has made the UK reliant on a single weapon system – the Royal Navy's Trident submarine system – for the strategic and sub-strategic roles performed by its several predecessors. The Trident system operates solely out of Scotland.

A Scottish declaration of independence which carried a commitment to rid Scotland of nuclear weapons, requiring the closure of the current nuclear bases, could therefore give rise to acute conflicts between

Edinburgh and London, potentially jeopardising efforts to bring about an amicable separation. Whilst satisfying Scotland's desire to achieve its own nuclear disarmament, the denial of basing rights to Trident would throw into question the ability of the state formed out of the rest of the UK (which we call rUK) to sustain a nuclear force.[1] As we shall find, Trident's relocation would be hard to justify in light of the enormous cost of establishing the present bases and the likely obstacles to opening new sites elsewhere in the UK. Scotland's independence might then be perceived as posing direct threats to rUK's prestige and security, just as rUK's insistence on the retention of Trident's bases would be regarded by many as an infringement of Scotland's sovereign right to decide its own security policy. The stakes are therefore very high. Only if the London Government had already decided to abandon the nuclear deterrent would the nuclear issue be easily resolved.

Even without the prospect of independence, the task of operating the nuclear deterrent out of a Scotland with devolved government has become distinctly more difficult. Running Trident and its facilities requires extensive co-operation between the UK Government and various public bodies in Scotland, including the Scottish Parliament and Executive; the boundaries of responsibility for such issues as safety and environmental regulation, emergency planning, transport protection, and land use planning either overlap or are not precisely defined; various disputes could arise over these boundaries which could end up in the courts; and protest groups see an opportunity to exploit the devolutionary arrangements to cause difficulties for the Ministry of Defence and the Royal Navy. The deterrent may therefore be politically vulnerable even in the current circumstances in which defence and foreign policy are held firmly under London's sway as 'reserved matters'.

Trident's replacement also raises significant questions. How, when and whether to replace it will probably have to be decided within the next ten to fifteen years. Once the internal debate begins to be joined, the prudence of continuing to locate Trident's successor in Scotland is likely to be questioned in London. Independence or no independence, a decision to keep the nuclear force indefinitely in the Clyde may not be politically sustainable without some form of Scottish political consent. Gaining that

1. The rest of the UK would probably claim and retain the right to continue calling itself the UK. However, a distinction has been made here, in the interest of clarity, between today's UK and the reduced state that would succeed it. Although clumsy, rUK (pronounced R-U-K) seems the best available title for our purposes.

consent, whether through the Scottish Parliament or by some other means, would raise serious constitutional issues and could be tantamount to giving Scotland a veto over a crucial aspect of the UK's security policy. Just the *possibility* of independence may therefore compel the UK Government to consider developing alternatives, alternatives which would have to encompass delivery systems, sites and even the option of abandoning the nuclear armament. The Scottish question could thus provoke a broader and earlier inquiry into the future character and existence of the UK nuclear force than would otherwise have occurred.

There is also the international dimension. The UK nuclear force is 'assigned to NATO', and has been an accepted part of European and transatlantic security arrangements for almost half a century. Whether it will continue to be valued abroad and for how long is an open question, especially in light of the great changes in security policies and structures that are currently under discussion (regarding NATO's and the European Union's future relations, missile defence and much else besides). Come what may, events in Scotland could disturb whatever emerges from these debates. If independence occurred, there would be strong foreign interest, including US interest, in Scotland and rUK reaching a nuclear and military settlement that was congenial to all parties and was fully consistent with international laws and norms. As a consequence, the concerns of other states might well colour attitudes towards Scotland's and rUK's membership of international treaties and organisations, including the EU and NATO. So the nuclear issue would probably be inseparable from wider questions of international recognition and responsibility.

It is conceivable that changes in international circumstances will, along with pressures to invest in other more novel military technologies, lead the UK to abandon its nuclear armament before any break-up is in prospect. In that event Scotland's and rUK's relations would be largely undisturbed by nuclear questions after their separation. If the UK still valued its nuclear force at the time of Scotland's independence, relations between London and Edinburgh would be much more difficult. But it is not inevitable that they would come to blows. Another possible outcome is that Trident would continue to be based in an independent Scotland in return for the London Government's support for various other Scottish ambitions, including immediate membership of the European Union and a generous division of economic assets, not least the oil and gas fields in the North Sea. That continued basing would require a close cooperation between the Scottish and rUK Governments and between their respective armed forces and security services. Although many obstacles would have to be overcome, although major concessions would be required from both sides, and although considerable political finesse and even statesmanship would be needed, such a settlement of nuclear differences could paradoxically lead Edinburgh and London into a more constructive, cooperative and stable relationship than might otherwise be attainable.

This study is intended to open up these issues for public discussion, and to enable governments and political parties to develop well-thought-out policies. Its timeframe is the next two to three decades. The study has stemmed from our own recognition that Scotland's independence is a possibility – and its increasing sense of political autonomy a reality – that has to be taken seriously. We have also become concerned over the general poverty of understanding of nuclear aspects of the UK's political fragmentation and the risks that could arise from it. Many Scots, including those with no affiliation to the Scottish National Party, have taken a principled stance, which we respect, against the presence of nuclear weapons in their country. But few have weighed the full political and military implications of that stance, or have examined the means of realising disarmament in the event of Scotland gaining its independence and having to establish its foreign credentials. Neglect of these issues has been even more pronounced outside Scotland. Except in a few corners of the Ministry of Defence, scant attention has been given in England to the nuclear ramifications of Scotland's growing political autonomy. Abroad, we have found widespread ignorance of the Scottish question, let alone of its nuclear implications.

The study opens with two historical sections: one on the evolution of UK nuclear policy (including the policy on basing), the other on the Scottish independence movement and its attitude towards nuclear weapons. Chapter 3 examines the implications of the recent devolution settlement for the management of the nuclear force and its politics. Chapter 4 addresses the complex legal questions concerning Scotland's and rUK's succession and accession to membership of international treaties and organisations, including the European Union, UN and NATO; and it considers the rules and obligations associated with membership of the Nuclear Non-Proliferation Treaty (NPT). Chapter 5 assesses the prospects for finding new bases for Trident, whether in the UK or abroad, in the event of the UK's disintegration, and Chapter 6 examines the option of continuing to operate Trident out of Faslane and Coulport after independence. Chapter 7 considers the option of disarmament and aspects of its implementation in the UK or rUK. Our conclusions on the main issues arising from Scotland's quest for political autonomy, and on the principal options available to Edinburgh and London, are presented in Chapter 8. Finally, the Postscript offers some brief thoughts on the broad question of the management of nuclear legacies in collapsing states, drawing on lessons from the former Soviet Union (which experienced a more dramatic and far-reaching disintegration in the early 1990s) and the findings of our study. Three Appendices cover safety and environmental regulation at HM Naval Base Clyde, the timetable for Trident's replacement, and the application of international nuclear safeguards including the vexed issue of safeguarding submarine fuel-cycles.

Although our study is wide-ranging, there are inevitably some topics which we have not been able to address sufficiently if at all. We have made no attempt to examine the future prospects for, and governance of, civil nuclear power in Scotland or the UK. It is apparent from the recent controversy over proposals to construct another nuclear power station in Scotland that civil nuclear policies could become just as controversial, not least because energy policy is a reserved matter under the Scotland Act whereas land-use planning and environemntal protection are devolved matters. We have also given less space than we would have liked to economic issues – this is essentially a *political* study. And we have not been able to address the moral aspects of nuclear weaponry that play such a prominent part in political debates in Scotland as elsewhere. While recognising that everything is open to change, we have assumed broad continuity in the structures and practices of international organisations, especially the UN, NATO, the EU and the NPT.

Before going any further, we should emphasise that we take no position in this book on the desirability of Scotland's independence. Nor do we take any position on the desirability of nuclear disarmament in general or the UK's (and Scotland's) disarmament in particular. The study has not been backed by any government or political organisation.

We hope that our analysis will be of interest and value, and will help to illuminate an issue that has been neglected by scholars despite its political potency. We also hope that the study will, in its own way, contribute to the broad debates about the political futures of the UK and its constituent parts, and about responses to the fragmentation of states that possess weapons of mass destruction.

Chapter One

The Evolution of UK Nuclear Weapon and Basing Policies

A brief history of the UK's involvement with nuclear weapons and of its basing decisions will be presented here before attention is concentrated on the Scottish question in subsequent Chapters. It will be suggested that *geography* has exerted a great influence on this history. The current military hardware and facilities at Faslane and Coulport will also be described, together with the bases' connection to other facilities in England and the United States.

Nuclear weapon policies and debates

The UK's involvement in nuclear weapons dates back to the early days of the Second World War, when its scientists were closely involved in the US-led Manhattan Project. The withdrawal of US cooperation after the end of the war provided a fresh stimulus to the development of Britain's own nuclear force, with the government making the final decision to go ahead in January 1947. In 1952, the UK became the third country (after the US and the Soviet Union) to conduct an explosive nuclear test.[1] In May 1957, shortly after the humiliation of the Suez

1. For the history of the UK nuclear force, see Margaret Gowing, *Britain and Atomic Energy, 1939–1945* (Macmillan: London, 1964); Margaret Gowing, *Independence and Deterrence* (Macmillan: London, 1974); Andrew Pierre, *Nuclear Politics: The British Experience with an Independent Strategic Force, 1939–1970* (Oxford University Press: Oxford, 1972); Lawrence Freedman, *Britain and Nuclear Weapons* (Macmillan: London, 1980); Peter Malone, *The British Nuclear Deterrent* (Croom Helm: London, 1984); John Simpson, *The Independent Nuclear State* (Macmillan: London, 1986); Roger Ruston, *A Say in the End of the World* (Oxford University Press: Oxford, 1989); Ian Clark and Nicholas Wheeler, *The British Origins of Nuclear Strategy, 1945–1955* (Clarendon Press: Oxford, 1989); Ian Clark, *Nuclear Diplomacy and the Special Relationship: Britain's Deterrent and America, 1957–1962* (Clarendon Press: Oxford, 1994); Robert Paterson, *Britain's Strategic Nuclear Deterrent: From before the V-Bomber to beyond Trident* (Frank Cass: London, 1997).

invasion, the UK exploded its first hydrogen bomb over Christmas Island in the Pacific. In the late 1950s, the UK also began to deploy its newly developed strategic 'V-bombers'. By the time of the October 1962 Cuban missile crisis, 140 V-bombers were in frontline service, providing the UK with the ability to destroy around forty major cities in the Western Soviet Union with one megaton weapons.[2]

Even as Britain's nuclear force began to be deployed in substantial numbers from the late 1950s onwards, however, the political consensus in its support began to erode. Local committees of protest against nuclear testing were formed, and were followed in 1958 by the formation of the Campaign for Nuclear Disarmament (CND), which grew rapidly over the next three years. The Liberal Party voted in favour of UK unilateral nuclear disarmament in 1958, although it never opposed US nuclear bases. In 1960, the annual conference of the Labour Party (then the major opposition party) also passed a resolution in favour of British unilateralism. This decision was reversed the following year, after an impassioned campaign by party leader Hugh Gaitskell. Despite this reverse, however, many party activists remained opposed to nuclear weapons, and the campaigns of this period, symbolised in the annual Easter marches from the Aldermaston Atomic Weapons Establishment (AWE), proved to be a breeding ground for many Labour politicians, including future leaders Michael Foot and Neil Kinnock, as well as Foreign Secretary Robin Cook and NATO Secretary-General George Robertson.[3]

Opposition to nuclear weapons in the UK has always had strong moral foundations, building on non-conformist and pacifist traditions that have played an important part in radical politics through modern British history (including Scottish history, as will be discussed in

---

2. Bomber Command is estimated to have had 140 Main Force bombers in service by the time of the Cuban missile crisis in October 1962, of which at least 110 could have been ready for action within twelve hours. Andrew Brookes, *V-Force: The History of Britain's Airborne Deterrent* (Jane's: London, 1982), p. 102. For further discussion of the primarily 'countervalue' – or countercity – strategic targeting policy during this period, see Ian Clark, *op. cit.*, pp. 125–135, and Lawrence Freedman, 'British Nuclear Targeting', *Defense Analysis*, 1, 2, 1985, pp. 81–99. Also see 'The British Nuclear Deterrent', ADM205/202, Public Record Office, Kew, 9 June 1960.
3. Future NATO Secretary-General George Robertson first became politically active, while still at school, in the campaign against the basing of US nuclear submarines at Holy Loch, Scotland. His anti-nuclear activism was, however, short-lived.

Chapter 2).[4] It also gained strength from the increasingly dependent nature of the UK's nuclear relationship with the US. By the mid-1950s, relations between the two countries had begun to warm, leading to the July 1958 US–UK Mutual Defence Agreement (supplemented in May 1959), which facilitated a wide exchange of technical expertise and nuclear matériel.[5] When the attempt to develop an indigenous ballistic missile ('Blue Streak') was abandoned in 1960, therefore, the Government turned to the US for an alternative means of sustaining its ability to overcome Soviet air defences: the Skybolt air-launched ballistic missile. When this in turn was abandoned by the US in 1962, Prime Minister Macmillan persuaded President Kennedy to sell its Polaris missile to the UK.

Purchase of Polaris, and subsequently Trident, missiles helped the UK Government to keep the costs of its nuclear force within acceptable limits. The consequence of buying this 'cut-price' force was increased dependence on the US. In addition to relying on the US for the supply of missiles and related support systems, the UK came to depend on the US for the testing of its nuclear warheads.[6] US support was also linked to the UK's continuing willingness to accept US nuclear bases on its territory.[7] More generally, this 'special relationship' in nuclear matters between the two countries reinforced, and was dependent upon, a continuing convergence of overall UK and US defence policies. For some Atlanticists (for example in the Labour Party leadership), the very

4. For accounts of the history of the UK peace movement, see John Minnion and Phil Bolsover (eds), *The CND Story* (Allison and Busby: London, 1983); April Carter, *Peace Movements: International Protest and World Politics since 1945* (Longman: London, 1992); Richard Taylor and Nigel Young (eds.), *Campaigns for Peace: British peace movements in the 20th century* (Manchester University Press: Manchester, 1987); James Hinton, *Protests and Visions: Peace Politics in 20th century Britain* (Century Hutchinson: London, 1989).
5. Andrew Pierre, *op. cit.*, pp. 140–141.
6. The UK's reliance on the US for supply of missiles has often led both domestic critics (such as the Labour Opposition) and foreign opponents (notably the French government) to criticise the programme on the grounds that it would leave the force operationally dependent on the US, for example for satellite guidance. Provided that the submarine commander knew his own position accurately, however, such assistance does not appear to be necessary (target co-ordinates were already available).
7. This linkage was perhaps most explicit at the Camp David meeting between Macmillan and Eisenhower in March 1960, at which the US agreed to supply the UK with Skybolt and the UK agreed to allow the US Polaris facilities in Scotland. Ian Clark, *op. cit.*, pp. 258–296.

closeness of the US relationship meant that there was no need for a separate UK nuclear force. For supporters (on both the Left and Right) of a more independent security policy, the dependent character of the nuclear relationship undermined national autonomy, making it more difficult for the UK to oppose the US in foreign and security policy more generally. Supporters of government policy argued, by contrast, that cooperation with the US allowed Britain to remain a nuclear power at reasonable cost, while also helping to maintain some continuing influence in Washington.

CND's ability to mobilise large-scale protests against nuclear weapons declined sharply after 1963, with the banning of atmospheric nuclear tests playing a significant role. Throughout the late 1960s and early 1970s, the attention of radical activists focused instead on opposition to the Vietnam War. CND gained an important success when the 1974 Labour Party Conference committed itself to the expulsion of the US nuclear base from Holy Loch. But this commitment was never taken seriously by the 1974–79 Labour government, which allowed the base to remain. Its continuing yet nervous attachment to nuclear deterrence was manifested by its secret financing of the modernisation of Britain's Polaris warheads and guidance system (the *Chevaline* programme).

The late 1970s saw a revival of the peace movement, both in the UK and in other West European countries. In part, this was a response to rising levels of international tension, with Western leaders expressing growing concern over Soviet expansionism in Africa and Afghanistan. It was given focus by NATO's 1979 decision to deploy a new generation of land-based missiles in five West European countries, including the UK. The election of Ronald Reagan as President a year later, and the subsequent rapid build-up of spending on both nuclear and conventional forces, further contributed to public fears of nuclear war.

Protests in response to these wider developments were given additional momentum in the UK by the Thatcher government's 1980 decision to order the Trident missile system as a replacement for Polaris. Although Prime Minister Callaghan had taken the first steps towards such a decision under the previous government, Labour quickly moved to adopt a strongly anti-Trident, and anti-Cruise, position once in opposition. It elected Michael Foot, a lifelong CND supporter, as its leader. The party as a whole swung sharply to the Left.

The adoption of unilateralism had disastrous consequences for the party. It helped precipitate the formation of the breakaway Social Democratic Party, which split the anti-Conservative vote and contributed to the massive Conservative victories in 1983 and 1987. Labour was also unable to convince the wider public of the merits of its policy. As a result, Neil Kinnock – himself once a strong CND supporter – persuaded his colleagues to abandon unilateralism. By 1992, the cross-party nuclear consensus had been restored.

Despite CND's second defeat, however, the intense nuclear debates of the 1960s and 1980s may have contributed to subsequent developments. With the end of the Cold War, Conservative Prime Minister John Major progressively reduced the size of Britain's nuclear force. The Army gave up its battlefield nuclear roles (which entailed using US warheads for artillery and Lance missiles). The government decided to scrap its WE–177 free-fall bombs, 'several hundred' of which had been in service in the RAF and Royal Navy in the late 1980s.[8] The dismantling of the last WE–177 took place in August 1998, leaving the UK reliant on only one delivery system, the Trident missile-armed submarine.[9]

The government also began to address concerns that Trident represented an unnecessary escalation of firepower, compared to the Polaris system which it would replace. In 1995, Conservative Defence Secretary Malcolm Rifkind announced that each submarine would be deployed with no more than 96 warheads. In the 1998 Strategic Defence Review, Labour Defence Secretary George Robertson went further, announcing that no more than 48 warheads would be deployed on each submarine, and that only one boat (on a reduced state of alert) would be on patrol at any time. This revised 'minimum deterrent' posture was also accompanied by increased commitments to transparency and arms control.[10] The UK's nuclear force is not covered by any treaty restrictions on its nuclear arsenal, and its policy of unilateral restraint is not subject to international verification. But the UK was the first nuclear weapon state (along with France) to ratify the CTBT. The 1998 Strategic Defence Review charged the AWE with developing capabilities for the verification of future nuclear disarmament treaties.[11] Most recently, at the 2000 review conference for the Non-Proliferation Treaty, the UK played a

8. Ministry of Defence, *The Strategic Defence Review: Supporting Essays* (London: The Stationery Office, 1998), p. 5–2.
9. 'All WE–177 nuclear bombs dismantled by the end of August 1998', Ministry of Defence, Press Release 200/98, 30 July 1998.
10. Malcolm Chalmers, 'Bombs Away'? Britain and Nuclear Weapons under New Labour', *Security Dialogue*, vol. 30, no. 1, March 1999, pp. 61–74.
11. An initial report on this work is published as *Confidence, Security and Verification*, Atomic Weapons Establishment, Aldermaston, 2000.

crucial role in pressing its fellow NWS to give a clear commitment to the long-term goal of nuclear disarmament.[12]

Short of the emergence of a major new external threat to the UK, this approach – a minimal, low-key, force posture combined with support for multilateral nuclear disarmament – now appears to represent a stable domestic consensus except in Scotland. Any attempt at major rearmament – for example through a renewed RAF nuclear role in addition to the Navy's – is likely to be strongly opposed, not least from the armed forces themselves. On the other hand, there are few pressures for further reductions. With the smallest nuclear arsenal of the five recognised NWS, the UK government is under little external pressure to do more, especially given the deterioration in strategic relations between the US, Russia and China that has occurred since the mid-1990s. Now that the Trident capital programme is complete, moreover, nuclear costs constitute only a small part of the total defence budget. Perhaps most important of all, the government is aware that a more radical policy – of either rearmament or disarmament – could threaten to reawaken the political controversies of the 1980s.

Geography and the basing decisions

Nuclear weapons have to be transported to their targets in distant places: they need delivery vehicles. For the UK, that has meant aircraft (armed with free-fall bombs or stand-off missiles) and submarines (armed with ballistic missiles). Nuclear submarines need bases of a very particular kind and complexity. Ever since the decision to base US Polaris submarines in the UK, geography has therefore been an important part of the nuclear story. It is the principal reason why nuclear weapons came to be based in Scotland. Information gleaned from the Public Record Office allows us to tell this story for the first time in any detail.[13]

The US base at Holy Loch

The history of nuclear missile submarines on the Clyde began in 1959, when the US Navy requested that the UK provide it with a forward

12. For an account of this conference, see Rebecca Johnson, 'The NPT Review: Disaster Averted', *Bulletin of Atomic Scientists*, July-August 2000.
13. None of the many historical accounts of the UK's nuclear force, some of which are cited above, gave any substantial attention to the geographical dimension of the nuclear force. But see Malcolm Spaven, *Fortress Scotland: A Guide to the Military Presence* (Pluto Press: London, 1983).

berth for its own Polaris submarines. During the 1950s, the US had relied on bombers to drop nuclear weapons on their targets. As concern grew (both in the US and UK) over the reliability of bombers against Soviet air defences, however, the US began to develop a range of alternative missile-based means of delivery. One of these was the Polaris submarine-launched ballistic missile, whose development was agreed in 1955 and which was first deployed on patrol in November 1960.

Polaris's great advantage was that it was invulnerable to attack from the growing force of Soviet ballistic missiles that was then beginning to be deployed. Yet it remained limited in range (only 1,200 miles for Polaris A–1), incapable of attacking the Soviet Union from locations adjacent to the continental United States. In order to maximise the time that Polaris-armed boats could remain within range of Soviet targets, therefore, the US Navy was eager to acquire forward operating bases which could be used for resupply and maintenance of their submarines.

Accordingly, the US Chief of Naval Operations approached the Royal Navy in November 1959 with a request to base a Polaris support ship (capable of providing repair and replenishment services) in the UK. A list of US requirements was tabled, which involved 'a sheltered anchorage with access to deep water and situated near a transatlantic airfield and a centre of population in which the American service personnel and their families could be absorbed'.[14] In response, the Admiralty forewarned Ministers and began a detailed study of possible locations. At this early stage, Prime Minister Macmillan was reported to have 'mentioned Invergordon as a possible base which might have political attractions'.[15] But this and other options on the east coast of Scotland were ruled out 'on grounds of shallow water and distance from noise ranging facilities'.[16] Other possible locations in Scotland were also ruled out because American domestic requirements could not be met, e.g. access to an airfield, housing and schools. This narrowed the field to the Clyde.[17] Options in the rest of the UK do not appear to have been seriously considered by the Admiralty at this stage.

14. 'Basing of US Polaris submarines in Northern UK: Memorandum by the Admiralty, 16 June 1960', ADM 27203, Public Record Office, Kew.
15. 'Note of a Meeting held by First Sea Lord to discuss basing of Polaris submarines in Northern UK, 26 November 1959', ADM 1/27609, Public Record Office, Kew.
16. 'Basing of US Polaris submarines in Northern UK: Memorandum by the Admiralty, 16 June 1960', ADM 27203, Public Record Office, Kew.
17. 'Extract from Secret and Personal letter dated 5 November from C.N.O. to CINCNELM', ADM 205222, Public Record Office, Kew.

The Government therefore instructed the UK Atomic Energy Authority (which still had responsibility for the nuclear weapon programme) to inspect four possible locations in the Clyde area, assessing them against a range of safety criteria, including their proximity to population centres and their water supplies, and the resulting differences in estimated levels of exposure to radiation in the event of a major accident. These were the Largs Channel, Rothesay Bay (on the isle of Bute), Holy Loch and Roseneath (Gareloch). All four sites were in deep water and could provide clear movement to the open sea. A comparative safety assessment led to the recommendation to shortlist two sites: **Holy Loch** and Largs Number 1 Buoy (on the west side of the **Largs Channel**).

The study also pointed out that 'a release of activity at Largs, Rothesay and Rosneath with a rising tide could carry activity further inland and cause contamination of considerable areas of the shore. At such a time, a release in Holy Loch would be restricted to the shores of the loch itself (a relatively small area)'.[18] Given recent controversy over the £5 million clean-up effort required even for Holy Loch, the wisdom of this advice has been confirmed.[19]

The final decision was taken against a wider range of criteria, but other studies came to the same conclusion: of the available bases in the Clyde area, Holy Loch was the best option. The possibility of locating the US base at **Rosneath** was opposed by the Admiralty on the grounds that 'one suitably aimed bomb could then destroy both the tender and the Third Submarine Squadron ... The shore facilities at Helensburgh and district are heavily loaded by the Third Submarine Squadron. The introduction of the American Squadron would result in heavy overloading'. Rosneath was also closer to a substantial population centre (Greenock). **Rothesay** was felt to be unsuitable because of the logistical problems involved in providing all necessary facilities by water. It was also the Global War Station for the UK element of the Eastern Atlantic Submarine Force.[20] Of the two remaining sites, Holy Loch was chosen 'for reasons of seamanship, Largs Channel providing only poor shelter'.[21]

18. 'Assessment of four proposed Admiralty sites', AHSB Memo 37 of January 1960, ADM 205222, Public Record Office, Kew.
19. 'Holy Loch clean-up begins', *BBC News Online*, 24 February 1998.
20. 'Report of Subcommittee into Basing of Polaris Submarines in Northern UK', February 1960, ADM 1/27609, Public Record Office, Kew.
21. 'Basing of US Polaris Submarines in Northern UK: Memorandum by the Admiralty', June 1960, ADM 27203, Public Record Office, Kew.

It has been widely reported that Macmillan agreed to the basing of US Polaris boats at Holy Loch at the March 1960 summit at Camp David. In fact, as the documents from the time make clear, Macmillan had only agreed to Polaris being based in Scotland, and both he and other ministers continued to have reservations about basing nuclear weapons so close to Glasgow, with its 'large number of agitators'. Spring 1960 was the zenith of popular support for CND in Scotland as elsewhere. In these circumstances, both the Prime Minister and Foreign Secretary intervened on 14 June ('at the last minute', according to a frustrated First Sea Lord) to seek an alternative location.[22] As Macmillan argued in a draft of the letter he was to send to President Eisenhower: 'The placing, so to speak, of a target so near to Glasgow would give rise to the greatest political difficulties and would make the project almost unsaleable in this country'.[23] In what appears to have been a last effort to persuade the US not to push their case, Defence Minister Watkinson even suggested that 'housing would be as big a problem (for US Polaris workers) in Glasgow as anywhere in the country, because of the poor housing conditions there already'.

In response to their political masters, the Admiralty had to be seen to rethink the alternatives. The Admiralty did so by producing a list of possible alternative bases in Scotland. Most of the suggestions (such as Shetland, Orkney, Loch Eriboll and Stornoway) were never serious alternatives. The Undersurface Warfare Division produced a short study on the prospects for using **Falmouth** or **Milford Haven** for Polaris, but given the commitment to a Scottish base made at Camp David, these alternatives also do not appear to have been seriously considered.[24]

Within two days of Macmillan's opposition to the Clyde becoming clear, it was agreed that the US should be offered a base almost opposite **Fort William** at the top of Loch Linnhe. This proposal was endorsed by Cabinet, and sent to the US. The Government made the case that this was an acceptable location from an operational point of view, sheltered yet with deep water and noise ranges relatively nearby. The

22. According to a report of a meeting of Ministers held on 15 June, 'The Prime Minister and Foreign Secretary will not wear at any cost the proposal of a Polaris base in the Clyde so close to Glasgow and therefore the Gareloch and Holy Loch are OUT'. [emphasis in original]. 'Siting of Lamachus Base', memorandum for First Sea Lord, June 1960, ADM 205222, Public Record Office, Kew.
23. 'Draft message from the Prime Minister to President Eisenhower', 16 June 1960, ADM 27203, Public Record Office, Kew.
24. 'Project Lamachus', 8 July 1960, ADM 205222, Public Record Office, Kew.

Atomic Energy Authority (AEA) was concerned that the base should not be too close to Fort William, which then had a population of 7,000 permanent residents. Provided that the base was at least two miles from the town, however, the AEA regarded Loch Linnhe as 'much better than Holy Loch because there are no other people around except those at Fort William'.[25]

While Fort William's remoteness counted in its favour in both political and safety terms, it was not viewed favourably by the US Navy. Road and rail links with Glasgow were better than at most alternative Highland locations. Compared with Clyde bases, however, it was remote from the nearest international airport (Prestwick on the Ayrshire coast), to which regular access would be required for the transport of equipment and personnel from the US. The main problem lay, however, in Fort William's lack of the houses, schools, recreation and other facilities needed for the expected influx of around 500 American families.[26] Acting on his Navy's advice, Eisenhower declined the UK offer, citing the need for 'greater shore facilities for logistical support, more immediate access to open seas and international waters, and the need for comparative ease and safety of navigation'.[27] Unwilling to call into question the 'special relationship' (or access to Polaris for UK use) on this issue, Macmillan then agreed, paving the way for deployment at Holy Loch in 1961. Until now, the existence of this dispute has, to our knowledge, never been publicly revealed. It is recounted here as an early illustration of the difficulties in balancing many factors (political, logistical, operational and safety) in decisions on base location.

Although Macmillan had failed to persuade the US to give way on the location issue, he did gain a concession on command arrangements that set an important precedent for study of possible future foreign basing arrangements in Scotland. After accepting Macmillan's concession on location, Eisenhower went on to confirm that 'on the question of control, we agree that our Polaris missiles would not be launched within your territorial waters without your consent'. At the same time, he

25. 'Loch Linnhe: Memorandum from Head of Military Branch II', 23 June 1960, ADM 27203, Public Record Office, Kew.
26. The US Navy was particularly concerned that it would be unable to retain the services of its Polaris technicians against competition from employment offers from US industry. Bringing the families of submarine crews and servicing teams to the base was deemed essential.
27. 'Prime Minister's Personal Telegram Serial T 381/60', 30 June 1960, ADM 205222, Public Record Office, Kew.

insisted that to 'extend any form of dual control beyond territorial waters would ... present us with a number of problems ... For example, the one hundred-mile proposal could form a most difficult precedent with respect to the utilisation of weapons in other waters, such as the Mediterranean and the Caribbean'.[28]

The first deployment of a Polaris submarine and submarine tender at Holy Loch took place in March 1961. Although more limited than a full-service base (warheads and missiles were not offloaded), and therefore not directly comparable to subsequent UK facilities, Holy Loch nevertheless became a major facility, with around 2,000 US personnel in place together with their dependants and the crews of visiting SSBNs. The base continued after Polaris was withdrawn from the US Navy in 1982, to be replaced by the 2,500-mile range Poseidon missiles. But with the progressive introduction of the 4,000-mile Trident C4 missile into service from 1981 onwards, the US no longer required forward bases for its SSBN force. The end of the Cold War further accelerated the rundown of the Poseidon-armed fleet, and Holy Loch was finally closed in March 1992.[29]

Polaris at Faslane/Coulport

In order to have the UK Polaris force in service before the V-bomber force became obsolescent, it was vital to begin work on it as early as possible. It was rapidly agreed that the US would guarantee supply of all the technical information and spare parts necessary to ensure that the missiles could be installed and serviced by the UK. Using this information, it was decided that the new Polaris submarines would be built in the UK, two at Vickers in Barrow-in-Furness and two at Cammell Laird, Birkenhead. A working party was established in February 1963 to review the possible options for locating the operating base and make recommendations for action within three weeks.[30]

The working party assessed a large number of possible locations against a list of criteria, of which it considered the most important to be operational suitability (including safe navigation and berthing, and secure

28. Letter to Prime Minister Macmillan from President Eisenhower, July 15 1960, ADM 27203, Public Record Office, Kew.
29. 'Dunoon US Navy', *Argyll on Line*, http://www.argyllonline.co.UK/pages/towns/dunoon/usnavy/dunusnavy.html
30. Sir Rae McKaig, 'Initial Tasks', in Captain J. E. Moore (ed.), *The Impact of Polaris* (Richard Netherwood: London, 1999), pp. 79–80. McKaig was Deputy Chief Polaris Executive 1963–65 and chair of the working party on location.

approaches), safety and cost.[31] In order to meet safety requirements, the Polaris missile storage and maintenance facility (in the RNAD) would have to be separated by at least 4,400 feet from the other elements, with its own berthing arrangements. At the same time, in order to avoid lost time in the vital three weeks available for maintenance between patrols, it was 'most desirable' that separation between the RNAD and the operating base should not exceed one hour's sailing.[32]

In the final draft of the study, the working party began by excluding: '(a) sites on the south and east coasts between the Firth of Forth and Portland due to their remoteness from deep water and adequate conditions for work-up facilities.[33]
(b) sites not on the mainland of Great Britain (i.e. island sites) due to their lack of accessibility for efficient logistics support, including the need for double-handling of stores and spares.
(c) sites in Western Scotland remote from rail and good roads on the same count as (b).'[34]

The group then dismissed a further 25 ports and bays westwards and clockwise from Falmouth to Invergordon without closer scrutiny. Seventeen of these sites were in Scotland. Of the remaining eight, six (St Ives, Newquay, Padstow, Barnstaple, Carmarthen Bay and Tremadoc Bay) were dismissed because of the lack of deep water. The remaining two possibilities (Fishguard and Holyhead) are discussed further below.

This left the working party with a shortlist of ten possible sites: Devonport, Falmouth, Milford Haven, Loch Ryan, Gareloch, Loch Alsh, Fort William, Invergordon, Rosyth and Portland. An individual study of each site was conducted in order to assess the work that would be needed to satisfy the requirements for an operating base. The reasons

31. Other criteria included: accessibility by land for sufficient external re-supply, relative naval manpower requirements, availability of land for base and armaments depot, existence of admiralty facilities, existence and proximity of amenities and labour, and expansion potential. *Naval Ballistic Missile Force: Report of Working Party established by SMBA 5268 dated 25 February 1963*, P.O.B./P. (63) 2. (henceforth 'Report of Working Party'), ADM 1/28965, Public Record Office, Kew.
32. *Ibid.*, Appendix A, p. 2.
33. In its analysis of possible locations for US Polaris submarines, the Admiralty pointed out that submarines needed 30 fathoms to dive to periscope depth, and they could not go fast in less than 100 fathoms of water. Shallow water, moreover, is more easily mined. 'Basing of US Polaris Submarines in Northern UK: Memorandum by the Admiralty', June 1960, ADM 27203, Public Record Office, Kew.
34. Report of Working Party, p. 3.

why alternatives to Faslane and Coulport were eventually rejected are worth summarising here as they are relevant to our later discussions:

- **Milford Haven** was rejected on safety grounds because of the dangers involved in handling and storing high explosives near major oil facilities.
- **Loch Ryan** was rejected because of the lack of basic pilotage facilities and the need for extensive dredging of the approaches.
- **Fort William**, which had previously been offered to the US Navy as a forward operating base, was rejected as a UK facility because 'the narrow channel and tidal streams at Corran Point make access to Upper Loch Linnhe unacceptably hazardous. Possible sites in Lower Loch offer little or no shelter from prevailing winds'.
- **Portland** was rejected on safety grounds because no safe site for the RNAD existed on the Isle of Portland or the immediate mainland. In order to supply the submarines, assembled nuclear weapons would have to be transported by road to and from the base through Weymouth, and this would be unacceptable. Weather conditions at the proposed operating base (an extension of the coaling pier) were also poor, with a high degree of exposure to gales from all directions.

Of the remaining six locations, **Devonport**, **Falmouth**, **Invergordon** and **Loch Alsh** were rejected on various grounds:

- There were concerns over reactor safety in the densely populated area surrounding the proposed base at Carew Point, Devonport. But the most serious difficulties arose over the location of the RNAD, for which it was agreed that the only possible location would be Antony Park at Wilcove, on the Cornish side of the Tamar River. This would provide only 'marginal explosive safety factor' for berths of adequate reactor safety.[35] In addition, 'local objections to siting RNAD close to a densely populated area likely to be very strong' and prospects for land acquisition were 'very poor'.[36] Although the second cheapest

35. The WRNS quarters, parts of the naval married quarters at St Budeaux, the bulk of the RN Thanckes Oil Fuel Depot, and the north-west corner of the Dockyard would lie within the 4,400-foot radius of major damage to housing in the event of the maximum credible explosives accident (involving 16 Polaris missiles).
36. 'Land has just been returned to owner (Lord Lieutenant of Cornwall). Likely delay before compulsory purchase and survey could take place 10–11 months.' Ibid., Appendix B, p. 7.

option, with the advantages of co-location with a refitting base, Devonport also suffered from its distance from the sound-ranging facilities in Loch Fyne, which could not be provided locally.

- Location near **Falmouth** was also seriously considered, with provisional plans involving an operating base at Carclase Point, an RNAD 600 yards south of Penarrow Point, near the small town of St Mylor, and a floating dock moored close to Messack Point. This option was estimated to have a good reactor safety rating, with the base located 1,100 yards from St Just and 1,500 yards from St Mawes. The weapon safety rating was judged to be 'fair' with only 'scattered housing and the small villages of Trelew and Trefussis' within the radius of major damage from the RNAD. This option was judged less favourably than Faslane/Coulport because of the problems involved in land purchase from the Duchy of Cornwall and the National Trust. The study's authors argued that 'a strong case would be required to justify spoiling a national beauty spot or vigorous sailing centre'. This was also one of the most expensive sites to develop.

Invergordon and **Loch Alsh** were thought to be generally acceptable, but they suffered from their remoteness and lack of amenities for off-duty sailors. Their exits would also be vulnerable to enemy anti-submarine attack.

The final choice was therefore between **Rosyth** on the Forth, and **Faslane** at Gareloch. Both locations had acceptable safety ratings, while construction costs at Rosyth (with the RNAD at nearby Crombie) were estimated to be lower.[37] Rosyth's proximity to Edinburgh and Dunfermline and to the Forth rail and road crossings does not appear to have been considered a disadvantage. According to the memoirs of Vice Admiral Sir Hugh Mackenzie, Polaris Chief Executive from 1963 to 1968, the Treasury and Ministries of Defence and Transport all favoured Rosyth.[38] **Faslane** was eventually chosen because of the strength of the Admiralty's arguments on operational grounds. **Gareloch** had the advantage of being sheltered, while also being close to exercise areas with deep water, as well as to the existing sound range at nearby Loch Fyne. Polaris submarines would have a choice of exits covered by well-used

37. Rosyth is ten miles from Edinburgh, well above the minimum safety distance used in the study.
38. Vice Admiral Sir Hugh Mackenzie, *The Sword of Damocles*, The Royal Navy Submarine Museum, 1995, p. 218.

shipping lanes and also used by conventionally armed submarines (which could be used for support). Protected territorial waters in the Clyde led into deep water from the Cumbraes and they could go dived on either side of Arran or down to St George's Channel, so the chances of evasion and deception of hostile surveillance were high. Rosyth, by contrast, was 500 miles from both the nearest attack submarine base and the Loch Fyne sound range, and its more exposed location meant that there was only a 'fair chance' of being able consistently to evade hostile surveillance.

Ability to conceal submarine movements in and out of operating bases was a vital consideration during the Cold War. On average, an estimated 15 Soviet submarines passed Scotland on patrol every month in the 1980s, often seeking to spot US or UK nuclear-armed submarines as they left the Clyde. A Soviet intelligence-gathering trawler was reported to have been frequently stationed off Malin Head (in Northern Ireland), just outside the 12-mile limit, using sonar to detect submarines in transit and alert Soviet submarines.[39] In addition to varying exit routes and timing, and deploying attack submarines as decoys, the Royal Navy deployed patrol ships and helicopters to check on Soviet naval activity. The Navy is adamant that no Polaris submarine was ever detected by the Soviet Union while on deterrent patrol.

During discussion of the possibility of a Faslane base in Gareloch, concern was expressed (from within both the US and the Royal Navy) that the proximity of the base to US facilities at Holy Loch would permit the Soviet Union to concentrate its own anti-submarine efforts. These objections were overruled, in part because it was assumed that the US Navy tender could be 'expected to leave Holy Loch during a period of tension'.[40] The study concluded that 'in any case the national requirement would be regarded as paramount'.

Having decided on co-locating the operating base with the third (conventional) Submarine Squadron at **Faslane**, the working party then agreed to locate the RNAD nearby at **Coulport**. The option of locating at Glen Douglas was rejected because of its proximity to a main public road and the potential problems of operating alongside the already-existing NATO facility. Metal Industries, a shipbreaking firm, readily agreed to sell the necessary land at Faslane, and most of Coulport was

39. Adela Gooch, 'The strange case of the 'invisible' submarine', *Daily Telegraph*, 14 December 1987.
40. Report of Working Party, p. 8.

already government-owned, being used for torpedo trials. According to a recent memoir, 'One farmer objected at first but soon became quite happy to be compensated by the Admiralty. Most of his family subsequently got jobs with the builders of the RNAD'.[41]

Once the basing decision was confirmed in March 1963, construction proceeded rapidly, with all essential facilities available in time for the first Polaris boat to begin patrol in June 1968.[42] It was the first new naval base in the United Kingdom since Rosyth was developed in 1909, making its rapid completion in time, and on budget, all the more remarkable.[43]

The total capital cost of the Polaris programme (at today's prices) came to some £4 billion.[44] The last Polaris boat, HMS *Repulse*, was withdrawn from service in August 1996.

Trident at Faslane/Coulport

Within a decade of Polaris entering service, civil servants and Ministers had begun to discuss what might replace it. In 1977, Ministers commissioned two internal studies, one on the broader implications of Polaris replacement and the other on alternative delivery systems.[45] The process accelerated after the election of the Conservatives in May 1979, and in July 1980 the Government announced its intention to replace Polaris with the Trident C4 missile system at an estimated cost of between £4,500 million and £5,000 million (£11–12 billion at today's prices).[46] In 1982, it was decided to switch to the more capable, and larger, Trident D5 missile in order to maintain commonality with the US

41. Ken Dunlop, 'Support Planning', in J. E. Moore (ed.), *The Impact of Polaris*, *op. cit.*, p. 169.
42. For further discussion of the Polaris programme, see John Simpson, 'Lessons of the British Polaris Project: An Organisational History', *Royal United Services Institute Journal*, March 1969, pp. 46–50; Peter Nailor, *The Nassau Connection: The Organisation and Management of the British Polaris Project* (HMSO: London, 1988).
43. Peter Nailor, *op. cit.*, p. 31.
44. 'Supplementary Memorandum by the Ministry of Defence', in *Strategic Nuclear Weapons Policy*, Fourth Report from the House of Commons Defence Committee 1980/81, May 1981, p. 229 estimates the capital cost of the Polaris programme to have been £330 million at 1963 prices. This is equivalent to £3,900 million at 2000/2001 prices (using the GDP deflator).
45. Lawrence Freedman, *op. cit.*, p. 60.
46. *The Future United Kingdom Strategic Nuclear Deterrent Force*, Defence Open Government Document 80/23, MoD, London, July 1980, p. 25.

throughout the system's lifetime. As a consequence, the total estimated programme cost rose to £7,500 million at 1981 prices (£16.7 billion at today's prices).[47]

In order to help contain the increased costs of the missiles, and the larger submarines that would be necessary to carry them, the UK agreed to an arrangement whereby the main servicing work on its Trident D5 missiles would be carried out in the US, rather than at Coulport as was the case with Polaris. By reducing the extent of new work necessary at Coulport, this decision reduced the capital cost of the programme by £1,200 million at today's prices.[48] Nevertheless, Coulport would still retain the ability to unload and store up to 16 missiles in case these had to be removed in a submarine emergency.[49]

Given the considerable cost savings involved in developing existing facilities at Faslane and Coulport, however, the discussion on where to locate the UK Trident force appears to have been relatively straightforward. The relative advantages of a base in the Clyde were further increased by the greater size of the Trident boats, which increased the premium on having adequate depth of water close to base, combined with shelter from wind and storm. Despite the controversy over devolution in the late 1970s, the possibility of future Scottish independence does not appear to have been mentioned in discussions of alternative locations.[50]

The construction programme at Faslane and Coulport was the largest and most complex building programme ever undertaken by the Ministry of Defence and the Property Services Agency. In contrast to the Polaris construction programme in the 1960s, the Trident works programme was plagued by delays and cost escalation. Its final total cost of £1.9 billion at 1994 prices (£2.2 billion at today's prices) was 72% over budget

---

47. *The United Kingdom Trident Programme*, Defence Open Government Document 82/1, Ministry of Defence, London, March 1992, Figure 3. As of 30 September 1999, 96% of expenditure on Trident acquisition had been completed. If all expenditure were brought up to 2000/2001 prices, Trident's total cost would now be £13.5 billion, or 20% less in real terms than originally estimated. *House of Commons Written Answer*, column 389, 10 May 2000.
48. Government evidence published in 'The Progress of the Trident Programme', *Fifth Report from the Defence Committee 1988/89*, June 1989, p. 31 estimates savings from the decision to process in the US at £784 million at 1988/89 prices.
49. William Hill, '384 warheads for UK Trident force', *Jane's Defence Weekly*, 9 June 1984, p. 916.
50. Interviews with several senior ex-officials.

in real terms.[51] One of the main factors contributing to the cost escalation was the significant tightening of nuclear safety standards that took place during the programme, which led to substantial redesign. In the case of the ship lift, for example, the safety case criteria were only finally agreed four years after construction commenced. In evidence to the Public Accounts Committee, the MoD confirmed that the 1986 Chernobyl incident, together with the recommendations of the 1987 Sizewell B enquiry, had led to major design changes being made for facilities at both Faslane and Coulport. It was decided, in particular, to redesign the ship lift to cope with a one in ten thousand year probability of an earthquake of a particular magnitude (7.5 to 8 on the Richter scale) occurring. According to the MoD's Chief of Defence Procurement, 'the nuclear safety requirements which were thought to be appropriate at the time when the Trident works were undertaken were very, very different from those which had been applied 20 years earlier when the Polaris system was at the same stage'.[52]

The UK's nuclear weapon infrastructure today

Located on Gareloch on the Firth of Clyde, some 25 miles from Glasgow, **HM Naval Base Clyde at Faslane** is now the only operating base for the UK's nuclear forces. The first Polaris patrol (by HMS Resolution) began from Faslane in June 1968, and the fourth Polaris submarine started its patrol in September 1970. The Polaris force was subsequently phased out of service between 1992 and 1996. Faslane is now home to four Trident ballistic missile submarines (SSBNs), the fourth (HMS Vengeance) having become operational in February 2001. After extensive modernisation and development during the 1980s and 1990s, the facilities

51. According to a trenchant critique of the programme's management by the National Audit Office, many designs were incomplete when construction commenced. Monitoring of contractors' performance was unsatisfactory. Inadequate management structures and practices resulted, at one stage, in the simultaneous employment of over 1,000 consultants, many of them on cost-plus contracts. Total consultancy costs alone amounted to £360 million at 1994 prices. 'Ministry of Defence: Management of the Trident Works Programme', *Twenty Sixth Report of the Committee of Public Accounts 1994/95*, June 1995, paragraph 2 and p. xi.
52. Evidence given by Dr Malcolm McIntosh, Chief of Defence Procurement, Ministry of Defence, *ibid.*, p. 12. The 1990 Drell Report to the US Congress, and the subsequent UK Oxburgh Report, re-examined the safety issues involved in loading and unloading Trident warheads. Their influence on subsequent technical decisions is unclear.

at Faslane now include a floating jetty as well as a massive ship lift, the height of an eleven-storey building and as long as Wembley Stadium, capable of raising the 15,900-ton boat out of the water.[53] The naval facilities at Faslane provide comprehensive engineering stores and support for the submarines themselves, as well as independent generating facilities that can provide, when necessary, secure electricity supplies for reactor cooling, control and instrumentation. The base also includes training facilities and accommodation for six Trident crews.

In addition, Faslane is currently used as the main operating base for five Swiftsure-class nuclear-powered attack submarines (SSN's), seven Sandown-class mine counter-measure vessels and three Northern Ireland Patrol Craft. It will be the operating base for the three Astute-class submarines that are due to enter service (replacing the Swiftsure-class) from 2005 onwards, and a new jetty will need to be built for this purpose. In total, the Clyde naval base houses a total of 7,000 personnel, including large contingents of MoD Police and MoD Guard Service personnel.[54] Part of the Fleet Royal Marine Protection Group, one of whose primary roles is to provide specialist services for the protection of the strategic force, is also included in this total.

The **Royal Navy Armament Depot (RNAD), Coulport** is integral to Trident's nuclear capability. Situated on Loch Long, Coulport is five miles from Faslane by road and 13 miles by sea. It contains a covered floating explosives handling jetty from which warheads can be safely loaded onto, and unloaded from, onboard missiles using overhead cranes. Weighing 85,000 tonnes, the jetty is as tall as Nelson's Column and as long as two football pitches.[55] Coulport contains secure facilities for warhead maintenance and storage, and for the storage and loading of conventional torpedoes, as well as a capability for removal and storage of Trident D5 missiles for minor repair or emergency work. It also has secure access roads between these facilities and the explosives handling jetty.

Coulport was used in the past for the complete servicing and refurbishment of Polaris missiles, using spare parts flown in from the US when necessary. In order to reduce the costs of the Trident programme, the Government decided in 1982 that the servicing of Trident missiles would

53. National Audit Office, *Ministry of Defence: Management of the Trident Works Programme* (HMSO: London, July 1994), p 1.
54. As of early 2001, HM Naval Base included 3200 naval personnel, 2500 civilians, 700 MoD Police, 400 Royal Marines and 300 MoD Guard Service.
55. National Audit Office, *op. cit.*, p. 1.

take place at the US's own Trident base in **King's Bay, Georgia**. When the last Polaris missiles went out of service in the 1990s, the Coulport workforce was therefore significantly reduced. Trident boats now begin their ten-year operational cycle by picking up missiles at King's Bay before sailing to Coulport to arm them with warheads. Shortly before the boats are due for long refit, the process is reversed. Warheads are offloaded at Coulport and missiles are returned to the King's Bay stockpile for refurbishment and repair. After refitting at Devonport (see below), boats sail to King's Bay to take on a new batch of missiles, after which they load warheads at Coulport and re-enter their Faslane-based operational cycle.[56]

In order to remain effective, nuclear warheads have to be regularly returned to Aldermaston for maintenance and refurbishment. This requirement is partly driven by the need to replenish the tritium in warheads and remove any americium that has built up in their plutonium cores.[57] Initial UK studies estimated that Polaris warheads and re-entry vehicles would have to be overhauled about every two-and-a-half years.[58] Information on the necessary frequency of refurbishment for Trident warheads at these sites is not publicly available, but it is thought that the time between overhauls at Aldermaston may now have been extended to as much as ten years.

It was originally planned that Trident boats would receive their regular refits (scheduled to be every ten years or so) at Rosyth Dockyard in the Forth Estuary on the east coast of Scotland, where Polaris refits had taken place in the past. This included refuelling the nuclear submarine reactors with enriched uranium. In a controversial decision, the Government announced in June 1993 that Trident boats would be refitted and refuelled at the **Devonport Dockyard** in Plymouth. The facilities for these operations are now under construction, and work on the first Trident boat (HMS Vanguard) in Devonport is scheduled to begin in early 2002. Thereafter, one of the four Trident boats will normally be

56. As of December 2000, seven Trident missiles had already been used for test firing, a further seven were due for future test firing, and there was a processing margin of four missiles. The total purchase was 58 missiles.
57. Tritium is used both as a neutron source for 'boosting' the primaries in thermonuclear weapons, and as a thermonuclear fuel. It has a half-life of 12.5 years. Americium results from the decay of the isotope plutonium–241. It is highly radioactive and diminishes the performance of nuclear warheads if allowed to accumulate.
58. Report of Working Party, p. 7.

undergoing a refit, each of which is planned to last between 18 months and two years.

Political considerations are suspected to have played an important role in the Devonport decision. Some commentators have speculated that the need to shore up Conservative support in the South-West of England was the key factor. Others have suggested that 'the possibility that Scotland might vote for independence at some point made it certain that the MoD would favour Devonport rather than Rosyth'.[59] These suggestions have been strongly denied by those involved in the decision which, they state, was taken purely on technical and financial grounds.[60] Even if this was the case, however, the speculation that other factors were involved illustrates the increasing political sensitivity of regional issues in nuclear basing decisions.

Other key components of the UK nuclear capability are also located outside Scotland. Trident warheads are regularly transported by road between the **Atomic Weapons Establishment (AWE) at Aldermaston and Burghfield** and Coulport. AWE is responsible for production, reconditioning, repair and dismantling of warheads and for nuclear weapons R&D work. While on patrol, Trident submarine commanders answer to the Commander-in-Chief Fleet, based in **Northwood, London**. Communications with the submarines are, *inter alia*, conducted through Ultra-Low Frequency (ULF) transmitters at **Rugby** in the Midlands. In an emergency, political control would be exercised through the Defence Secretary and the Prime Minister of the UK Government.

The acquisition of nuclear materials for Trident and its predecessors has had a complicated history.[61] The plutonium used in warheads was mainly produced in the Calder Hall reactors at Sellafield in England and the Chapelcross reactors at Annan near Dumfries in south-west Scotland. Highly enriched uranium (HEU) used in warheads has been acquired from the US under barter arrangements (involving the exchange of HEU and tritium for plutonium) set out in the US–UK Mutual Defence Agreement.[62] Additional HEU has been purchased from the US under separate arrangements in order to fuel the submarine reactors.

59. Allan Massie, 'Rosyth survival helps keep UK afloat', *Sunday Times*, 18 February 2001.
60. Information from interviews.
61. See David Albright, Frans Berkhout and William Walker, *Plutonium and Highly Enriched Uranium 1996: World Inventories, Capabilities and Policies* (Oxford University Press: Oxford, 1997), Chapters 3 and 4.
62. John Simpson, *The Independent Nuclear State*, *op. cit.*, Chapter 7.

Tritium was both bartered with the US and produced in the Chapelcross reactors. **Chapelcross** remains the only facility in Scotland involved in a significant way in production for the UK's nuclear warhead arsenal.

The Government announced in early 1995 that there would be no further production in the UK of plutonium and HEU for nuclear weapons. The UK nuclear arsenal will be supported henceforth by recycling material held in unsafeguarded stocks. Tritium is not a fissile material and its production has continued at Chapelcross. The acquisition of HEU to fuel submarine reactors, whether through domestic production or purchase from the US, is not covered by the announcement.

Entrenchment on the Clyde

It is evident that a formidable political, economic and operational commitment grew over a 40-year period around the permanent basing of the UK's nuclear forces on the Clyde. We return to the basing issue in Chapter 5 which shows that this very entrenchment on the Clyde, and the political and economic obstacles to opening new bases elsewhere, make it extraordinarily difficult to relocate Trident.

It is also evident that the prospect of Scottish independence seldom if ever troubled the decisions that led to these commitments. As we shall now see, the Scottish question may loom large in years ahead, whether or not independence occurs.

Chapter Two

Scottish Nationalism and Nuclear Weapons

Only the briefest account of Scottish political and constitutional history can be given here. But some historical background is necessary, especially for those unfamiliar with Scottish history and politics, for our later discussions. It will be followed by an account of Scottish nationalist attitudes towards nuclear weapons, Trident and NATO.

Scotland's constitutional history

Scotland was a self-governing kingdom for four hundred years after its unification under a single Crown in the late thirteenth century. It lost its political autonomy in 1707 when its Parliament was voluntarily dissolved and the United Kingdom, with its political centre in London, was formed with England and Wales. After the defeat of the last Jacobite rebellion in 1745, the governance of Scotland was not at issue for well over a century.[1] Although the rise of Scottish nationalism began in the late nineteenth century, the movement for full independence only became a significant political force in the 1960s.[2]

This political quiescence had many reasons, among them the economic and cultural dynamism of eighteenth- and nineteenth-century Scotland, the expansion of the British Empire in which Scots were prominent as administrators, manufacturers and traders, the rise of Socialism and the Labour movement which attracted much political support in Scotland, the lack of a trauma on the scale of the Irish famine, the unifying and

1. For accounts of Scottish history and of the processes by which 'Britishness' was formed, see Christopher Smout, *A History of the Scottish People, 1560–1830* (Collins: Glasgow, 1969); Michael Lynch, *Scotland: A New History* (Pimlico: London, 1992); Linda Colley, *Britons: Forging the Nation, 1707–1837* (Vintage Press: London, 1996); and Norman Davies, *The Isles: A History* (Macmillan: London, 1999).
2. On the background to and history of Scottish nationalism, see Christopher Harvie, *Scotland and Nationalism* (Routledge: London, 1998); Alice Brown, David McCrone and Lindsay Paterson, *Politics and Society in Scotland* (Macmillan: London, 1998); Tom Nairn, *After Britain: New Labour and the Return of Scotland* (Granta: London, 2000); Alan Taylor (ed.), *What A State! Is Devolution for Scotland the End of Britain?* (HarperCollins: London, 2000).

centralising influence of two World Wars, and the presence of Scots in UK governments. Scotland's acceptance of England's political supremacy was also eased by its retention of an autonomous Church and separate legal and educational systems, and by Westminster's gradual granting of concessions to Scotland in the administrative and political fields. In contrast to Ireland, concessions to Scottish nationalism were wrung and have continued to be wrung by peaceful means. The nationalist movement in Scotland has always been secular and pacific, lacking the militancy and religious identification of Irish nationalism.

Thus, when members of the Scottish elite began to press for Home Rule in the late nineteenth century, partly in imitation of Irish demands for the same, a Scottish Secretary was appointed to represent Scottish interests in the UK Cabinet in London, a post that has been in existence ever since. Legislation to grant Scotland Home Rule was set aside only after the outbreak of the First World War (the Gladstonian proposals to develop a federal structure for Britain, with home rule for each region, died when the Irish Free State was established in 1921).[3] Although policy continued to be decided in London, the administration of health, education and some other social services was transferred in the 1930s from London to a Scottish Office in Edinburgh, and its responsibilities were extended during the Second World War.

The strong growth of Scottish nationalism in the 1960s and 1970s, led by a rejuvenated Scottish National Party (founded in 1934), had many causes. They included the collapse of empire, Britain's industrial decline, the discovery of North Sea oil, and a new cultural self-awareness and assertiveness north of the Border. In response a devolved Parliament for Scotland was proposed by the UK Labour Goverment.

The proposal's failure in a referendum in 1979 proved temporary. Supported by the Scottish Labour and Liberal Democrat Parties, the Scottish Constitutional Convention met between 1989 and 1995 and laid the foundations for the creation of a new Scottish Parliament. Its main recommendations featured in the Labour Party's manifesto for the May 1997 General Election as part of a broad programme of constitutional reform, including the establishment of a Welsh Assembly and reform of the House of Lords among other things. The Scottish Parliament was duly established after a decisive referendum in September 1997 called by

3. On Scotland and Home Rule, see Christopher Harvie, *op. cit.*, pp. 16–17; and Robert McLean, 'A Brief History of Scottish Home Rule', in Gerry Hassan (ed.), *A Guide to the Scottish Parliament* (The Stationery Office: London, 1999).

the Labour Government soon after it assumed office in May of that year. The Scotland Act gained Royal Assent in November 1998 and the Parliament was opened on 1 July 1999.[4]

As well as having its own Parliament, Scotland is today disproportionately represented in the UK Government, with five out of 21 Members of Parliament in the Cabinet currently coming from Scottish constituencies, including Chancellor Gordon Brown. It also continues to benefit from a formula for distributing public funds (the 'Barnett formula') that supports around 23% more spending per capita than in England.[5] As a result, the Scottish Parliament has been able to finance services (for example in education and care for the elderly) that are significantly better than those available in England.

Yet even under these relatively favourable conditions, and with a popular Labour Government at Westminster, the predicted decline in the SNP's fortunes has not taken place. The SNP's share of the Scottish vote in the 2001 UK election amounted to just over 20% of the total and, although disappointing to the Nationalists, was only slightly lower than its share in 1997. In the 1999 Scottish Parliament elections (the SNP is always likely to do better in Scottish elections) it gained 27% of votes cast, and recent opinion polls suggest that it could gain around a third of the popular vote in the next Scottish elections in 2003.

With the steep decline in the Conservative vote in Scotland in the 1990s, the SNP has become the main opposition party in the Scottish Parliament.[6] It may therefore be the main beneficiary of any future

4. On the history and constitution of the Scottish Parliament, see Gerry Hassan (ed.), *op. cit.*
5. Total identifiable government expenditure in Scotland in 1999–2000 was £5,271 per head, compared with £4,283 in England, £5,052 in Wales and £5,939 in Northern Ireland. See *Public Expenditure Statistical Analyses 2001–2002*, HM Treasury, Cm 5101, April 2001, Table 8.1. A further £637 per head of UK expenditure was not identifiable by country, of which £435 was for defence and overseas services (see Table 8.8). For a detailed description of how the Barnett formula works, see *Funding the Scottish Parliament, National Assembly for Wales and Northern Ireland Assembly*, HM Treasury, March 1999. The SNP does not dispute that spending per capita in Scotland is higher than in England, but suggests that this would be heavily outweighed, in an independent Scotland, by much higher revenues per head (notably from North Sea oil revenues). See *Scotland's 21st Century Opportunity: Government Expenditure and Revenues in Scotland 2000–2002*, Saltire Paper, Scottish National Party, December 2000.
6. Michael Dyer, 'The Evolution of the Centre-right and the state of Scottish Conservatism', *Political Studies*, vol. 49, no. 1, 2001, pp. 30–50.

discontent with the Labour/Liberal Democrat coalition which has exercised power in Edinburgh since 1999. At the same time, however, it is unlikely to gain an absolute majority. Partly to minimise the chances of the SNP dominating a future Parliament, a system of proportional representation was adopted in the Scotland Act. In sharp contrast to the 1997 and 2001 UK elections, whose 'first-past-the-post' system gave Labour a massive majority of seats despite obtaining just over 40% of votes, the Labour Party was obliged to make a deal with the much smaller Liberal Democrat Party in order to lead the first Scottish Executive. Even if it were to become the largest single party, therefore, the SNP would be obliged to seek coalition partners if it wished to form a government.

It remains to be seen whether devolution will be sufficient to stem the drift towards full independence. Andrew Marr, now the BBC's chief political commentator, concluded a recent book by expressing his 'profound belief in the likelihood of the British Union dissolving within a decade'.[7] A spate of other books and articles have come to the same conclusion, mainly but not only on the grounds that Scots are unlikely to remain satisfied with the limited autonomy and tax-raising powers granted them in the devolution settlement.[8] Other commentators have been sceptical, a common view being that the Scots will draw back from independence when the full risks of separation, including the international risks, are revealed to them. The romantic appeal of independence will diminish, they claim, when the hard practical realities have to be faced.

Still others argue that developments in England rather than in Scotland (and Wales) will decide the fate of the Union. Its dissolution could be triggered, for instance, by pressures to revise the Barnett formula and to remove the economic advantage enjoyed by Scotland over the English regions. Although a Conservative Party revival in England currently appears unlikely after its hefty defeats in recent elections, it too could trigger the UK's fragmentation, especially if the Party were denied office by the weight of Labour and Nationalist MPs from Scotland and Wales. That would fuel demands for an English Parliament or a substantial curtailment of Scottish and Welsh MPs' rights in the UK Parliament, just as it would raise questions about the rights of the Government in London to decide policy in Scotland if the Conservative Party had little electoral support

7. Andrew Marr, *The Day Britain Died* (Profile Books: London, 2000), p. 245.
8. See, for example, John Redwood, *Stars and Strife* (Palgrave: London, 2001) and *The Death of Britain?* (Macmillan: London, 1999); Peter Hitchens, *The Abolition of Britain* (Quartet Books: London, 1999); Tom Nairn, *After Britain: New Labour and the Return of Scotland, op. cit.*

there.[9] Equally, diverging policy preferences in London and Edinburgh, especially on vital issues such as Europe or social welfare, could create a 'let's go it alone' outlook in either place. One implication is that the Union's survival may now rest upon either the Labour Party's perpetual sway in both England and Scotland (a sway reinforced by tacit or actual coalitions with the Liberal Democrats), upon a remarkable revival of the fortunes of the Conservative Party as an electoral force north of the Border, or upon a marked decline of the Nationalist vote.

Developments in the European Union will also influence the outcome. Again there are many possibilities. An expanding European Union which welcomed many new member countries, including small countries which lacked Scotland's economic and democratic credentials, might encourage Scots to seek similar rights. Against this, a Union that was becoming more integrated politically (with the backing of its major players) while giving its regions more room to oversee their economic and cultural development could discourage rather than encourage nationalist movements. European political integration that fomented anti-European nationalism in England might, by contrast, encourage Scotland to seek its own position on its own terms in the European Union. So there are many possibilities, all of which would be taking place against the background of the tremendous changes being wrought by globalisation, which may or may not encourage nationalism and the formation of new states, depending on context.

The future of the Union is therefore very uncertain. If it did not hold together, how might the process of break-up take place? It would probably involve the SNP becoming the largest party in a Scottish election and able to obtain enough support from other Members of the Scottish Parliament for an independence referendum. One recent opinion poll suggested that, despite the continuing popularity of Labour

9. Scottish MPs at Westminster still vote on legislation in the many areas (such as education, legal reform and social services) where competence in Scotland has been devolved to Edinburgh. In 2000, Party leader William Hague promised that Scottish MPs would lose this right within weeks of a Conservative government coming to power. He argued that such a move would 'strengthen our common identity' and prevent the emergence of 'a dangerous English nationalism'. Andrew Sparrow, 'Hague would curb Scots MPs' votes', *Daily Telegraph*, 14 November 2000. Labour ministers have suggested, by contrast, that the Hague proposal 'fans separatist sentiment and, if ever implemented, would lead inexorably to the breakup of the United Kingdom'. Michael Wills, 'Why we are now the party of Britain and the Union', *Daily Telegraph*, 3 January 2001.

in Scotland, 45% of voters would vote for independence in such a referendum, with 49% against.[10] The SNP would probably require evidence of much stronger popular support for independence before risking a referendum. It already fears a 'Quebec scenario', with the Scottish people drawing back from the radical implications of full separation once the question is put to them and those implications are explained.

Once secured by referendum, a vote in favour of separation would provide the Scottish Parliament with the democratic authority to complete its powers, effectively countermanding the Westminster Parliament's claim to supremacy. But before the Scottish state could function effectively, there would have to be intensive negotiations between the Edinburgh, London and other governments on a wide range of issues. These talks would entail negotiation with the London Government on 'domestic' issues such as the division of assets and liabilities, and with overseas governments on membership of international treaties and organisations (especially the UN, European Union and NATO). The SNP has estimated, perhaps optimistically, that these negotiations could be concluded within a year. With its various domestic and international dimensions, the nuclear question could turn out to be one of the most complicated and controversial of all the issues to be settled.

Complicating the discussion further, it cannot be assumed that the post-referendum Scottish Government, responsible for negotiating the terms of independence, would necessarily be dominated by the SNP. A 'Yes' vote would be likely to lead to a wide-ranging realignment of Scottish politics, in ways that cannot be predicted in advance, but could significantly constrain the freedom of manoeuvre of the Scottish negotiating team. When the various options for dealing with the nuclear question are considered in subsequent chapters, therefore, it is important to remember that the Scottish negotiating team (like its London counterpart) would be unlikely to be a unitary actor. In seeking to discuss how such a team might behave, it is important to consider the evolution of Scottish political opinion as a whole, rather than simply the current views of one particular party.

10. 'Support for SNP falls as budget boosts Labour', *The Sunday Times*, 11 March 2001. Trends in Scottish opinion on independence, devolution and other political matters are surveyed in a recent book by Lindsay Paterson and his colleagues at Edinburgh University. See Lindsay Paterson, Alice Brown, John Curtice, Kerstin Hinds, David McCrone, Alison Park, Kerry Sproston and Paula Surridge, *New Scotland, New Politics* (Polygon at Edinburgh University Press: Edinburgh, 2001).

Scotland and the defence of the UK

Throughout the history of the Union, Scotland has had no right to develop its own foreign and defence policy, only having the status of a region in a unitary state. Nor has it had any special involvement in the conduct and shaping of UK policy. Scotland's military contribution to the Union has nevertheless been substantial, even disproportionate, in the three centuries since 1707.[11] Scottish regiments were prominent in countless colonial wars and in the two World Wars in which they bore more than their share of the casualties. Out of the Army's current 40 infantry battalions, six are identifiably Scottish, their soldiers mainly recruited within Scotland.[12] The presence of naval and air force bases in Scotland, of the Army's northern headquarters in Edinburgh,[13] and of naval shipyards on the Clyde, all sustain the tradition of Scotland being an active contributor to the UK's defence and a significant beneficiary of the MoD's largesse.[14]

It needs emphasising that the growing political and institutional estrangement of Scotland and England has at no time been evident in the armed forces. There has been no questioning of their primary loyalty to the Crown and Parliament in London. Indeed, the armed forces remain one of the strongest sources of political unity in the UK, even if this does not discourage significant numbers of their members from voting for the SNP. Whether in Northern Ireland, Kosovo or other areas of conflict, there is no sense in which Scottish or English or Welsh regiments are operating under separate banners. Regimental loyalties remain cultural rather than political.[15]

---

11. For a discussion of the origins of the 'Scottish Empire', see Linda Colley, *op. cit.*, pp. 122–140.
12. The Royal Scots, Royal Highland Fusiliers, King's Own Scottish Borderers, Black Watch, the Highlanders, and the Argyll and Sutherland Highlanders. Scotland also has one cavalry (armoured) regiment and two artillery regiments (the 'Lowland Gunners' and the 'Highland Gunners'). See Jack Hawthorn, *Some Thoughts on an Independent Scottish Defence Force*, Scottish Centre for War Studies Occasional Paper 1, University of Glasgow, 1997.
13. The 1998 decision in preference to York was widely seen to be motivated by a desire to 'ensure Scotland plays a major role in the nation's defence'. See Kirsty Milne, 'Spinwatch', *New Statesman*, 6 November 1988.
14. In a further example of this relationship, the Rosyth dockyard was recently given a £75 million contract to refit five Type 23 frigates. 'Royal Navy rescues Rosyth', *The Guardian*, 31 March 2001.
15. This said, the recruitment difficulties being experienced by the British Army, and especially by the Scottish regiments, suggest that the Army's attractions for the young may be diminishing.

This unity of policy and purpose is also upheld by the significant presence of Scots in the UK's foreign and defence policy establishments. Scotland continues to be 'unusually well represented in Britain's foreign office, in its diplomatic service and, it would seem, in the upper echelons of its secret service' as well as in the Ministry of Defence.[16] NATO's Secretary-General (Lord Robertson) is also a Scot and a committed Unionist.

As a result, the reservation of foreign and security policy to the government in London has, with the single exception of nuclear policy, been one of the least controversial elements of the Scotland Act. Moreover, the UK Government's assertion of pre-eminence in this field has not been significantly dented by international trends that might have strengthened the case for Scotland developing its own security policies and structures. The Government in London has not had to justify its monopoly against the vanishing need to police a worldwide empire, the diminished threat to UK security after the end of the Cold War, the greatly reduced danger of war with other European states (an external danger which played an important role in the formation and maintenance of the Union in times past), and the lesser resources required by small European states to mount an effective defence, albeit in cooperation with other states, in the new international circumstances.[17]

These realities have presented the Scottish National Party with obvious problems. While pledged to establish a sovereign Scottish state with its own foreign and defence policies and its own armed forces, the Party has been loath to ruffle the feathers of the military establishment in Scotland and has had difficulty assembling a convincing case for Scotland being better able to look after its own security. It has responded in three ways. Firstly, it has tried to avoid a full debate in Scotland and in the Party on what the defence and security policies of an independent Scotland would entail, preferring to give prominence to social, economic and other issues. Secondly, it has stressed that a Scottish government would commit substantial resources to conventional defence and has proposed budgets that would allow a newly established Scottish Defence Force to absorb the full Scottish 'share' of the UK conventional defence budget.[18] In

16. Linda Colley, *op. cit.*, p. 139.
17. UK armed forces are currently around 60% of their 1985 level. Large numbers of defence bases have been closed and industrial employment dependent on UK defence expenditure has fallen sharply.
18. In the late 1970s, the SNP's defence policy group (led by economist Gavin Kennedy) proposed a Scottish defence budget of £450 million a year,

addition, it has cast itself as protector of the Scottish infantry regiments when they have been threatened with merger or dissolution during the UK Government's efforts to rationalise the Army. Thirdly, the SNP has proclaimed that Scotland would play an active and distinctive part in emerging security structures in alliance with other states. In recent years it has given particular emphasis to Scotland's potential role in UN peace-keeping and in nascent European defence institutions, and has invited comparison with the contributions that Denmark, Ireland, Norway and other small European states have made, in their various ways, to collective security.

The SNP and nuclear weapons

Nuclear weapons have provided the one field of defence policy where the SNP and other groups in Scotland have consistently taken a stand against UK commitments. The nuclear issue has helped the Party to claim that it has a distinctive defence policy and that a Scottish state would enhance rather than diminish Scotland's security, and it has usefully diverted attention from awkward questions about Scotland's and the UK's conventional defence. This focusing of attention on nuclear weapons has been safe politically because of the special nature of nuclear weapons, the increasing concentration of UK nuclear forces in Scotland, the currents of opposition to nuclear weapons that have run through English as well as Scottish society, and the moral authority the SNP has been able to claim from the identification of nuclear disarmament as the supreme aspiration in the Nuclear Non-Proliferation Treaty and other international treaties (see Chapter 4).

However, the SNP's stance has not been primarily opportunistic. It has drawn upon genuine moral concerns and a long pacifist tradition in Scotland (especially strong in Glasgow) which, if less pronounced than the martial tradition, still has political resonance. The 1961 deployment of US missile submarines at the Holy Loch in the Clyde, followed by the 1963 decision to base the UK's Polaris force at Faslane – both bases within 30 miles of the centre of Glasgow, Scotland's largest city – guaranteed strong feelings about nuclear weapons in Scotland. The SNP's nuclear

equivalent to 8.5% of UK defence spending at the time, but roughly six times the defence budget of Ireland. See Christopher Harvie, *op. cit.*, p. 195. Recent SNP policy documents assume a Scottish defence budget of 8% of the UK level, only slightly below its 8.6% share of non-oil GDP. See *Scotland's 21st Century Opportunity*, *op. cit.*

policy has also been strongly rooted in a nationalist depiction of England as Scotland's exploiter.[19] The Government in London is commonly accused of locating the nuclear submarine bases in a 'non-essential' area of the UK, and of treating the Scottish people as if they were expendable. Such accusations may overlook the vulnerability of densely populated regions of southern England to nuclear strikes on Aldermaston and London, but they have been politically telling nonetheless.

The Labour Party's support for nuclear deterrence has waxed and waned. After famous battles in the late 1950s, it supported the deterrent in the 1960s and 1970s, swung to a policy of unilateral disarmament in the early 1980s, and reverted to a policy of supporting Trident late in the 1980s from which it has not since departed. In contrast, the SNP has consistently set itself against the UK and NATO policies of deterrence and against the basing of nuclear weapons in Scotland. Its advocacy of nuclear disarmament has been uncompromising. To cite some SNP declarations over the years:

> On Scotland regaining her independence all governments responsible for Nuclear Weapon Bases and nuclear weapons on Scottish land, waters or airspace, will be required to remove these ... Scotland will also sign the Nuclear Weapons Non-Proliferation Treaty [sic], and will ban any manufacture of nuclear weapons on Scottish soil. Scotland will seek the co-operation of neighbouring non-nuclear states: Iceland, Norway, Sweden, Finland and Denmark to initiate consultations with the USA and other NATO allies and with the USSR on the establishment of a nuclear-free zone in the North Sea/North East Atlantic and Scottish territorial waters.
>
> *SNP statement of defence policy, December 1976*

> Scotland is covered with nuclear bases and military installations, making us a number one target in the event of nuclear war. Nuclear weapons have been placed on our soil by both Labour and Conservative governments, without the consent of the Scottish people ... A Scottish government will
>
> - cancel the Trident nuclear programme ...;

---

19. For one of the few discussions of Nationalist anti-nuclearism, see Isobel Lindsay, 'CND and the Nationalist Parties', in John Minnion and Phil Bolsover (eds), *The CND Story* (Allison and Busby: London, 1983), pp. 134–136.

- remove all nuclear weapons and foreign nuclear establishments from Scottish soil and territorial waters;
- promote nuclear disarmament by seeking agreement ... to the creation of nuclear-free zones in Europe;
- divert resources to strong and efficient conventional forces.

SNP election manifesto, 1983

The SNP is committed to a non-nuclear Scotland. An independent Scotland will immediately withdraw from the UK's Trident programme, and will order nuclear weapons and installations off our soil ... Both of the UK parties want to base Trident on the Clyde, far away from London. The SNP will not tolerate Scottish waters being used as a dumping ground for weapons of mass destruction. The existing Polaris nuclear weapons fleet will be removed from Scotland as soon as possible.

SNP election manifesto, 1992

The SNP have a long-standing objection to nuclear weapons. We will negotiate a phased but complete withdrawal of Trident from the Clyde and invest our savings from this costly, deadly and unnecessary nuclear deterrent in conventional defence as well as other priorities including health and education ... The Scottish Navy will require both surface and submarine craft based at Faslane and Rosyth ...

SNP election manifesto, 1997

On independence, we will negotiate the safe removal of Trident from Scotland and an independent Scotland will work to eliminate nuclear, biological and chemical weapons worldwide. Pre-independence, we will continue to be part of the coalition against Trident in the UK, but while we have the risk of Trident we should get the benefits of jobs at Rosyth and will fight any government proposals to remove refitting work from Scotland.

SNP election manifesto, 2001

It is evident from these statements that the SNP has shifted its ground on how to implement Scotland's disarmament and on how to create a favourable security environment for an independent Scotland. The Party's recent acceptance that Trident's withdrawal from Scotland would have to be negotiated and phased is especially significant. But the policy has not changed in its fundamentals. If anything, the political risks in Scotland of taking this hard line have diminished as reliance on the income from the nuclear bases, and from the repair and maintenance works that have flowed from them, has been reduced. The closure of Holy Loch, the removal of missile maintenance to the United States, the transfer of the submarine servicing facilities from Rosyth to Devonport and other moves have reduced Scotland's economic dependence on the presence of nuclear forces on its territory. Scotland also played little part in the manufacture of the Trident submarines, its reactors and major weapon systems, and would presumably be little involved in any programmes of refurbishment. Although the employment consequences of Trident's removal would still be significant, they would be very localised and carry minor electoral risks for the SNP. On top of this, the end of the Cold War has raised fresh questions about the UK's need for a nuclear deterrent: having it on Scottish soil cannot easily be depicted as an essential sacrifice.

Other Scottish attitudes towards nuclear weapons

The SNP has not been alone in opposing nuclear weapons in Scotland. Although the UK Labour Party has supported a policy of maintaining Trident (while striving for successful multilateral disarmament) since the early 1990s, its Scottish wing has consistently voted in favour of unilateral nuclear disarmament at its annual conferences, as has the Scottish Trades Union Congress. Likewise, there are Liberal Democrat MPs and MSPs in Scotland who openly dissent from the Party's support for the British nuclear deterrent, and MSPs representing the small Scottish Socialist and Green Parties have all declared themselves against nuclear weapons. Now that the Scottish Conservative Party's electoral support has been so diminished (it alone has been consistently pro-nuclear and pro-NATO), the majority political opinion in Scotland appears to favour Trident's removal.

It is also significant that the Scottish churches, which have retained greater political influence in Scotland than their counterparts in England, have unequivocally set themselves against the possession of nuclear arms. The General Assembly of the Church of Scotland has declared that 'nuclear arms, including the readiness to use them, are by nature morally and theologically wrong', and in May 1999 it passed a resolution 'noting the result of a recent national opinion poll which suggested that 85 percent of the Scottish people opposed nuclear weapons, and while reaffirming the Church of Scotland's opposition to the possession and deployment of nuclear weapons, this assembly calls upon Her Majesty's Government to abandon its nuclear defence policy'. Representing the Catholic Church, which has the second largest following in Scotland, the Catholic Bishops of Scotland repeated in February 2001 their statement of 1982 that 'if it is immoral to use nuclear weapons it is also immoral to threaten their use'.[20] The strongly anti-nuclear stance of the Iona Community, an influential ecumenical group based on the island of Iona and in Glasgow, should also be noted.

Opposition to nuclear weapons in Scotland has been given further bite by protest groups which have mounted active and well- publicised campaigns against Trident. They have been gaining in strength and effectiveness in recent years. Notable among them have been Scottish CND, which is now stronger and better funded than its English counterpart, and Trident Ploughshares which has mounted numerous actions at Faslane since 1998. Trident Ploughshares is international (if predominantly northern European) in membership and has drawn on the models of direct action that proved so effective, at least in terms of raising public awareness, at Greenham Common in the 1980s. Like its predecessor, the movement has a strong feminist and idealist slant.[21] It gained national and international notoriety almost immediately after its formation. In 1999, three members of Ploughshares (Ellen Moxley, Ulla Roder and Angie Zelter) gained access to a Trident submarine test facility on Loch Goil and were charged in Greenock Sheriff Court with having caused malicious damage. The MoD's case against them was dismissed by Sheriff Gimblett on the unusual grounds that, as nuclear weapons had been pronounced illegal by the International Court of Justice (ICJ) in its 1996 Advisory Opinion, the defendants were not committing a crime when taking actions against an illegal installation.[22] This verdict attracted widespread international attention among groups who saw it as endorsing the illegality of nuclear weapons, and as establishing a precedent that

20. Press Statement, Catholic Media Office, Glasgow, 12 February 2001.
21. See Angie Zelter, *Trident on Trial: the case for people's disarmament* (Luath Press: Edinburgh, 2001). Of the 179 pledgers to Trident Ploughshares on 30 March 2001 listed in Zelter's book, 95 were from England, 43 from Scotland, 7 each from Belgium and the Netherlands, 5 from Sweden, 4 each from Ireland and Wales, 3 from Australia, Germany and Japan, 2 from Finland, and one each from Denmark, Israel and the US.
22. The ICJ had been asked by a group of states in the UN to give an Advisory Opinion on the Use or Threat of Use of Nuclear Weapons.

could be cited in other court cases involving direct action against nuclear facilities.

The Lord Advocate of Scotland then referred the matter to the High Court of Justiciary in Edinburgh (Scotland having its own legal system), asking for a clarification of the ruling. In late March 2001, three judges ruled that Sheriff Gimblett's interpretation of the ICJ Advisory Opinion was incorrect, as were her court procedures, and that the UK's deployment of Trident was not contrary to international law.[23] Whilst those involved in direct action against Trident will probably be unable to use the same defence again, this episode demonstrates the particularity of nuclear politics in Scotland.

Whether public antagonism to nuclear weapons in Scotland is as strong as activists claim is open to question. Some observers have suggested to us that, in their experience, Scottish opinion on the nuclear issue is divided more or less as it is elsewhere in the UK, belying claims of a uniquely Scottish radicalism. What is not in doubt is that the opposition to Trident now has a political potency in Scotland that is largely absent south of the Border, although it is possible that the US missile defence proposals will re-ignite the anti-nuclear movement in England and in the Westminster Parliament. It has been the combination of a resurgent protest movement in Scotland and political devolution, the subject of the next chapter, that has made the nuclear Navy's life significantly more uncomfortable since 1998.

Where electoral politics are concerned, Trident has not been a decisive vote winner or loser in Scotland. The SNP has focused its campaigns in general elections on the usual terrain of the economy and social welfare, and on the failure of the UK to serve Scottish interests. But Trident retains its powerful symbolism and capacities for tapping into a strain of Scottish idealism and for stirring up feelings of national resentment. In party politics it also continues to serve the SNP's purpose of creating 'blue water' between itself and Labour on security issues, while challenging the allegiances of anti-nuclear Labour supporters who find themselves wedded to a pro-nuclear party. This is especially important in Glasgow where feelings on Trident ride highest and where

23. Opinion of the Appeal Court, High Court of Justiciary (the Lords Prosser, Kirkwood and Penrose) in Lord Advocate's Reference No. 1 of 2000 by Her Majesty's Advocate, Edinburgh, 30 March 2001. For a critique of the judges' opinion, see Charles Moxley, 'The unlawfulness of the United Kingdom's policy of nuclear deterrence: the invalidity of the Scottish High Court's decision in 'Zelter'', *Disarmament Diplomacy*, Issue Number 58, June 2001.

the SNP has to increase its support if it is to become the largest party in the Scottish Parliament.

At present, opposition to Trident is therefore perceived as helping the SNP's electoral ambitions and its wider goal of securing Scotland's independence. If Trident and independence were to come into conflict, however, it is less clear how SNP policy would develop. Some SNP supporters concede privately that, if Trident became an obstacle to a smooth transition to independence, they might have to back away from disarmament and accept some form of base leasing arrangement, albeit a temporary one, as the price to be paid for international recognition and a settlement with rUK. We shall return to these trade-offs in later chapters. Others argue that Trident's departure is non-negotiable, and that 'London will have to work out whether keeping Trident is worth the cost of finding it a suitable base elsewhere'.[24]

The SNP and NATO

There remains the question of the SNP's stance on NATO. Whereas the Party shifted its ground on the European Union in the 1980s from rejection to enthusiastic support, it has had much greater difficulty arriving at a credible and settled policy on NATO, largely due to the Alliance's continuing attachment to a strategy in which nuclear weapons play a prominent part. It has not been easy to reconcile the Party's principled opposition to nuclear weapons with its desire not to exclude Scotland from the institutions of collective security in which the UK currently participates with the United States and most of its European neighbours. Equally, the Party has been aware of the armed services' strong allegiance to NATO and their discomfort with a political movement that advocates Scotland's removal from it. Sensitivities were increased on all sides by the SNP's outspoken opposition to NATO's bombing of Serbia in 1999 and the unpopularity that it brought the Party.

Until the late 1960s the SNP held to the position that an independent Scotland 'would not apply for membership of NATO in its present form' while it would support 'mutual [non-nuclear] arrangements with England and other European states for defence against aggression'. In 1970, a defence policy committee established two years earlier changed tack by recommending that Scotland should seek NATO membership

24. 'SNP can rid Scotland of Trident', SNP Press Release by Defence Spokesperson Colin Campbell MSP, 11 February 2001.

in recognition of its Western and democratic orientation and its geographical position. Through the 1970s, the Party's policy was to adopt the 'Norwegian' position whereby NATO membership would be accompanied by refusal to allow the siting of nuclear weapons on Scottish soil. In the early 1980s, the policy again became aggressively anti-NATO, partly in response to the Cold War's intensification and the plans to expand missile deployments in Europe. Armed neutrality, along Swedish lines, instead became the objective.[25]

Later in the 1980s and into the 1990s, the policy again shifted. The SNP's 1992 election manifesto stated that:

> An independent Scotland will inherit the Treaty obligations of NATO membership but membership of a nuclear weapons based alliance system is inconsistent with the SNP non-nuclear defence policy. As long as NATO strategy remains based on nuclear deterrence the SNP will negotiate to disengage from the NATO command structure in a manner which does not destabilise the defence interests of Scotland or of Europe.

In the 1997 manifesto, that statement was modified to:

> An independent Scotland will have a Treaty obligation to NATO. However our opposition to nuclear defence will make our continued participation in nuclear alliances difficult. We therefore propose to negotiate a phased withdrawal from NATO but will retain military cooperation with NATO nations as a result of our other proposed international involvements ... An independent Scotland will contribute to, and benefit from, international cooperation especially in peace-keeping, training, and conflict resolution. In addition to the SNP's support for an EU Common Security and Defence Policy we would participate in the WEU, the Organisation for Security and Cooperation in Europe, the North Atlantic Cooperation Council, and Partnership for Peace.

The equivalent passage in the 2001 manifesto began with the same two sentences as the 1997 manifesto, followed by:

> ... We therefore propose to negotiate a phased withdrawal from NATO but will retain military co-operation with NATO nations through a variety of international involvements. We will contribute

25. The information in this paragraph has been drawn from interviews with former members of the SNP Defence Council.

to international security, conflict resolution, peacekeeping and disaster and humanitarian relief through the European Union Common Foreign & Security Policy and European Rapid Reaction Force, the OSCE, EAPC/PfP and the UN. An SNP government will promote the study of the theory and practice of peacekeeping, and will make its skills available to Scottish Defence Force personnel and to the forces of democratically elected nations.

The SNP's policy on NATO membership has therefore shown little consistency. The Party has hoped against hope that its problems might be resolved in due course by NATO changing its nuclear strategy (especially by adopting the no-first-use doctrine advocated by some leading politicians in Germany and other member countries), and by the development of other defence approaches and structures in Europe into which an independent Scotland could slot more easily. Talk of an EU defence capability is now greeted with enthusiasm in the SNP. In practice, however, defence structures and policies have been moving in directions that are making the SNP's choices more rather than less difficult. NATO has not adjusted its nuclear strategy (and Russia has abandoned its no-first-use policy in the meantime), and under American pressure the Alliance is having to consider the future role of controversial ballistic missile defence systems. What is more, the decision to develop a Common European Security and Defence Policy, following the Franco-British initiative at St Mâlo in 1998, seems likely to result in a closer political and military collaboration between NATO and the European Union.[26] The SNP's long-standing assumption that EU and NATO membership could be approached separately, without political linkage, currently seems mistaken.

Against this background, a resolution is expected to be submitted to the SNP's annual conference in autumn 2001 which will again seek support for NATO membership on the 'Norwegian' model.[27] The Party leaders now appear determined to separate the nuclear and NATO issues, and to overcome the problems of domestic and international credibility that have flowed from the SNP's stance on NATO. However, the Party has yet to work out how to persuade NATO members to admit Scotland to the Alliance if it were simultaneously committed to expelling from

26. For the debates on European defence structures, see François Heisbourg (ed.), *European defence: making it work*, Chaillot Paper 42, WEU Institute for Security Studies, Paris, September 2000.
27. 'SNP warms to NATO membership', *The Scotsman*, 3 July 2001.

its territory one of the only two nuclear forces allocated to NATO (the other being that of the US). As will be very evident in the next chapters, the options available to an independent Scotland would, when it came to the crunch, be heavily constrained by the interests of much more powerful states.

Chapter Three

Devolution and Trident

Although the Scottish Parliament only opened its doors in 1999, much has already happened and been achieved. Formally initiated by the UK Parliament's passage of the Scotland Act in 1998, devolution has so far involved the establishment of the Scottish Parliament and Executive, adoption of a novel electoral system and the consequent practice of coalition government, and the working out of ways in which the new institutions will function and relate to the UK Parliament and Government in London.

Yet it has now become commonplace to describe devolution as a process rather than an event or an end point, and this process looks set to affect much more than the organs of government in Scotland. A distinctive set of Scottish policies, reflecting Scotland's identifiable political culture, is beginning to emerge on education, health care, social justice and other issues. The political parties appear to be changing, the Scottish Labour and Conservative Parties becoming more distinct from the UK Parties, and the Scottish National Party becoming a more conventional political party rather than a political movement, shedding some of its radicalism on the way. As many have observed, the sense of 'Britishness' which underlay the political and cultural unity of the UK is also being profoundly affected by Scotland's devolution and by the parallel developments in Wales and Northern Ireland. In response, England has itself embarked on a painful search for identity and for means of giving the English regions their own greater autonomy. It is evident that much energy and imagination will have to be devoted to keeping the Union intact and functioning, irrespective of what happens within Scotland.

Devolution is thus both a process internal to Scotland and a process that envelops the entire UK. Matters are complicated by its interaction with another process – the developing political architecture of the European Union. How far will the EU's enlargement go, and how will it affect attitudes in Scotland, Catalonia and other 'constitutional regions' that have more developed economies and administrations than a number of the countries that are bidding for membership?[1] Will those advocating greater political integration win new powers for Brussels, or will the forces of national assertion loosen the EU instead? Where will the debates about multi-level governance, due to be the subject of the Intergovernmental Conference in Berlin in 2004, lead the Union? How will all this be affected by the still more fundamental processes of globalisation?

Where devolution will lead is therefore very unpredictable. It could mean Scotland acquiring greater autonomy and distinctiveness but remaining part of the sovereign state that is the United Kingdom, a state that may develop a more federal or confederal structure while retaining its international personality and its centre of power in London. But it could also involve Scotland slipping or tipping towards independence, whether through its (or England's) nationalistic preferences or through an inability of political institutions in Scotland and the UK to withstand the divergence of interests and policies and the tensions created by the devolutionary settlement. Intended to preserve the Union, devolution will inevitably enhance Scotland's capacities to function autonomously, and gradually (or possibly quite quickly) to develop more of the attributes of a state. The unanswerable question is whether it will at some stage cross the line into full statehood.

The next chapters will discuss the nuclear implications of full independence. Here we are concerned with the handling of nuclear weapons policy, and the management of the nuclear force, under devolution. As we shall see later, Scotland's emergence as a sovereign independent state would give rise to the starkest questions. Even so, the politics and operation of Trident in a devolved Scotland will be far from straightforward, in ways that highlight the ambiguities in and frailty of the current devolutionary arrangements. The sources of difficulty can be summarised as follows:

- political elites in Scotland are distinctly more sceptical of the merits of nuclear deterrence, and of the prestige afforded by the possession of nuclear weapons, than their counterparts in England;
- Scottish interests are not recognised in Whitehall as special and distinct from UK interests in the nuclear field, notwithstanding the entire nuclear force's location in Scotland where they often do appear special and distinct;

1. On the regions and the European Union, see Eberhard Bort and Neil Evans (eds), *Networking Europe: Essays on Regionalism and Social Democracy* (Liverpool University Press: Liverpool, 2000).

- the representative political institutions of Scotland have no say, under current arrangements, over the deployment and management of nuclear weapons on Scottish territory, yet their extensive cooperation is required so that the nuclear force can operate effectively and safely;
- there are several fuzzy areas where the boundaries of responsibility between London and Edinburgh have not been clearly drawn by the Scotland Act, and that might give rise to 'devolution issues' that would have to be settled in the courts;
- the possibility of full Scottish independence will inevitably cast a shadow over nuclear politics and policy-making under devolution, whether or not it becomes a reality.

This is not to suggest that nuclear relations *cannot* be managed successfully by London and Edinburgh over the long term. But they will require a flexibility, a completely clean safety record, and a degree of participation in decision-making that extend beyond what is currently regarded as within the bounds of political legitimacy and acceptability. Otherwise, the nuclear deterrent could be politically vulnerable even without Scotland becoming independent.

The Scotland Act and the Memorandum of Understanding

The Scotland Act of 1998 determines the powers of the Scottish Parliament and Executive which it founded.[2] The Parliament's legislative scope is defined not directly but indirectly by describing (in Schedule 5) the fields in which it *cannot* intrude – the fields that are 'reserved' to the UK Parliament in Westminster. The 'devolved' matters are therefore those that are omitted from Schedule 5.

A first point to emphasise is that the Act preserves the ultimate supremacy of the UK Parliament. The Scottish Parliament can make laws, but only on matters within the fields of legislative competence and responsibility conferred (through exclusion from the list of reserved matters) by the Act. Nothing in the Act prevents the UK Parliament from making laws for Scotland on any subject; and the UK Parliament also retains sole powers to modify the Scotland Act and the Act of Union. Likewise, the Scottish Executive can develop policy only in those areas where the

2. An excellent discussion of the Scotland Act and its background is provided by P. Lynch, *Scottish Government and Politics: An Introduction* (Edinburgh University Press: Edinburgh, 2001).

Scottish Parliament has been granted legislative responsibility. The Act therefore simultaneously creates and confines the powers of the new political institutions, while the legislative powers of the UK Parliament remain formally undiminished. In political practice, however, they *are* diminished by the Act and its derogation of powers to Edinburgh.

A second point to emphasise about the Act is that 'devolution issues', that is questions over whether competences and functions properly reside in Edinburgh or London, are to be referred for judicial decision if they cannot be settled through discussion by the two administrations. This is a departure from the tradition of governance in the UK which shies away from judicial control.[3] Under the Act, matters in dispute may be referred to either the Scottish or the English and Welsh judiciary (procedures are described in Schedule 6), even if the expectation is that most issues will be settled in the Scottish courts. The final arbiter is the Judicial Committee of the Privy Council.

The Scotland Act reflected the expectation that London and Edinburgh would develop a strong cooperative relationship, take care to avoid encroaching on each other's political territory, and endeavour to settle differences before they came anywhere near the courts. That expectation was spelt out in a Memorandum of Understanding agreed by the UK Government and the Ministers who headed the Scottish Executive, the Cabinet of the National Assembly of Wales and the Northern Ireland Executive Committee.[4] The Memorandum commits the administrations to 'the principle of good communication with each other'; to 'give appropriate consideration to the views of the other administrations'; 'where appropriate, to establish arrangements that allow for policies for which responsibility is shared to be drawn up and developed jointly between the administrations'; and 'to work together, where appropriate, on matters of mutual interest'. It also states that:

> The United Kingdom Parliament retains authority to legislate on any issue, whether devolved or not. It is ultimately for Parliament to

3. Judicial control was adopted on Scottish insistence that the UK Government should have nothing resembling a governor-general role on policy issues. In addition, whenever the UK set up a federal constitution within former colonies (e.g. Canada and India), it was the courts, and ultimately the Privy Council, which decided disputes about the proper distribution of powers. Also influential was the role which the UK Government was prepared to give to the courts in the Human Rights Act to determine constitutional-type issues.
4. The 'Memorandum of Understanding and supplementary agreements' can be found on http://www.scotland.gov.uk/library2/memorandum/mous–02.htm

> decide what use to make of that power. However, the UK Government will proceed in accordance with the convention that the UK Parliament would not normally legislate with regard to devolved matters except with the agreement of the devolved legislature. The devolved administration will be responsible for seeking such agreement as may be required for this purpose on an approach from the UK Government.[5]

As things have turned out, the boundaries of responsibility set out in the Act have proved less clear-cut than anticipated. Significant changes to the Scottish Parliament's and Executive's powers have already taken place, if mainly on the fringes of the reserved policy areas. The changes have been introduced partly through Orders to amend Schedule 5 (which defines the matters that are reserved to London), and partly through the device of the Sewel Motion.[6] Prepared by the Scottish Ministers, such Motions invite the Scottish Parliament to agree that a UK bill (or part thereof) affecting a devolved area of policy should extend to Scotland once enacted. Sewel Motions preserve the proprieties of devolution while deferring to London on the legislative front where a common interest is served. They also have the effect, sometimes to the chagrin of London, of asserting that certain policy matters are devolved when UK Ministers and Departments may not take the same view of the boundaries of responsibility as set out in the Scotland Act (the Motion on the Ministry of Defence Police cited below was one such instance). By July 2001, no fewer than 23 Sewel Motions had been adopted by the Scottish Parliament.

To give just one example, a Sewel Motion was approved by the Scottish Parliament on 8 March 2001 when the Armed Forces Bill (a Westminster Bill) would have extended the jurisdiction of MoD Police beyond defence land and property in certain circumstances (in the event, the provisions were dropped from the Bill to secure its passage before the General Election). The Motion brought before the Parliament proposed:

> That the Scottish Parliament agrees the principles contained in the

5. 'Memorandum of Understanding and supplementary agreements', paragraph 13.
6. The Motion was named after Lord Sewel who, when Under-Secretary of State in the Scottish Office, announced in Westminster that the UK Parliament would not normally legislate on devolved matters without the consent of the Scottish Parliament. Section 30 of the Scotland Act provides the powers to amend the boundaries of reserved matters. Any changes require the consent of both Parliaments (under Schedule 8 of the Act).

provisions of the Armed Forces Bill as they relate to the Ministry of Defence Police in Scotland and that the Scottish Ministers should consent to the measures on jurisdiction being commenced in Scotland, and agrees that the relevant provisions to achieve these ends in the Bill should be considered by the UK Parliament.

The scope and implementation of the Scotland Act are therefore intended to be elastic, although they can only be as elastic as the political authorities in London and Edinburgh – and ultimately the courts – will allow. There is a common assumption in Scotland that the Scottish Parliament's legislative powers will gradually be extended, and might have to be quite substantially extended if the UK Government were faced with a rising nationalist tide. The SNP now talks explicitly about 'completing the powers' of the Scottish Parliament. Defence and foreign policy would probably be among the last fields in which significant powers were transferred to Edinburgh. We shall see below, however, that the operation of Trident and its bases requires support from civil as well as military agencies, some of which already answer to the Executive in Edinburgh. An extension of powers in the civil field might therefore increase London's dependence on the cooperation of the Scottish Parliament and Executive, and by the same token increase their scope for influencing nuclear activities in Scotland.

Reservation of defence and foreign policy: the Concordats

Defence and foreign policy is unequivocally reserved to the UK Government in the Scotland Act. Where foreign policy is concerned, the Act reserves to London 'international relations, including relations with territories outside the United Kingdom, the European Communities (and their institutions) and other international organisations, regulation of international trade, and international development assistance and cooperation'.[7] This has not prevented the Scottish Parliament and Executive from taking some steps, with London's consent, to increase their international profile and representation. The entitlement to do so is elaborated in the Concordat on International Relations which commits the Foreign and Commonwealth Office to promote Scottish interests where

7. Scotland Act 1998, Schedule 5, Part I, Paragraph 7 (1). The same paragraph states that 'observing and implementing international obligations, obligations under the Human Rights Convention and obligations under Community law' are *not* reserved matters.

appropriate, commits the UK Government to consult with Scottish Ministers where international developments have a bearing on devolved matters, and creates the space for some participation by the Executive in foreign policy-making (notably where devolved matters such as education, fisheries and the environment have international dimensions). Other international initiatives since 1998 have included the opening of Scotland House in Brussels with a full-time staff to handle EU affairs, the appointment of a full-time Scottish representative at the UK Embassy in Washington, and the Executive's joining the Flanders Group and endorsement of its 'Political Declaration of the International Regions' in Brussels in May 2001.[8]

On defence policy, the Scotland Act's pronouncements are still more emphatic. The reserved matters identified in the Act include:

(a) the defence of the realm,
(b) the naval, military or air forces of the Crown, including reserve forces,
(c) visiting forces,
(d) international headquarters and defence organisations . . .[9]

Whereas the Concordat on International Relations runs to just over one page, the Concordat between the Scottish Ministers and the Secretary of State for Defence runs to eleven. It emphasises that 'all matters relating to the defence of the UK remain the direct responsibility of the UK Government' and enjoins Scottish Ministers to 'take into account the need for the unimpeded conduct of the defence of the UK, and the interests and responsibilities of the Secretary of State for Defence and the Armed Forces, when framing and implementing Scottish legislation or otherwise undertaking actions and functions within their competence', while enjoining the Secretary of State to take similar account of the interests, rights and responsibilities of the Scottish Ministers.

Unlike the Concordat on International Relations, the Defence Concordat devotes considerable space to an elaboration of the 'matters

8. The members of the Flanders Group are Bavaria, Catalonia, Flanders, North-Rhine Westphalia, Salzburg, Wallonia and now Scotland. The declaration demanded *inter alia* that the 'constitutional regions' be allowed to participate directly in the preparatory work for the Intergovernmental Conference in Berlin in 2004, and generally sought to promote discussion of multi-level governance in the European Union.
9. Scotland Act 1998, Schedule 5, Part I, Paragraph 9 (1).

thought likely to be included within the reservation'.[10] Twenty-eight fields of reserved activity are described in some detail in an Annex. They range from command and control to training, from the conduct of military courts to the management of war graves, from the disclosure of information to the use of civilian installations, from the Ministry of Defence Police to the deployment of armed forces, and from the power to requisition property in emergencies to 'the installation, operation and decommissioning of any nuclear installation or device for the purposes of the armed forces of the Crown'.[11]

This first section of the Annex is followed by a second which identifies 'areas of cooperation between the MoD and the Scottish Executive'. Its five pages are subdivided into 'Matters affecting defence activities', 'Organisations and Personnel', 'Information' and 'Ownership of Land and Property'. The headings include:

- radioactivity, explosives and other dangerous materials (use, storage, carriage, disposal);
- nuclear accident response and other emergency planning;
- matters affecting training;
- general policing and security matters;
- shipping;
- re-organisation of defence establishments;
- freedom of information legislation, and exemptions from the provision of information or powers of entry on grounds of national security;
- environmental issues;
- land-use planning; and
- building control and safety.

The Defence Concordat therefore indicates the wide range of activities in which cooperation is required between the Ministry of Defence and the Scottish Executive and the various organisations under their jurisdictions.

10. The tentative nature of this stipulation reflects the Concordat's status as a non-binding 'guide to normal working practices'.
11. 'Concordat between the Scottish Ministers and the Secretary of State for Defence', Annex: Section 1, undated. This and other concordats can be found on http://www.scotland.gov.uk/concordats

The reality is that the UK nuclear force cannot now be operated without the cooperation of a wide range of public authorities in Scotland, including the Scottish Executive and Parliament. The Concordat also confirms that there are large areas of policy and activity where the boundaries of responsibility between the Scottish and UK authorities are not clearly defined. On such an apparently mundane issue as land-use planning, responsibility for the planning process may lie in Scotland while the policies leading to an application are reserved to London, giving rise to plenty of scope for dispute.[12] There is the added complication that the Ministry of Defence enjoys exemptions from legislation enacted in either the Scottish or the UK Parliaments, and the further complication that Scottish and English law are distinctive. As the Concordat itself acknowledges:

> In view of the special circumstances of defence, legislation has conferred a large number of exemptions, privileges and powers on the Secretary of State for Defence, the Ministry of Defence, the Armed Forces or other defence organisations. It is recognised that there will be cases where legislation enacted in the Scottish Parliament will also need to take similar account of these special circumstances. Many of these are in fields of responsibility devolved to the Scottish Parliament (for example, environmental law, building and fire regulations, land use and access and road safety).[13]

The nuclear force and its bases are the most substantial and complex military assets north of the Border. As such, they require the most wide-ranging cooperation from the Scottish Executive and the institutions that answer to it (such as police, fire, medical and local authorities). Responsibility for the nuclear force and for the policies underpinning it is nevertheless thoroughly ring-fenced by the Scotland Act. The Scottish Executive has no involvement in the running of Trident and its bases, nor in the development of nuclear policy; and the Executive has no office in NATO, or participation in UK delegations to NATO, to parallel its growing engagement with the European Union. Nuclear weapons are a reserved matter, and the Ministry of Defence has shown little desire to bring Scottish institutions into the policy fold.

---

12. A current issue that is perplexing administrators and lawyers is the construction of mobile telephone masts in Scotland. Proposals to build nuclear power stations could be even more problematic. 'Telecommunications and wireless telegraphy' and 'energy policy' are reserved matters.
13. 'Concordat between the Scottish Ministers and the Secretary of State for Defence', paragraphs 7 and 8.

In principle, specifically Scottish interests in the nuclear as in other reserved fields of policy are represented in the UK Government by the Secretary of State for Scotland who has retained a seat in the UK Cabinet.[14] This does not appear to mean much in practice, although it will be evident below that the Secretary of State has a nominal role in nuclear safety and environmental regulation. The Secretary of State is not a member of the Defence Overseas Policy (Official) Committee, the Cabinet Committee which is the prime mover on nuclear policy in the UK Government. Membership of the Cabinet is no substitute as nuclear decisions are rarely brought before it.[15] Nor does the Ministry of Defence involve the Scotland Office in nuclear planning.[16]

Given the extraordinary character of nuclear weapons, it is natural that any state will seek to exert absolute control over their deployment and usage, even if that causes difficulties in relations with the regions or countries where they are located. The UK Government's monopoly is reinforced in the Scotland Act which grants it 'sole control of nuclear, biological and chemical weapons of mass destruction', the only weapons singled out for attention in the Act. But the determination to centralise political control extends into aspects where there are indeed pronounced Scottish interests pertaining to public health and safety. As the nuclear force's presence in the Clyde is often seen as placing the Scottish people at particular risk, those interests are less easily sidelined.

14. For a discussion of 'Scotland at Westminster' after 1998, see Peter Lynch, *Scottish Government and Politics, op. cit.*, Chapter 8. There is an expectation in London that the posts of Secretary of State for Scotland, Wales and Northern Ireland will be amalgamated into a single post of Secretary of State for Devolved Governance (or some such title) if and when peace in Northern Ireland is finally secured.
15. A recent government document states that: 'within the United Kingdom, constitutional responsibility for the formulation of nuclear weapons policy resides with the Cabinet. In practice, however, policy decisions relating to the acquisition, deployment and potential use of nuclear weapons were often taken by small groups of senior ministers meeting in ad hoc Cabinet committees ... Once political approval for a project had been granted, other government departments were involved on a 'need to know basis''. See *Operational Selection Policy on Nuclear Weapons Policy 1967–1998*, Public Record Office, Kew, April 2001, paragraph 3.1. A draft circulated for public consultation in December 2000 contained more forthright observations on internal secrecy.
16. The Scotland Office is based in London. A small part of the former Scottish Office (most of which was spun off into the Scottish Executive), it provides administrative support to the Secretary of State for Scotland.

The complex measures applied to safety and environmental regulation at Faslane and Coulport are described in Appendix A. It shows that such regulation is primarily handled by the Ministry of Defence in conjunction with regulatory bodies located south of the Border where the main competences reside; and that the London-based Secretary of State for Scotland, rather than the Edinburgh-based First Minister, is given primacy in protecting Scottish interests where safety is concerned. This follows the Scotland Act's limitation of the Scottish Parliament's and Executive's roles in regard to public health to 'matters which are not reserved', and its reservation to London of matters pertaining to 'nuclear energy and nuclear installations, including ... nuclear safety, security and safeguards' and to the transport of radioactive material.[17]

However, London's sway is not total in these respects. The Scotland Act makes an exception of radioactive emissions from nuclear sites for whose regulation the Scottish Environment Protection Agency (SEPA), a Non-Departmental Public Body answering to the Scottish Executive, has responsibility.[18] Here it is worth quoting the relevant paragraph in Annex A:

> The discharge of radioactive material is regulated by the Scottish Environment Protection Agency (SEPA). The discharge and exposure criteria are identical to those applied in the civil field. As MoD is exempt from the Radioactive Substances Act of 1993 (RSA93), there is no statutory requirement to honour its procedures. In practice, however, MoD behaves 'as if' it were subject to the Act, and discharges are agreed with SEPA using letters of consent.[19] One consequence is that changes to discharge agreements are now put out to full public consultation as if there were no Crown exemption to RSA93.

This description reveals that two trends have been affecting regulatory

17. Scotland Act 1998, Schedule 5, Sections H2, D4 and E5.
18. SEPA is 'sponsored' by the Environment Protection Unit in the Scottish Executive's Environment and Rural Affairs Department. Its functions at Faslane, Chapelcross, Coulport, Rosyth and Dounreay are briefly described in *Radioactivity in Food and the Environment, 1999*, RIFE–5, Food Standards Agency and Scottish Environment Protection Agency, September 2000. This Report also provides information on radiation levels at these sites.
19. Because the Crown has exemption from the law, MoD is not criminally liable if it fails to comply with RSA93. However, SEPA can make it suffer the embarrassment of the Court of Session in Edinburgh declaring 'unlawful any act or omission of the Crown which constitutes such a contravention'. See RSA93, section 42, paragraph 3.

practices at nuclear sites. One is the passage of certain regulatory responsibilities to a devolved institution. The other is the application of civil regulatory standards and procedures to military sites, and the MoD's *de facto* waiving of Crown exemption so that this can happen. The second trend has in recent times been much the more significant for the MoD. Beginning in the 1970s, the MoD's rights to regulate itself have been progressively narrowed in an attempt to raise standards, increase regulatory efficiency and limit its exemptions from the law. Appendix A shows that this 'civilianising' of regulatory activity involves the work carried out by the Nuclear Installations Inspectorate (NII) as well as SEPA, despite both organisations having to agree special arrangements with the MoD in order to perform their duties.

The evidence presented to us during interviews suggests that a great strengthening of safety and environmental standards and practices at the nuclear sites has taken place as a result. While accepted as necessary, the cost to the Ministry of Defence and the Armed Services has been felt in a certain loss of autonomy, in the resources and time required to comply with the new regime, and in exposure to greater public scrutiny. There is a sense in which they have suffered a double whittling away of their powers of exemption: they have had to concede ground to civil authorities in the UK administration; and they have had to accept some encroachment (albeit still minor) in consequence of the devolution of regulatory responsibility to the Scottish Executive.

The role of the Scottish Parliament

The Scottish Parliament opened its doors in July 1999. In terms of party representation, its complexion is both similar to and different from the UK Parliament.[20] Labour is the largest party in both Parliaments, gaining 40.7% of the 2001 UK-wide vote for Westminster and 38.8% of the 1999 vote for the Scottish Parliament. A plurality of the vote was enough to give Labour an overwhelming Commons majority on the 'first past the post' system, but the system of proportional representation north of the Border deprived it of a majority (it holds 55 out of 129 seats), forcing it into coalition with the Liberal Democrat Party (17 seats). Whereas the Conservative Party was much the largest opposition party in the UK Parliament, its place was taken in the Scottish Parliament by the Scottish

20. Out of 659 seats in the UK Parliament, the Labour Party won 413 in the June 2001 General Election, the Conservative Party 166, the Liberal Democrat Party 52, and others 28.

National Party (35 seats, the Conservatives holding 19). Three seats won by the Green and Scottish Socialist Parties and an Independent made up the remainder.

The balance of opinion in the Scottish Parliament is more clearly anti-nuclear than in Westminster. The SNP has maintained an unremitting hostility towards nuclear weapons, and there are individuals in both the Labour and Liberal Democrat Parties who share its views. Indeed, it is not easy to find strong advocates of nuclear deterrence anywhere in the Scottish Parliament outside the Conservative Party. Insofar as Trident has Scottish political support, it is to be found amongst MPs in the UK Parliament rather than MSPs in the Scottish Parliament.

The strong opinions in Scotland on Trident and nuclear weapons have inevitably spilled over into the Scottish Parliament. Motions on Faslane and Trident have become commonplace, and a Cross-Party Group on Nuclear Disarmament with membership drawn from all Parties (excepting the Conservative Party) has been formally recognised by the Parliament.[21] Despite this, the Parliament has not been as active on nuclear issues as might have been expected from the strength of feeling among some of its Members. The Parliament possesses the right to debate reserved issues, but it has so far kept nuclear weapons off its agenda. Why is this the case?

The most important reason is that the Parliament has been preoccupied with other immediate issues that do fall within its competence – establishing its working practices, debating and legislating on devolved matters such as education and social welfare, and generally settling into the novel business of running a Parliament and engaging in parliamentary politics in Scotland. Another reason is that the UK Labour Party's policy is to retain the nuclear deterrent and all that goes with it, including the bases in Scotland. As the Labour Party currently dominates the Scottish as well as the UK Parliament, the Party in Scotland will not promote debates on policies on reserved matters which it has established at the UK level. On devolved matters the Scottish Labour Party has on occasion been prepared to row its own boat, but not so far on reserved matters. The same applies to the Liberal Democrat Party, Labour's coalition partner, which is mildly if uncomfortably supportive of Trident in Westminster. Both Parties may also be fearful that a nuclear debate would expose divisions in their ranks; and they will be aware that, while opinion polls

21. The Group currently has 18 MSPs amongst its members (12 SNP, two Labour, two Liberal Democrat and one each from the Green and the Scottish Socialist Parties).

regularly show a majority of the public opposed to Trident, nuclear issues are unlikely to be influential in elections in normal circumstances.

Even the SNP has been reluctant to press for a debate on nuclear weapons, mainly for tactical reasons (it has not been shy of using its allotted Parliamentary time to mount debates on other reserved matters – 19 had been held by July 2001). It has not wished to provoke a debate that could result in Labour and Liberal Democrat MSPs voting on party lines, thereby undermining its claim that political opinion in Scotland strongly favours Trident's removal from the Clyde. It is aware that it can only prevail in debates on reserved matters where there is a powerful common interest across the Scottish political spectrum in defying London (one such bone of contention may be the redrawing of constituency boundaries – a reserved matter – when the Boundary Commission next addresses its task).[22] Furthermore, a threat of sorts hangs over the Scottish Parliament: although it has rights to debate reserved matters, it would risk retaliation from the UK Government on other fronts if it made a habit of doing so. Yet another reason for the SNP leaders' hesitancy in highlighting the nuclear issue at this time may be their desire to have NATO membership adopted by the Party before it addresses Trident frontally. If NATO membership had not already become Party policy, it would face accusations of being weak on security and out of touch with 'the real world', even if this latter accusation could still be levelled at a policy that supported NATO membership while seeking Trident's early and unconditional expulsion.

Having been unsuccessful in pressing for Parliamentary debate on a reserved issue, anti-nuclear groups have tried to engage the Scottish Parliament by filing petitions. The Parliament, in its keenness to be accessible to the public and responsive to public concerns, has established procedures for allowing petitions to be brought before it (there are no equivalent mechanisms at present in the UK Parliament).[23] The petitioner can request the Parliament to 'take a view on a matter of public interest or concern; or amend existing legislation and introduce new legislation'.

---

22. It is predicted that the Boundary Commission will recommend reducing the number of UK parliamentary constituencies in Scotland from the current 72 to 57. Under a rule laid out in the Scotland Act, the number of Scottish parliamentary seats would be reduced in consequence (from 129 to just over 100). There is a broad interest in the Scottish Parliament in holding the number of MSPs at or close to the present number.
23. On the submission of public petitions, see http://scottish.parliament.uk/official_report/cttee/petit99–00/pg-c.htm

Petitions are submitted to the Parliament's Public Petitions Committee which may, among several courses of action, forward the petition to the relevant Parliamentary Committee for its consideration, forward it to the Scottish Executive for consideration or response, or recommend to the Parliamentary Bureau that it be debated at a meeting of the Parliament.

By July 2001, five petitions had been submitted on issues relating to Trident and Faslane. The first three were submitted in late 1999 in the wake of Sheriff Gimblett's acquittal of the three protestors on the grounds that they were not committing a criminal act when damaging a Trident-related facility when nuclear weapons had, in the court's view, been pronounced illegal by the International Court of Justice (see Chapter 2).[24] After seeking clarification of the legal position from the Lord Advocate, resulting in the High Court's opinion that Sheriff Gimblett was incorrect, the Petitions Committee decided that no further action was warranted.

In February and May 2001, two petitions were submitted by the Scottish Campaign for Nuclear Disarmament (CND), the first 'calling for the Scottish Parliament to ask the Scottish Executive to initiate a review of Emergency Planning measures for nuclear submarine accidents in Scotland to ensure there is adequate protection for the local population and the environment.' The Committee forwarded it to the Scottish Executive which responded by tabling a copy of the 'Faslane safety plan' (see Appendix A) that Argyll and Bute Council had drawn up with the Navy's assistance.[25] The Committee then decided to submit materials received from outside bodies to the Parliament's Justice 2 Committee for consideration.[26] The second petition followed on from the first, calling on the Parliament to 'investigate the adverse consequences of the location and operation of Trident and associated nuclear weapon systems in Scotland in relation to its powers, and in particular to examine the Faslane Safety Plan and to publicise its findings'. The Petitions Committee again passed it to the Justice 2 Committee, asking 'whether it would wish to carry out an investigation of the nature requested by the petitions'.

This is where matters stand at present. Scottish CND is here probing

24. Petitions PE31, PE34 and PE35.
25. The Committee also sought the views of responsible local authorities and of the Steering Group of the Nuclear-Free Local Authorities.
26. There are two Justice Committees, formed to share the workload, with the identical remit to 'consider and report on matters relating to the administration of civil and criminal justice, the reform of the civil and criminal law and such other matters as fall within the responsibility of the Minister for Justice'.

an issue in which the Parliament and Executive have a recognised interest – that of emergency planning. That interest was acknowledged by the UK Government in the Concordat between the Health and Safety Executive (a UK body) and the Scottish Executive. The Concordat states that nuclear safety 'is a reserved matter. However, the Scottish Ministers have an interest arising from the part they would play in the event of a nuclear incident – they have, for instance, policy responsibility for the civil emergency services in Scotland – and because of the connection between nuclear safety and the protection of the environment, which is a devolved matter'.

The more we have studied the Scotland Act, the more we have become aware of Whitehall's deliberate attempt to clad it in a suit of armour that prevents any Scottish intervention in nuclear policy. One piece of that armour which has yet to be mentioned is the Secretary of State's right to prohibit a Bill from the Scottish Parliament being submitted for Royal Assent if he or she 'has reasonable grounds to believe [that it] would be incompatible with any international obligations or the interests of defence or national security'. This is one of only two circumstances in which matters in the Act are subject to political rather than judicial control, and where the UK Government has retained a 'governor-general' role.[27]

Yet there are chinks in the armour, and finding and exploiting these chinks has become a priority for Trident's opponents. Whether they will have any joy with their petitions remains to be seen. One doubts that the Justice Committee has much 'wish' to carry out an investigation, not least because it might expose the Parliament's difficulties in compelling the responsible persons and organisations to give evidence. But if it chose to do so, the Scottish Parliament and Executive would be drawn inexorably into the nuclear debate. There is currently no great appetite in Edinburgh for getting into an argument with London on nuclear issues, but the Parliament's discharge of its public responsibilities could lead to this outcome.

The role of the UK Parliament

There is, however, another established route that can be followed to open such issues to public scrutiny. This is for Scottish and other MPs

27. The political powers to prohibit are defined in Section 35 of the Act. The second field in which the UK Government has retained powers of intervention concerns modification of the law on reserved matters.

to persuade Select Committees of the UK Parliament to conduct an inquiry. Throughout the 1970s and 1980s, the UK nuclear weapons programme was the subject of repeated inquiries by Select Committees, on which Scottish MPs were usually well represented.[28] A recent and pertinent example of Scottish interests being represented in Westminster was the Inquiry conducted by the specially constituted Select Committee on the Armed Forces Bill which was chaired, probably coincidentally, by a Scottish MP (Rachel Squires).[29] As noted earlier, provisions in the Bill proposed extending the MoD Police's powers of arrest outside MoD property. The Select Committee recommended several amendments to the Bill on this count, partly in response to evidence given by Colin McKerracher, Assistant Chief Constable of Strathclyde Police. As things turned out, these particular proposals were dropped from the Bill, but the Committee's actions illustrate the scope for attending to Scottish interests through the UK Parliament which has, after all, a responsibility to protect them.

This brings us to the broader issue of the UK Parliament's role in regard to Trident's location in Scotland. Policy on the nuclear force is reserved to London, and it is the Westminster Parliament's responsibility to hold the UK Government and the Ministry of Defence to account in this as in other reserved fields. The Westminster Parliament exists to represent and protect the interests of *all* the peoples of the Union, including the Scottish people. Yet it can often seem a distant place when viewed from north of the Border, and that feeling of distance seems to be growing as the UK Parliament becomes less involved in Scottish affairs, and as the Edinburgh Parliament takes charge of devolved matters. The expected reduction in the number of Scottish MPs, and the ending of the temporary practice whereby Scottish politicians have held seats

28. The House of Commons Defence Committee published reports on an annual basis into the progress of the Trident programme between 1981 and 1995, including written memoranda from the MoD, evidence presented by outside experts and interested parties, and transcripts of written oral evidence given by Ministers and senior officials. These enquiries ranged widely, examining strategic and arms control implications as well as considerations of safety and cost-effectiveness. See, for example, 'Progress of the Trident Programme', *Eighth Report from the Defence Committee* (1994–1995) (HMSO: London, July 1995). The Public Accounts Committee published a further four reports on aspects of the Trident project during the same period. See, for example, 'Ministry of Defence: Management of the Trident Works Programme', *Twenty Sixth Report of the Committee of Public Accounts 1994/95* (HMSO: London, June 1995).
29. 'Special Report from the Select Committee on the Armed Forces Bill' (The Stationery Office: London, March 2001).

in both Parliaments, can only reinforce this trend. The Westminster Parliament will have its work cut out to maintain trust that it is indeed representing the interests of the Scottish people, especially on an issue like Trident where Scots perceive that they have special concerns.

Much will depend on factors that are outside the formal division of powers between the two Parliaments. The UK Parliament and Government are already reacting in unanticipated ways to the anomalies created by devolution. In UK Government departments whose remit is limited to England (or England and Wales), Scottish MPs are now rarely appointed as Ministers; and Scottish MPs appear to be becoming more hesitant, in informal response to Tam Dalyell's West Lothian Question, about voting in Westminster on issues pertinent just to England and Wales.[30] A similar trend may increasingly be seen in the membership of Select Committees. Although such a limitation has not (to our knowledge) been institutionalised in any way, it may nevertheless have important long-term consequences. It could, for example, make Westminster increasingly unattractive to aspiring Scottish politicians, for whom Edinburgh may be seen as offering more opportunities. An expectation that further powers will be devolved to Scotland could only accelerate this trend.

Yet the presence of a contingent of high-quality Scottish MPs (of all parties) at Westminster is now more important than ever if Scotland is to be properly represented in those areas (including defence and foreign affairs) that remain a UK responsibility. Scotland has been well served in this regard in recent years, with figures such as Malcolm Rifkind (Conservative), Menzies Campbell (Liberal Democrat), Robin Cook and George Robertson (both Labour) all making a prominent contribution to UK debates on defence and security policy. In a Parliament in which Scottish MPs hold only 9% of the seats, it will be hard to maintain the level and quality of contribution represented by this generation. If Scottish MPs were seen to be marginalised in Westminster, the Scottish political community might be more inclined to turn to the Edinburgh Parliament as a voice for its concerns, even on matters such as defence which were outside its formal remit.

The Scottish MPs of the future will therefore have a particular responsibility to ensure, whether through the Select Committee system or by other means, that the UK Parliament is casting a wakeful eye over the

30. The West Lothian Question refers to the inequities caused when Scottish MPs have rights to vote on English and Welsh issues in the Westminster Parliament, but English and Welsh MPs have no rights to vote on Scottish issues in the Scottish Parliament.

management of Trident and its bases in Scotland, that it is alert to any difficulties that may arise between the administrations in London and Edinburgh, and that it is generally sensitive to Scottish concerns. Could they even establish mechanisms for sustaining a dialogue with MSPs on nuclear issues where the boundaries of responsibility are not clearly drawn, or where particularly close cooperation is required between the administrations in London and Edinburgh? Might MPs and MSPs even find ways of bringing the Committee systems together to inquire into such matters as safety and emergency planning at Faslane and Coulport? Somehow, confidence has to be established that Parliamentary accountability is functioning effectively in regard to both reserved and devolved matters and in the margins between them.

Trident's vulnerability in a devolved Scotland

We have seen that the Memorandum of Understanding and the Concordats commit the Scottish and UK administrations to work together, within the framework of the Scotland Act, to implement policies and laws. 'Effective and efficient relationships between the administrations ... must be an everyday part of the business of government across the UK.'[31] Trident and its bases cannot function without that effective and efficient relationship. Although devolution has complicated the task of running the nuclear deterrent, it has not yet frustrated it. If present trends continue, cooperation rather than confrontation will probably remain the hallmark of relations between Edinburgh and London in the nuclear field.

There are two circumstances in which this could all change. The first is the occurrence of a serious accident or 'incident' involving nuclear matériel at or in the vicinity of Faslane or Coulport. If that happened, the Scottish Parliament and Ministers, of whichever political complexion, would come under intense public pressure to intervene and to open Trident's stay in Scotland to public debate. The recent uproar in Gibraltar over the docking of a damaged British nuclear hunter-killer submarine has shown how rebellious local and regional governments can become if they feel unable to guarantee their citizens' protection from harm, and if they believe that they are being denied accurate information about the risks to which people are being subjected.

In particular, the realisation is beginning to dawn in some government

31. 'Devolution in Practice: A Checklist for Officials', brochure prepared by The Cabinet Office, Scottish Executive, National Assembly of Wales, Northern Ireland Executive, undated.

circles that, independence or no independence, Scotland's tolerance of Faslane and Coulport is now contingent upon the very highest levels of safety in the operation of the nuclear installations and of the Trident force. What is more, a serious incident could do more than jeopardise the deterrent. It could open deep rifts between Edinburgh and London, strengthening nationalist sentiment amongst the general public, perhaps to the extent of threatening the Union itself (it is worth recalling the effects of the Chernobyl accident on the Ukraine's determination to gain self-government). This is why the efforts discussed earlier to establish the highest possible standards of safety at HM Naval Base Clyde – although strictly speaking a reserved matter – are so crucial to future relations between the two capitals.

The second circumstance in which Trident would become vulnerable is if the political complexions of the Scottish and UK Parliaments changed, ending the near-unity of interests brought about by the Labour Party's dominance of both places since 1999. Agreement would become more difficult on a swathe of issues in a period of 'cohabitation', for example involving a Labour-led administration in Edinburgh and a Conservative administration in London, or an SNP-led administration in Scotland and a Labour or Conservative administration in London. In such circumstances, one or both administrations might seek to exploit their differences for party-political advantage. Areas where boundaries between reserved and devolved matters are not clearly drawn could be a particular focus of such disputes, and many issues could be deliberately brought before the courts. The Scottish Executive (especially but not only if SNP-led) might even seek to challenge the legitimacy of the UK Government on fully reserved matters, hoping among other things to gain further transfers of authority to itself.

It would nevertheless be a mistake to assume that confrontation on nuclear issues would inevitably follow if the SNP were in government north of the Border while lacking sufficent support to risk a referendum on independence. One can envisage it being torn in two directions. On the one hand, its priority would be to establish itself as a Party able to govern effectively. Even while arguing for the Scotland Act's amendment, it would still have to govern under its aegis. Reserved matters would remain reserved matters. Furthermore, if the SNP wished to use its time in office to build its domestic and international credentials, it would have to be careful not to break legal commitments under the Act or take steps that might ruffle feathers abroad.

On the other hand, the SNP would probably be sorely tempted, short of confronting the UK Government on Trident, to make life as difficult as possible for it. It could, to give just two examples, initiate a debate in the Scottish Parliament on the UK's – and Scotland's – international obligations under the Nuclear Non-Proliferation Treaty (see Chapter 4), or on the legality of the use or threat of use of nuclear weapons. Or it could authorise the independent review of safety at Faslane and Coulport for which Trident's opponents have been pressing.

There is therefore likely to be less certainty over the stability of the nuclear arrangements if Party mixes change substantially in one or both of the two Parliaments. It would be surprising, given the see-saws in Party fortunes in Britain's parliamentary history, if this did not happen more than once during Trident's lifetime.

Trident's replacement and Scotland's consent

There remains the question of how Trident's replacement might be handled in a Scotland with devolved government. Whether, when and how to replace Trident will depend on many factors, some internal to the UK, some external (the replacement timetable is examined in Appendix B). They include the nature and severity of threats to UK and European security, technical performance of the submarines and their proneness to wear and tear, the outcome of international debates about nuclear deterrence and missile defence, and the decisions taken by the United States on the replacement of its own Trident missile systems (especially relevant due to the servicing there of UK missiles which we discussed in Chapter 1). Because of the long time required to plan, design, manufacture and test such complex weapon systems, initial replacement decisions may have to be taken up to a couple of decades before the weapons are deployed. If Trident had an operational lifetime of 30–40 years, as has often been anticipated, a choice would have to be made around 2010.[32]

The Scotland Act places no obligation on the UK Government to involve or consult with Scottish Ministers when decisions are being taken on reserved matters that affect Scottish interests. The Memorandum of Understanding enjoins the Government to consult with Scottish Ministers in advance of such decisions, but it is not binding. Where nuclear weapons are concerned, the Memorandum provides grounds for waiving even that injunction when it states that 'it is recognised that there are

32. See Appendix B for further discussion.

certain areas of Government action – Budget proposals and national security are two examples – in which, as a matter of existing practice, advance notification does not take place or is very limited. These practices are unaffected by devolution'.

In our view, it would be very risky to make a decision to replace Trident with an equivalent system on the Clyde merely through a process of Ministerial consultation, still less through Whitehall's fiat. Too much has changed for the closed and centralised procedures followed in the 1970s (for both Chevaline and Polaris replacement) to be repeated without substantial political fallout. A procedure would therefore have to be found which would bind the Scottish polity into supporting the new system over its lifetime, while at the same time not eroding the principle that nuclear policy is a reserved matter.

This would not be easy, and much would depend on the party composition of the two Parliaments at the time that a decision was taken. The Scottish Parliament has rights to mount its own debate on Trident's replacement, and it might be particularly prone to reject any proposals that came from a Conservative-led government in Westminster. Any UK Government would be extremely reluctant to concede to Scotland a *de facto* veto over the replacement decision, even if it could be assured in advance that the vote would be favourable, for fear of the precedent it might set for all reserved matters. If Scotland were to be given a veto over Trident replacement, it might also seek such a veto over other matters of critical importance to the Scottish people such as whether or not to go to war, or whether to transfer new powers to the European Union. Yet, in contrast to most other issues of foreign policy, the siting of the UK's nuclear force at Faslane gives Scotland a unique interest that is not shared by the other regions and nations of the UK. Moreover, the existence of a distinct (but not separate) Scottish political community, now being consolidated by the formation of the Scottish Parliament, means that there could be considerable pressure to ensure that this unique position is recognised in some way.

The Scottish Parliament could have no legal standing in relation to a Trident replacement decision. If it were to come out in opposition to such a decision, however, and if it were to have the backing of a large section of Scottish public opinion, the UK Government would be ill-advised simply to override its stance. Such a response would play into the hands of those who would seek to portray the decision as another instance of London's willingness to impose policies – and in this case risks – on Scotland against the democratic wishes of its people. The Thatcher

Government's decision to impose the unpopular poll tax on Scotland in the late 1980s, despite the Labour majority in Scotland, played an important role in galvanising support for a Scottish Parliament at that time.[33] A comparable stand-off over Trident replacement could not be ruled out.

The attitudes brought to such a debate in Scotland would, of course, be strongly influenced by experiences with Trident and its bases over the previous years, not least in regard to their safety records. But we would make two other observations. The first is that the Scottish Parliament could not be expected to have a 'balanced' debate, in which the security benefits for Scotland, the UK and their allies were fully weighed against the costs, if the Scottish political elites had been totally excluded from the nuclear policy loop. This is one of the traps in the current devolutionary settlement. By giving London exclusive responsibility for such matters, it prevents development of the expertise in strategic nuclear issues and, more broadly, in defence and foreign policy, required to mount a persuasive case for Trident's successor. One cannot expect a 'mature' debate in Scotland on such matters if no habit of thinking about security policy has been allowed to take root.

The second observation is that a Scottish Parliament would be unlikely to adopt a positive attitude towards a proposal to replace Trident with an equivalent system in the Clyde if the UK Parliament had not already scrutinised, debated and voted on the matter. The corollary is that the Scottish Parliament would find it much more difficult to reject a proposal that had Westminster's solid backing, including the backing of Scottish MPs. Such involvement of the UK Parliament would, however, itself be an innovation as it played little or no part in previous replacement decisions, even if it did on occasion debate the principles behind them (as in the debate on nuclear deterrence held on 14 January 1992).[34] Notoriously the UK Cabinet, let alone the Parliament, was not informed

33. Harvie has described the imposition of the poll tax on Scotland as 'seemingly in breach of the Act of Union'. Christopher Harvie, *Scotland and Nationalism* (Routledge: London, 1998), p. 235.

34. The UK Parliament's involvement in investment decisions is unusual but not unprecedented. In 1978, for instance, the Labour Government of the time sought Parliament's endorsement of its decision to allow British Nuclear Fuels to build the THORP reprocessing plant at Sellafield. The proposal and its implications were debated in a first debate before being put to the House for a vote in a second debate. Parliament again was called upon in 1993 to give its consent to the start-up of the plant. See W. Walker, *Nuclear Entrapment: THORP and the Politics of Commitment* (Institute for Public Policy Research: London, 1999).

of the decision to develop the Chevaline system which replaced the warheads and guidance systems on Polaris missiles.

What this implies is that the political approach adopted for Trident's replacement would have to be radically different to those adopted on prior occasions. The 'Scottish question' impels this, although wider democratic pressures in the UK also lead in the same direction. The decision-making process would in all likelihood have to be more open, and the UK Government would have to demonstrate that it had weighed all the options, including the option of abandoning the nuclear deterrent and investing in other military capabilities.

This would encourage the Ministry of Defence and its military planners to draw one of two conclusions, assuming they remain wedded to nuclear deterrence. The first is that the submarine-based missile force's life should be extended if possible through periodic refurbishment and modular replacement rather than a large and visible programme for complete replacement.[35] Instead of a 30- or 40-year lifetime, such an approach would spread capital spending more evenly, thereby minimising the political controversy that has surrounded major replacement decisions (in 1963 and 1980) in the past. Lifetime extension would probably have the added advantage of being the most economical option.

Such an approach – which may be regarded as the most probable – would be tantamount to making a commitment to retain Trident in Scotland over the long term. The UK Government would not thereby escape the need to deepen support and cooperation amongst the Scottish political institutions. Indeed, such a decision would increase the pressure to recognise a distinctive Scottish interest in the nuclear deterrent and to increase Scottish involvement in its oversight.

The MoD's second possible conclusion is that long-term options should be explored for enabling it to replace Trident with another nuclear weapon system (such as air-launched missiles) that could be more easily based south of the Border. Yet this option currently seems unattractive. It would be much more expensive than Trident's refurbishment and would have its own technical and other uncertainties.[36] In addition, an

35. For example, the missiles could be replaced at a different time from the submarines, and/or the submarines could be replaced one at a time, rather than all at once. Such a system would be more comparable with the French practice, which is characterised by continuing modernisation rather than by a single replacement decision. See Appendix B for further discussion.

36. Many of the factors that led to the demise of the V-bomber as the strategic force in the 1960s would remain relevant. In particular, measures designed to

overt decision to replace Trident with another system could, if not taken on technical or strategic grounds, be interpreted as a declaration of no confidence by the UK Government in the stability of devolution. Whichever way it looks, the Ministry of Defence will find it hard not to take the Scottish dimension into account when it comes to consider its Trident replacement options.

The need for political engagement

The devolved Parliament is only two years old. On the streets in Scotland it is commonly spoken of as ineffective and spendthrift – an opinion encouraged by sections of the press. Yet it has quickly established itself as the centre of Scottish political life, and few want it to be disbanded. If one looks closely at what has taken place in the Parliament and Executive and in their dealings with the outside world, it is remarkable how quickly these new institutions have taken root. A recent book concluded that 'the Scottish Parliament has become the main forum for Scottish politics. It may or may not evolve eventually into an independent state, but people in Scotland expect it to become stronger as time goes on'.[37] It appears to be becoming *the* representative political institution in the minds of most Scots, whichever parties they vote for in elections.

In the political imagination, the Scottish Parliament has therefore already been assigned rights and responsibilities to promote Scottish interests and safeguard Scottish welfare. Nuclear weaponry is one of the areas where those rights and responsibilities cannot be exercised in line with expectations. It remains the UK Government's exclusive charge, inevitably so as the UK and not Scotland is the sovereign state. Even without independence, there is therefore a tension which will need to be managed with political skill and energy if it is not to become a source of serious difficulty between Edinburgh and London.

Currently, the UK Government and the Scottish institutions only engage through administrative channels where the nuclear force is con-

secure a strategic air force against possible surprise attack (such as maintaining a dedicated force of strategic bombers, keeping a large proportion of aircraft on high alert, and maintaining a wide range of dispersal sites) would prove very expensive, as well as being politically controversial and difficult to reconcile with modern safety requirements.

37. Lindsay Paterson, Alice Brown, John Curtice, Kerstin Hinds, David McCrone, Alison Park, Kerry Sproston and Paula Surridge, *New Scotland, New Politics?* (Polygon: Edinburgh, 2001), p. 167.

cerned. The Scottish Ministers and Executive have responsibility under the Scotland Act and its associated agreements to implement UK policy, not to devise it. In our view, the engagement will have to become more political and more policy-infused if it is to have lasting stability. To date, the Ministry of Defence has maintained a strict exclusion zone around nuclear policy. It would be prudent to reconsider its approach. The kinds of questions it should be asking are: How can an effective dialogue be established with the Scottish Parliament and Executive on nuclear policy, insofar as it has particular effects on Scotland? How can a 'culture of international security' be nurtured in Scotland? How can the UK Government best establish confidence in Scotland in the safety of its nuclear forces and facilities? Should Parliamentary Committees in Westminster or Edinburgh be positively encouraged to conduct investigations into such matters? These questions may seem heretical in London, not least because they imply intrusion into reserved matters and the opening of nuclear policy to a wider debate than has been the convention. But that is the price that may have to be paid to sustain a UK nuclear force in Scotland.

If the nuclear relationship between the Scottish and UK political institutions develops – and is allowed to develop – in a constructive manner, and if no serious mishaps occur to sully it, Trident's stay in a devolved Scotland will probably be politically uneventful. Were Scotland then to gain independence, a prior history of constructive engagement would increase the prospects for extending that stay. Efforts to deepen cooperation would therefore provide an insurance of sorts against rainier days. If, however, the relationship soured under devolution, the pressure to expel Trident after independence could become irresistible in Scottish politics. There are two implications for believers in nuclear deterrence in London: there can be no major accidents in the Clyde; and too jealous a guarding of reserved matters by the UK Government and Parliament could block off the option of deploying nuclear forces in Scotland over the long term.

Chapter Four

EU and NATO Membership and International Nuclear Law

We now turn to a future in which the Scottish people choose independence. It is commonly assumed that they would seek to establish a state which was a member of the European Union and the United Nations and a non-nuclear weapon state in practice and in law (see Table 4.1). It seems likely that the SNP will soon come into line with all Scotland's other major parties in supporting NATO, while still opposing the deployment of nuclear weapons on Scottish territory. It is also reasonable to assume that the rest of the United Kingdom would seek continuity in all regards: it would strive to keep its current membership of the EU, the UN and NATO, to remain a permanent member of the UN Security Council and – at least in the immediate aftermath of Scottish independence – to remain a nuclear weapon state.

Table 4.1. Post-independence aspirations

	Status			
Country	*Nuclear*	*EU*	*NATO*	*UN*
Scotland	NNWS	Member state	Member state? (non-nuclear)	Member state
rUK	NWS	Member state	Member state (nuclear)	Permanent member, UNSC

However, states cannot simply announce their arrival on the international stage and decide for themselves how they will engage with the existing community of states. They have to be accepted into that community and its institutions through various rites of passage of both a political and legal nature. Our concern in this chapter is primarily with the legal rites of passage – with the international legal issues that would have to be addressed if Scotland sought independent statehood, and with the effects of international law on the choices that would be available to the governments of Scotland, the rest of the UK (rUK) and other states. Inevitably, the interpretation of international law is often highly political in nature. We will therefore be obliged to make some tentative judgements as to how international law might be interpreted on key questions.

There are two bodies of international law relevant to our case. The first concerns the standing, rights and obligations of states being formed when a prior state fragments. Which, if any, of the emerging states can claim recognition as 'successors' to the original state, and in which regards? How is the legal situation affected if fragmentation takes place through secession from, as distinct from dissolution of, the original state? What is the standing of emerging states in regard to international treaties and to membership of international organisations? This body of law is pertinent to Scotland's and rUK's international recognition, and to their respective rights to succeed to the UK's membership of the European Union, NATO and the United Nations (and UN Security Council).

The second body of international law concerns the possession of nuclear weapons, especially as expressed through the Nuclear Non-Proliferation Treaty of 1968 (NPT).[1] Which states have rights to possess nuclear weapons, and what are the obligations of states exercising and renouncing those rights? This body of law has obvious relevance to the choices facing Scotland and rUK concerning the nuclear weapons and capabilities on their territories. The legal situation has here been clarified in some but not other respects by the experience of the break-up of the Soviet Union, a much more substantial nuclear power, in the early 1990s. The great complication in our case arises, of course, from the entire UK nuclear force's presence in Scotland, the country that wishes to disarm, and outside rUK, the country that will probably try to retain a nuclear arsenal. In the event of independence, these circumstances would inevitably prompt a search for a political settlement that would allow Scotland and rUK's interests to be served in a fashion that was consistent with international law and did not offend against the interests of other states. That settlement would have to go hand-in-hand with clarification of Scotland's (and rUK's) role within NATO and within whichever European military arrangements applied at the time of independence.

Although only the second body of international law has a direct bearing on the nuclear question, both have to be considered here. One reason is that the two bodies of law are interconnected and are even at

1. We assume in the following pages that the NPT will survive. Although currently threatened, in particular, by the apparent disdain of many in the Bush administration for arms control, it would still be surprising if this foundation of international nuclear order lost its authority.

variance with one another (in regard to the NPT) where the law of succession is concerned. The other reason is that legal processes and interpretations in either context will inevitably become entangled at a political level. Indeed, the very lack of clarity that we shall find over Scotland's (and rUK's) legal rights to EU membership provides room for all sides to engage in political linkage. A satisfactory settlement of the nuclear and other contentious issues could thereby become a condition for Scotland's membership of the EU, just as any frustration of Scotland's claim to EU membership could encourage it to be obstructive on nuclear matters. Although the Ukrainian and Scottish situations are very different, the political resort to using nuclear weapons as a bargaining card could become equally significant in our context.[2]

The chapter begins with discussions of Scotland's (and rUK's) prospective standing in the UN, the EU and NATO. Why is the law so often unclear on these matters? We then examine the bearing of international law on the nuclear situation after independence and the new states' standing in the NPT. The chapter ends by revisiting the vexed issue of secession and its ramifications, especially when Trident is taken into account.

Before proceeding, we should stress that the devolution settlement of 1998 raises no issues under international law pertinent to our case. From an international perspective, Scotland remains part of the state that is the United Kingdom. This state remains the same member of the United Nations, European Union and NATO, and the same nuclear weapon state under international law. Scotland currently has no separate identity, and no separate rights and obligations, from an international political and legal perspective.

2. In 1993–94, the Ukraine threatened to lay claim to the nuclear weapons deployed on its territory, and to back out of its commitment to join the Nuclear Non-Proliferation Treaty as a non-nuclear weapon states, if the terms of the political and economic settlement with Russia were unsatisfactory and if it were denied security guarantees by Russia and the United States in particular. Although Scotland is very unlikely to claim title to Trident submarines, it could use access to the nuclear bases as a bargaining card. A fascinating account of the development and resolution of the 'crisis' over the Ukraine's nuclear stance is provided by Mark Skootsky, 'An annotated chronology of Post-Soviet nuclear disarmament', *The Nonproliferation Review*, Spring-Summer 1995.

International recognition and EU membership

There is already an extensive literature on an independent Scotland's relations with the European Union.[3] The central question has been whether Scotland would have immediate rights to membership of the EU, with no discontinuity, or whether it would have to join the group of states seeking admission. Some have argued that EU membership would be automatic, others that it would have to be won the hard way, still others that Scotland's future standing within the EU could only be decided, after a vote for independence, through the weighing of political and legal arguments at the time. Having considered much of the literature, we are most persuaded by this last assertion – that Scotland's membership of the EU would depend on the collective political decision of the EU's member states after it had become clear that independence would take place. Membership rights cannot therefore be prejudged.

The principal complications may be summarised as follows.

Succession to international treaties and to UN membership. There is no consistent and generally accepted body of international law relating to the succession of rights and obligations when new states are formed out of old states.[4] The Vienna Convention on Succession of States in Respect of Treaties of 1978 provides some guidance, but it has not come into force and has yet to be ratified by members of the European

3. See, for instance, Robert Lane, '"Scotland in Europe": an independent Scotland and the European Community', in Wilson Finnie, C. Himsworth and Neil Walker (eds), *Edinburgh Essays in Public Law* (Edinburgh University Press: Edinburgh, 1991), pp. 143–157; Scottish Centre for Economic and Social Research, *Scotland's Government – the transition to independence* (SCESR: Peterhead, 1996); Matthew Happold, *Scotland Europa: independence in Europe?*, Centre for European Reform Working Paper, April 1999; David Sinclair, *Issues around Scottish independence*, The Constitution Unit, University College London, September 1999; Neil MacCormick, 'Is there a constitutional path to Scottish independence?', *Parliamentary Affairs*, vol. 53, 2000, pp. 721–736; S. Schieren, 'Independence in Europe: Scotland's choice?', *Scottish Affairs*, no. 31, Spring 2000, pp. 111–127.
4. For discussions of state succession, see Oscar Schachter, 'State succession: the once and future law', *Virginia Journal of International Law*, vol. 33, 1993, pp. 252–260; and Edwin Williamson and John Osborn, 'A U.S. perspective on treaty succession and related issues in the wake of the breakup of the USSR and Yugoslavia', *Virginia Journal of International Law*, vol. 33, 1993, pp. 261–274. Robert Lane observes that the various precedents around which international practice has developed 'indicate that it is not the intention of the successor state which is definitive but rather the recognition granted to that intention by third parties'. See Robert Lane, *op. cit.*, p. 148.

Union.[5] This said, international practice usually begins with three presumptions. Firstly, states that are forming through secession from established states will usually have lesser rights to succession than those that are forming through the consensual dissolution of states. Secondly, new states will continue to be bound (unless they are escaping colonial domination or the clutches of a pariah state) by pledges made by their predecessors under international law, whether or not they are emerging through secession or dissolution: there is a general presumption of continuity of treaty obligations.[6] Thirdly, new states have to apply afresh for membership of international organisations, although states whose territories are redrawn through acts of secession but whose personalities survive intact will normally retain their membership.

The implication is that Scotland and rUK would both continue to be bound by treaties to which the UK is party (the Nuclear Non-Proliferation Treaty and the Treaty on European Union are special cases to which we return below). In addition, an independent Scotland would have to apply to become a member of the UN and other international organisations. Whether rUK would also have to apply to join the UN, or could claim automatic succession to the UK's membership, including its permanent membership of the UN Security Council, is less clear, at least on paper. Could it justifiably claim to be the UK's sole successor state for these purposes?

In 1947, the UN's Sixth (Legal) Committee offered the following advice:[7]

As a general rule, it is in accordance with principle to assume that a

5. Treaties that are signed by states may still not enter into force. Entry into force usually requires ratification (i.e. endorsement by national legislatures) by a defined number of states. Although the US and most EU member states have not ratified the Vienna Convention, US and European governments have recognised the Convention as customary international law and thus as an important source of guidance on these matters.
6. Article 34 of the Vienna Convention on Succession of States in Respect of Treaties contends that: 'When a part or parts of a territory of a State separate to form one or more States, whether or not the predecessor States continues to exist ... any treaty in force at the date of succession of States in respect of the entire territory of the predecessor State continues in force in respect of each successor State so formed ...'.
7. See UN GAOR 6th Committee, 2nd Session, 43rd meeting at pages 38–39 (1947). The advice was given after a decision to allow India to retain all the rights to UN membership, and Pakistan none of those rights, after the division of India was contested by Argentina on the grounds that the decision was discriminatory.

> State which is a Member of the United Nations does not cease to be a Member from the mere fact that its constitution or frontiers have been modified, and to consider the rights and obligations which that State possesses as a Member of the United Nations as ceasing to exist only with its extinction as a legal person internationally recognised as such.

The central question is therefore whether the UK would have suffered 'extinction as a legal person'. The Scottish nationalist argument is that the UK would be dissolved, and its international personality fundamentally altered, if either of the Act of Union's founding parties decided to reconstitute itself as an independent state. The unionist response is that the UK has over three centuries become more than the union of England and Scotland, and that Scotland's economic and demographic weight are too slight to upset the UK's international standing. Its personality could therefore survive Scotland's departure.

Whatever interpretation might be put by the different domestic parties on the Act of Union, the UN Legal Committee's advice is that any decision on these matters would rest with the international community, and not with Scotland and rUK. In particular, its recommendation implies that if the UN's member states decided 'on its merits' that a state should sustain the legal personality of its predecessor, then its membership would not lapse.[8]

Such an outcome must be considered likely where rUK is concerned. It is difficult to imagine that the international community would consider that the UK had become extinct as a legal personality because of the loss of a part of its territory that accounted for only 8% of its population (though a much larger proportion of its landmass). Nor is it easy to see what political motives the international community would have for denying rUK such recognition. Even if Scotland and rUK were in dispute over the succession question (and it is far from clear from our later discussion that they would be), other countries would be more wary of offending the latter, which would remain one of Europe's major powers. States facing separatist forces of their own (including China and Russia, as well as EU members such as France, Italy and Spain) could be expected to insist that the UK should not become extinct as a legal personality. They would probably have little patience with arcane disputes over interpretations of the 1707 Act of Union.

A precedent of sorts has been provided by the Soviet Union's

8. The UN 6th Committee also advised in 1947 that 'each case must … be judged on its merits'.

disintegration into 12 separate states. As the Soviet Union ceased to exist when it broke up, the Russian Federation had no superior *legal* right to inherit its mantle as a UN member state, not least because the Soviet Union's demise was precipitated partly by Russia's own secession.[9] The Russian Federation nevertheless inherited the Soviet Union's position in the UN because President Yeltsin's demand for this privilege was not contested by other members of the UN Security Council, by other ex-Soviet states, or by the wider community of states (it helped that his demand was positively supported by the US President).[10] They took this position for a number of reasons. Russia was the largest and most powerful of the new states; its capital Moscow had been the capital of the USSR; and it had vowed to shoulder the USSR's debts and treaty obligations. In addition, the UN Charter names the five permanent members of the UN Security Council: acceptance of Russia's succession to the Soviet Union's legal personality avoided any questions of amending the Charter to allow a different state to take the USSR's seat.

The political leadership of rUK would doubtless make similar claims to occupy the UK's seat. Much would depend on the international circumstances at the time of the UK's break-up. But the natural inclination of the US and its fellow members of the UNSC, and of other states, would still be to accept rUK's inheritance of the UK's permanent seat for rather similar reasons to those noted above for Russia. In the long term, reform of the UN Security Council could lead to a reconfiguration of the permanent membership.[11] Yet other states are unlikely

9. See Yehuda Blum, 'Russia takes over the Soviet Union's seat at the United Nations', *European Journal of International Law*, 1992, pp. 354–361.
10. The Ukraine and Belarus alone had legal rights to continuing UN membership because, despite having no independent statehood, they had belonged to the organisation since its foundation. Rhinelander points out that President Bush had the constitutional power to recognise, on behalf of the US, Russia as successor state to the USSR without need for the consent of the US Senate. See John Rhinelander, 'The legal status of the ABM Treaty: alive, but under the usual attacks', *National Institute for Public Policy*, Washington, DC, June 2000.
11. Proposals have frequently been made for Germany, India and Japan to join the permanent membership of the Council, but few have suggested that they should replace any of the five current members. If a permanent EU seat became a serious possibility, the case for a separate UK seat might eventually be questioned. In this context, UK withdrawal from the EU would be more likely to pose a threat to the UN Security Council seat than would Scottish independence. For it would undermine the UK's claim (along with France) to be representing the EU as a whole.

to see the UK's break-up as the right time to be pursuing such a reform, not least because of the far-reaching damage it would do to relations with a state that would continue to be a significant global power.[12]

Succession within the European Union. Scotland's right to membership of the EU has often been approached as if it would be determined by reference to the broad principles of international law alluded to above. Although those principles would have considerable relevance, it cannot automatically be assumed that succession to EU membership would follow any of the rules or practices applied in other contexts. The EU is more than a treaty and more than an international organisation: it has a scope and a distinctive legal order that give it a personality and authority all of its own. Various procedures have been established through which states can be admitted to the Union from outside the existing set of member states. But there are no recognised procedures for dealing with the fragmentation of a member state, simply because there has been no call for them so far. Other events that are often cited in the literature, such as Greenland's departure from the EU and East Germany's absorption into it, are sufficiently different to provide no useful precedent.[13]

Because of the UK's membership of the EU, Scottish law is already fully consistent with that of the EU. Provided that Scotland's future government was clearly committed to liberal political and economic values and could demonstrate administrative competence, it would therefore satisfy the 'Copenhagen Criteria' set down in 1993 to determine whether a state was fit to join the EU.[14] Scotland's evident fitness for

12. This claim would not rest only on its possession of nuclear weapons. The UK is also a significant contributor of conventional forces to international peacekeeping missions, the world's fourth largest provider of development assistance, and the sixth largest contributor to the UN budget. Even after Scottish independence, rUK would remain one of the world's eight largest economies.
13. Greenland left the European Communities in 1985, but only after long negotiations. This has been taken by some to imply that an independent Scotland could only negotiate its way out of the Union – it could not be 'expelled'. However, Greenland is still part of the Danish state, the core of which has remained in the EU. East Germany effectively joined the EU after absorption by West Germany in 1990 through the political decisions of member states not to oppose this process, showing that member states can change their borders without affecting the continuity of their membership.
14. The Copenhagen Criteria require the candidate country to achieve: (a) stability of institutions guaranteeing democracy, the rule of law, human rights and

membership has not prevented some from arguing that it would have to begin with a 'clean slate', effectively taking its place at the back of the queue of states seeking EU membership.[15] This is a dubious claim. But it also seems unlikely that Scotland would be granted membership without any questions being asked or conditions being attached. However warm the regard for Scotland in European capitals, the secession from or dissolution of an EU member state would raise serious concerns about the precedents that might be established if EU membership were granted too readily (Belgium, France, Italy and Spain all have secessionist movements). Although EU member states could not dismiss out of hand an application from a Scotland that was politically mature and that supported the EU's fundamental principles and norms, the need for Scotland to negotiate a treaty of accession with the EU would give the member states (each of which would have veto powers) the opportunity to review the case and be awkward if they felt so inclined.[16]

Writing in 1991, Robert Lane observed that:

> ... neither the United Kingdom nor Scotland (or any other successor state) can by unilateral action compel the Community and its law to recognise a member state or member states different from the United Kingdom as presently constituted. The proposition that Community

respect for and protection of minorities; (b) the existence of a functioning market economy as well as the capacity to cope with competitive pressure and market forces within the Union; (c) the ability to take on the obligations of membership including adherence to the aims of political, economic and monetary union; (d) the conditions for its integration through the adjustment of its administrative structures, so that European Community legislation transposed into national legislation is implemented effectively through appropriate administrative and judicial structures.

15. See, for example, Matthew Happold, *op. cit.*
16. For example, it would be necessary to decide on how many votes to allocate to Scotland and rUK in the Council of Ministers and European Parliament, and on whether this could be achieved without a wider redistribution. Matters would be complicated because votes are distributed to give disproportionate weight to smaller countries. As a result, rUK would almost certainly maintain the UK's 29 votes on the Council, and thus its equivalence with France, Germany and Italy. In addition, Scotland would be entitled to 7 votes, the number to which Denmark (population 5.3 million) and Ireland (population 3.7 million) are currently entitled, and to which Slovakia (population 5.4 million) and Lithuania (population 3.7 million) will be entitled if they become member states. The combined voting power of Scotland and rUK would therefore be greater than that of the UK today: a situation with which other member states might not be entirely comfortable.

> membership could be 'claimed' by an independent Scotland or 'refused' by the remainder of the United Kingdom is based upon fundamentally misconceived assumptions. Independence in Europe for Scotland (and for England) can be brought about only if action at the national level proceeds concurrently with action at the Community level, thus producing, at the end of the day, an agreed result which necessarily includes the concurrence of the Community institutions and all member states. A Scotland bent on independence grounded in the clear democratic support of the Scottish people would create a moral and, given the international law principle of self-determination, probably a legal obligation for all member states to negotiate in good faith in order to produce such a result, *but this solution lies essentially within the domain of politics, not law.*[17] (emphasis added)

Lane is surely correct. 'Action at the national level must proceed concurrently with action at the Community [now Union] level' implies that the EU's decision, and that of its individual member states, would be unlikely to be immediate, and that they would be strongly influenced by the ability and willingness of Scotland and rUK to reach their own settlement on all the issues of concern. Again, the future of UK nuclear forces might count among the issues upon which the European Union and its member states would expect agreement before Scotland's accession was accepted.

Would rUK also have to negotiate a fresh treaty of accession? That too would come down to political rather than legal choice. The EU's natural inclination would be to treat rUK as the UK's successor state, whose 1973 treaty of accession might need minor adjustment but not re-negotiation. Matters could turn out differently if England (specifically) adopted a strongly anti-European policy, and if England (specifically) had its own hand in the UK's disintegration, as Russia did with the Soviet Union. The EU might then decide to suspend judgement until the character of rUK and of its settlement with Scotland became clearer.

Both Scotland and rUK would have a strong interest in ensuring continuity and stability, given the high degree of economic disruption that a period of prolonged uncertainty could bring. Yet scenarios of confrontation in the run-up to independence can be readily imagined. The emotions engendered by a referendum campaign could strengthen the hand of more confrontational leaders. In the flush of victory, one cannot assume that Scotland's nationalist-led government would demonstrate

17. Robert Lane, *op. cit.*, pp. 154–155.

the sensitivity necessary to pilot the country to independence without an escalation of conflict. In the event of a close-run vote, moreover, opponents of independence (both in Scotland and in rUK) might still harbour hopes of reversing the initial verdict. Commitments made in the referendum campaign by both Scottish and UK political parties could hinder a smooth resolution of the major issues facing negotiators.

In these uncertain circumstances, Scotland's position on Trident basing could be decisive in shaping the direction of negotiations. If Scotland insisted on the prompt removal of Trident from its territory, there must be a real possibility that the rUK would then oppose its EU membership, and other EU member states (most of whom are also in NATO) would probably take the rUK's side in such a stand-off. By contrast, it seems unlikely that the rUK would block a claim to EU membership from a Scotland that was prepared to negotiate a Trident basing agreement and was willing to cooperate on other essential matters. By so clearly symbolising the mutual interdependence of the two states, therefore, the issue of Trident basing could paradoxically be a catalyst for an independence settlement that recognised their necessary interdependence across a wider range of areas. The particular implications for defence cooperation are discussed further in Chapter 6.

Scotland and NATO membership

An independent Scotland's relationship with NATO would be inextricably linked to whether it agreed to Trident basing on its territory (assuming rUK wished to maintain a nuclear deterrent). As discussed in Chapter 2, the SNP's opposition to NATO membership has been rooted in its opposition to membership of a nuclear alliance. If an independent Scotland were to accept that Trident would stay at Faslane, albeit temporarily, the arguments against NATO membership would be significantly weakened. Indeed, it is hard to envisage Trident remaining in Scotland without Scotland's full membership of NATO.

There is considerable common ground between the issues raised by accession to NATO and the EU. There is no precedent for parts of a fragmenting state seeking succession to membership of NATO, and accession would ultimately depend upon the consent of member states. Yet acceptance of rUK's rights to NATO membership would probably be well-nigh automatic given the UK's prominent role in NATO and its substantial military assets. The involvement of nuclear forces, and of a government that had for decades played a significant role in NATO nuclear planning, would make it even more important to maintain continuity in the UK's NATO membership.

Scotland's position would be more problematic. It could claim to have long demonstrated that it satisfied the economic and political criteria by which eligibility is judged. It might have more difficulty meeting the military criteria depending on the nature of the settlement it had reached – on both nuclear and conventional forces – with rUK. The process by which the accessions of the Czech Republic, Hungary and Poland were managed is instructive in this regard.[18] They began with the issuance, at the Madrid Summit of NATO Heads of State in July 1997, of invitations to the three governments to open talks on accession. After five months of negotiation, a Protocol of Accession was signed by foreign ministers in December 1997, followed in early 1998 by the beginnings of ratification procedures in the fifteen countries. By April 1999, the Protocol's ratification had been secured in all countries, including crucially the US President's ratification after the US Congress had provided its consent.

The need for US backing and consent deserves emphasis. Without it, there would be no chance of Scotland acceding to NATO. Given the strong military ties between the US and UK, in both the nuclear and conventional fields, the US would doubtless take a keen interest in the military settlement that was being negotiated by the rUK and Scottish Governments. Its preparedness to welcome Scotland into NATO would surely depend on the existence, nature and clarity of the military settlement which would probably have to be concluded before formal accession talks could begin.

However, NATO would surely be loath to lose the membership of a country that had played a significant part in European security and that had assets of considerable importance to NATO on its territory (they include naval exercise areas as well as Trident). In normal circumstances, there would be a strong collective interest in securing the membership of both states, and thus in encouraging the Scottish and rUK Governments to reach a settlement with which all parties could live.

The SNP's current policy (as of July 2001) is to join Partnership for Peace (PfP) and the Euro-Atlantic Partnership Council (EAPC), emulating the Irish position. If a future Scottish Government adhered to

18. See Gebhardt von Moltke, 'Accession of new members to the Alliance: what are the next steps?', *NATO Review*, vol. 45, July-August 1997, pp. 4–9; and Klaus-Peter Klaiber, 'The Membership Action Plan: keeping NATO's door open', *NATO Review*, vol. 47, Summer 1999, pp. 23–25.

this policy, it would still have to apply to join these institutions and to gain the approval of their members. However, the SNP's NATO policy is currently under review (see Chapter 2) and will probably be overtaken by support for full NATO membership.

Scotland, the UK and international nuclear law

The legal issues posed by Scotland's independence have greater clarity in the nuclear field. Under international law as it has come to be interpreted, especially since the break-up of the Soviet Union, two or more states cannot succeed to the rights of a single nuclear weapon state. Furthermore, the steps required for Scotland to become a non-nuclear weapon state are well defined. This said, the various complications discussed below for Scotland and especially for rUK mean that solutions would have to lie (paraphrasing Lane) essentially within the domains of *both* politics *and* law. Furthermore, those solutions would have to be found *both* within the global frameworks of arms control, non-proliferation and disarmament policy *and* within the regional frameworks of European and transatlantic security arrangements.

The possession and deployment of nuclear arms have been subjected to increasing legal constraint since efforts to establish a co-operative framework of nuclear arms control began in earnest in the early 1960s. Arms control treaties have subsequently taken two main forms: the bilateral treaties between the US and Soviet Union (latterly Russia) intended to stabilise deterrent relations by limiting deployments of missiles and bombers; and the multilateral treaties, several with universal intent, which constrain the development and spread of nuclear weapons and of the materials and capabilities used in their manufacture. The Nuclear Non-Proliferation Treaty of 1968 (NPT) occupies a special position amongst these multilateral treaties. Besides determining how states should act to prevent the spread of nuclear weapons, the NPT establishes the legal principles by which states may or may not possess nuclear weapons, formalises certain bargains between nuclear and non-nuclear weapon states, and asserts that complete nuclear disarmament is the goal that all states must work towards.

The UK is bound by no treaties of the first kind: it is party to no agreements with other nuclear powers which constrain the numbers and types of warheads and delivery vehicles that it can deploy. Successive UK Governments have stated that the UK will submit itself to legally binding limits only when the US and USSR/Russia have brought the sizes of their arsenals nearer to those of the lesser nuclear powers (usually implying a few hundred weapons apiece). The UK has, however, substantially reduced its arsenal over the past decade through unilateral actions, paralleling the reductions made by the US and Russia.

The UK has also been active in multilateral regimes and has willingly accepted the restraints associated with them. It played an important part in the negotiation of the NPT and the Comprehensive Nuclear Test-Ban Treaty (CTBT) and has promoted them strongly since their conclusion.[19] Unlike the US and China, but like France and Russia, the UK has ratified the CTBT. Moreover, it has enthusiastically advocated another multilateral treaty – the Fissile Material Cut-off Treaty (FMCT) – whose negotiation is still awaited.[20] By promoting these and other measures, by reducing its nuclear arms, by terminating in 1995 its production of fissile materials for weapons, and by ending nuclear testing, the UK has committed itself by various means to a substantial limitation of its nuclear weapon capability.

One can go further. Although continuing to rely on nuclear deterrence, the UK has arguably gone further than any other nuclear-armed state in lending its support to the project of global nuclear disarmament. The desirability and necessity of that project have been expressed in various government statements, including the Strategic Defence Review of 1998,[21] and the UK Government played an important part in drafting and negotiating the 'Final Document' at the NPT Review Conference which was held in New York in May 2000.[22] The Final Document contained

19. The CTBT was concluded in 1996, but will not come into force until ratified by all 44 states who possess nuclear power reactors. The 13 states that have not yet ratified include China, North Korea, India, Iran, Israel, Pakistan and the US. If it enters into force, the CTBT will institute a total ban on nuclear explosive testing, replacing the Partial Test Ban Treaty of 1963 which allowed States Parties to continue testing underground.
20. The FMCT would ban the production of fissile materials for weapons purposes. Proposed by the UN General Assembly in 1993, and brought before the Conference on Disarmament for negotiation, it has become entangled in various disputes between the US, China and India (in particular) which have hindered its negotiation.
21. 'The Government is committed to the goal of the global elimination of nuclear, biological and chemical weapons. We will work to create conditions in which even a minimum level of nuclear deterrence is no longer necessary.' *Strategic Defence Review: Supporting Essays* (London: HMSO, 1998), page 5–17, paragraph 55.
22. The NPT requires that its Parties convene a conference every five years to review the Treaty's progress. The 2000 Review Conference had particular

the strongest *political* commitment yet made by the five nuclear weapon states to pursue nuclear disarmament.[23] In it, they gave their 'unequivocal undertaking ... to accomplish the total elimination of their nuclear arsenals leading to nuclear disarmament', and together with other States Parties they identified a set of steps that should be taken in pursuit of that aim. This moved them some way beyond the vague undertaking in Article VI of the NPT to 'pursue negotiations in good faith on effective measures relating to ... nuclear disarmament'.[24]

The sincerity of the nuclear weapon states' commitment to the pledges contained in the NPT Final Document is nevertheless open to question.[25] The Final Document lacks the status of a treaty, and the agreements expressed therein have already been jeopardised by the US refusal to ratify the CTBT, by the Bush administration's denigration of multilateral arms control, and by the actions and reactions of Russia and China. Together they are casting doubt over the genuineness of the nuclear powers' commitment to nuclear disarmament. What is more, any commitment to disarmament has always essentially been a joint commitment: it is conditional on all of the nuclear armed states moving down this path. So the UK Government's support for disarmament does not extend to the UK's own unilateral disarmament. On the contrary, it is UK policy – which is now accepted by all major political parties aside from the Scottish National Party, Plaid Cymru and the Green Party – to pursue multilateral but not unilateral disarmament.[26]

Nevertheless, the obligations to pursue nuclear disarmament that are expressed in the NPT Final Document, and in the NPT itself, have considerable relevance to our case. Four points are worth making.

---

significance since it was the first to be held after the 1995 Conference which had given the Treaty an indefinite lifetime (it initially had a 25-year life, beginning with its entry into force in 1970) and agreed the 'Principles and Objectives for Nuclear Non-Proliferation and Disarmament' which expanded the NPT's scope and purpose.

23. The Final Document does not have the status of an international treaty. Although an intergovernmental agreement with substantial prestige, it lacks the form of a treaty and has not been endorsed by national legislatures.
24. It also breaks the link in the same Article of nuclear disarmament to complete disarmament (that is, the elimination of all weapons of war).
25. A discussion of the Final Document and its negotiation can be found in Tariq Rauf, 'An unequal success? Implications of the NPT Review Conference', *Arms Control Today*, vol. 30, no. 6, July/August 2000, pp. 9–16.
26. There are, however, dissenters from this position in both the Liberal Democrat and Labour (especially the Scottish Labour) Parties.

First, Scotland's nuclear disarmament would be fully consistent with the objectives of the NPT and the Final Document.

Second, whilst inheriting the UK's status of nuclear weapon state under the NPT (see below), rUK would also inherit the UK's commitment to pursue nuclear disarmament, including its own disarmament.

Third, if an independent Scotland refused to accept Trident's deployment on its territory and thereby made it difficult, even impossible, for rUK to sustain its nuclear deterrent, neither rUK nor any other state could contend that Scotland was acting unlawfully within the framework of the NPT. Although a Scottish government might be politically unwise to press for rUK's disarmament, it could present a reasonable case that it was acting lawfully by pushing rUK in this direction.

Fourth, Scotland's *and* rUK's disarmament would be the outcome that was most consistent with the spirit and letter of international law and that was least open to being contested on legal grounds. Furthermore, the legality of rUK's retention of nuclear arms would hinge on foreign powers' acceptance of its right to succeed the UK as a nuclear weapon state under the NPT.

Scotland, rUK and the NPT

The Nuclear Non-Proliferation Treaty (NPT) of 1968 provides the main statement of international law on the possession of nuclear weapons. The Treaty recognises two classes of state – nuclear and non-nuclear weapon states (NWS and NNWS) – both of which are encompassed by the Treaty. An NWS is defined in Article IX. 3 as one 'which has manufactured and exploded a nuclear weapon or other nuclear explosive device prior to January 1, 1967'.[27] This Article limited to five the number of states (the US, Soviet Union, UK, France and China) which could claim the rights and obligations of an NWS under international law. The Article IX principle's entrenchment was demonstrated when NPT Parties unanimously refused to acknowledge India's demand for recognition as a 'nuclear weapon state' after it conducted its nuclear tests in 1998, a refusal that has been sustained to this day.

The NPT has nothing to say about the circumstance in which one

27. 'NNWS' is not defined by the NPT. It is taken to refer to a state which does not qualify under Article IX. 3 to bear the rights and obligations of an NWS, which has renounced nuclear weapons and accepted the various restrictions imposed by the NPT, and which has opened its territory to full international safeguards.

of the five NWS breaks apart. The outcome of the Soviet Union's dissolution in 1991 grew naturally out of a realisation that acceptance of more than one successor state would confound the non-proliferation norm that gives life and meaning to the Treaty. As Williamson and Osborn observe:

> ... the fundamental purpose of the [NPT] would be vitiated were the 'nuclear' category expanded to encompass all of the former republics [of the Soviet Union] simply to maintain the consistency of the rule of continuity in matters of treaty succession. Any attempt to allocate the indivisible and unrecreatable rights, or to enforce the concomitant obligations set forth in the Non-Proliferation Treaty, would indeed be inconsistent with the object and purpose of the treaty itself.[28]

Although enshrined in no treaty law, it is now generally accepted that there can be no departure from this limitation to a single successor state for the inheritance of the rights and obligations accorded to an NWS by the NPT. This does not prevent more than one successor state being named to ensure continuity of compliance with other arms control treaties (always providing such actions would not compromise the NPT's fundamental principles), as happened when Belarus, Kazakhstan and the Ukraine became Parties to the START I and ABM Treaties in 1992–93.[29]

It is also worth noting that the NPT does not explicitly address the possibility that one or more NWS might yield sovereignty to a new state becoming an NWS in their stead. But nor does it rule it out. Indeed, this possibility was considered during the NPT's negotiation in reference to the possible future formation of a unified European state. It was broadly accepted at the time that:

> [The NPT] would not bar succession by a new federated European

28. Edwin Williamson and John Osborn, *op. cit.*, p. 267. The Vienna Convention on Succession of States in Respect of Treaties allows for departure from the normal presumption of succession by declaring in Article 34.2 that treaty succession will not apply 'if it appears from the Treaty or is otherwise established that the application of the treaty in respect of the successor State would be incompatible with the object and purpose of the treaty or would radically change the conditions for its operation'.
29. The inclusion of Belarus, Kazakhstan and Ukraine as Parties to START I through the Lisbon Protocol of December 1992 was made possible by the Protocol's simultaneous declaration that they were renouncing nuclear weapons and would accede to the NPT as NNWS.

state to the nuclear status of one of its former components. A new federated European state would have to control all of its external security functions including defence and all foreign policy matters relating to external security, but would not have to be so centralised as to assume all governmental functions. While not dealing with succession by such a federated state, the treaty would bar transfer of nuclear weapons (including ownership) or control over them to any recipient, including a multilateral entity.[30]

Another aspect of the NPT needs highlighting here. The Treaty was designed to inhibit the acquisition of nuclear weapons by states beyond the five that already possessed them. However, it did not bar the NWS from basing nuclear weapons on the territories of non-nuclear weapon states (as practised, for instance, by the US in Germany) provided that the weapons remained under the NWS's sole and total control. The corollary was that the nuclear weapon states were forbidden to transfer control over nuclear weapons to any NNWS.[31] rUK would thus be permitted by the NPT to site Trident on the territory of a disarmed Scotland (assuming it had gained recognition as the UK's successor under the Treaty), but only on condition that a Scottish government asserted no control over the weapons.

The term 'control' is not defined by the NPT. It is usually taken to refer to operational control over nuclear weapons (everything from storage to firing, including command and control) and to their protection against theft and sabotage. It does not encompass consultation on and planning of nuclear strategy by allies as occurs, for instance, within NATO's Nuclear Planning Group. A dialogue on nuclear strategy would therefore be permitted between the Governments in London and Edinburgh. Nor do the NPT's prohibitions on transfer extend to the 'dual-key'

30. 'Letter of submittal' on the NPT sent to the US President by the Secretary of State, Dean Rusk, on 2 July 1968. The letter was shown to the Soviet Union and the Eighteen-Nation Disarmament Conference which raised no objection. See Mohamed Shaker, *The Nuclear Non-Proliferation Treaty: Origin and Implementation, 1959–1979*, Oceana Publications, 1980, vol. I, pp. 234–235. The prohibition of transfers to multilateral entities mentioned in the quotation was a response to Soviet concerns about the attainment of control over nuclear weapons by the US–European Multi-Lateral Force which had recently been proposed for Europe.
31. Article I of the NPT states that 'Each nuclear-weapon State Party to the Treaty undertakes not to transfer to any recipient whatsoever nuclear weapons or other nuclear explosive devices or control over such weapons or explosive devices directly, or indirectly ...'.

arrangements (in place for several European NATO members) through which nuclear weapons are controlled in peacetime by US forces but can be designated for use on nuclear-capable aircraft deployed by NNWS in wartime. But control over the weapons and the decision to arm them would still remain in the hands of the nuclear powers.[32] As dual-key arrangements are unlikely to be applied in nuclear submarines, they are in any case irrelevant in the Scottish context.

Five possible NPT outcomes of the UK's break-up

The above discussion implies that there are five *legally* permissible outcomes to the break-up of the NWS that is now the United Kingdom. Some are implausible but they are worth listing nonetheless:

1. Scotland becomes the sole successor state to the United Kingdom under the NPT and takes on the mantle of NWS; rUK would dismantle its nuclear weapon capabilities and join the NPT as a non-nuclear weapon state.
2. Both Scotland and rUK join the NPT as non-nuclear weapon states. This might occur (a) after the UK had already abandoned its nuclear force, or (b) when the UK still possessed it.
3. The current British nuclear capability is subsumed into the capability of a federated European state which replaces the UK and France as an acknowledged NWS under the NPT.
4. The UK remains a single undivided state for nuclear and possibly broader security purposes, at least during a transition, but divides into Scotland and rUK for other purposes, including EU and UN membership (a confederal solution).
5. rUK becomes the sole successor state to the United Kingdom under the NPT and takes on the mantle of NWS; Scotland would dismantle any nuclear weapon capabilities and join the NPT as a non-nuclear weapon state. This seems by far the most plausible outcome. It would

32. The transfer of control to Germany – or Scotland – would be in breach of the NPT. The peacetime planning for either is still legal, but all bets are off in nuclear war, as US Secretary of State Dean Rusk made clear during Congressional Hearings on the NPT in June 1968: 'in a condition of general war involving the nuclear powers, treaty structures of this kind that were formally interposed between the parties would be terminated or suspended'.

be permissible for Trident to continue operating out of Faslane under this scenario providing it remained under the sole control of rUK.

Taking each possibility in turn:

1. **Scotland as the sole successor state**

Although legally admissible, and possessing a certain logic given the location of the Trident submarine base in Scotland, this option can be dismissed for obvious political and practical reasons. No politician or political grouping in Scotland has ever advocated that an independent Scotland should inherit the UK's nuclear force; it is hard to imagine that a Scotland which was trying to establish itself as a sovereign state, and to create good foreign relations inside and outside Europe, would compete with rUK for recognition as the successor NWS; and it is implausible that rUK would accede to Scotland becoming the sole inheritor of the British nuclear force.

The possibility that Scotland would seek to maintain or establish a nuclear force outside the NPT, as the Ukraine briefly contemplated in the early 1990s, can also be dismissed. Besides the great political costs and dubious security benefits, Scotland has no infrastructure capable of manufacturing and servicing nuclear warheads. Furthermore, the weapons in the Ukraine were land-based ICBMs, rather than submarine-launched systems that could easily be removed by the UK government from Scottish territory if there were any risk that they would be claimed by a Scottish state.

2. **Scotland and rUK both join the NPT as non-nuclear weapon states**

a) The UK had already disarmed prior to Scotland's independence

Especially if Scotland's independence did not occur in the next ten or twenty years, it is possible that independence would have been preceded by a decision by the UK to abandon its nuclear arms. This could follow *inter alia* from strong international movement towards complete nuclear disarmament, or from a British calculation that its security interests were better served by investments in other military capabilities and strategies.

The political, legal and instrumental tasks involved in bringing Scotland and rUK into the NPT as non-nuclear weapon states would be greatly simplified if the UK had already disarmed. There is, however, an intriguing legal twist to the UK's disarmament. As a state that exploded nuclear devices before 1 January 1967, the UK is defined as a nuclear weapon state in perpetuity by Article IX of the Nuclear Non-

Proliferation Treaty. It will be accorded this status so long as the Treaty survives as the primary source of international law in this field.[33] Some device would therefore have to be sought for 'de-legalising' or nullifying the UK's status under the Treaty and giving it recognition as a non-nuclear weapon state, even though it would formally remain a NWS under Article IX.

For example, in an article published in 1987, one of us argued that 'the only plausible way for Britain to give force under international law to a renunciation of nuclear weapons is to enter into an agreement with the IAEA and Euratom to apply full-scope safeguards to the nuclear fuel-cycle' (these safeguards are discussed in Appendix B). The UK's legal renunciation could be emphasised in a modified 'Basic Undertaking' to the safeguards agreement.[34] Although there has been no precedent, the means for cancelling the effects of Article IX and changing the UK's status under the NPT could certainly be found.[35]

If the UK had already gained legal recognition as a non-nuclear weapon state, the accession of Scotland and rUK to the NPT as separate non-nuclear weapon states would presumably be straightforward.

b) The UK had not disarmed prior to Scotland's independence

A joint decision to abandon the UK nuclear armament would not be legally problematic, although the issue of rUK's recognition as an NWS in terms of Article IX of the NPT would still have to be dealt with. The scale of the disarmament task after independence (involving the verified dismantlement and/or destruction of weapon capabilities) would be increased, rUK having most of the pertinent capabilities. One can imagine considerable political, legal and practical advantage in Scotland and rUK co-ordinating their political and instrumental approaches to nuclear disarmament. The whole process could be fraught, however, if rUK felt that it had been bounced into disarmament by Scotland.

---

33. As has often been discussed, a successor to the NPT might take the form of a Nuclear Weapons Convention outlawing nuclear weapons just as the Chemical Weapons Convention and Biological Weapons Convention have outlawed chemical and biological weapons.
34. Norman Dombey, David Fischer and William Walker, 'Becoming a non-nuclear weapon state: Britain, the NPT and safeguards', *International Affairs*, vol. 63, no. 2, Spring 1987, p. 204.
35. Any continuing presence of nuclear-fuelled submarines would be a particular complication, since the fuel cannot be kept under safeguards while the submarines are at sea. We discuss this below. Hitherto, the issue has not arisen because no non-nuclear weapon state has deployed nuclear submarines.

3. European integration

As discussed above, the NPT makes provision for a federated European state, with centralised control over armed forces, to take control of the nuclear forces of the UK and other EU states. Such an eventuality seems very unlikely in the medium term, even if it cannot be altogether excluded during the lifetime of Trident's successor.

That aside, cooperation between France and the UK on the development and management of their nuclear forces has been talked about for many years. As we discuss in Chapter 5, extending this cooperation through new basing arrangements would be one (remote) possibility for rUK if bases in Scotland were no longer available and Trident could not be relocated elsewhere in rUK. Provided that no transfers of ownership and control were entailed, the NPT would not stand in the way of such an arrangement, which is in principle no different from the foreign basing of nuclear weapons that is already common practice within NATO.

4. The confederal solution

The break-up of the Soviet Union created a precedent of sorts for the adoption, in the nuclear field, of a confederal approach to the break-up of the UK. When the Soviet Union was dissolved in December 1991, the emerging states formed the Commonwealth of Independent States (CIS) to manage their security relations. Control over the nuclear forces was formally vested in the CIS until Russia had unambiguously gained title to all of the nuclear weapons dispersed across the Soviet Union's territories. However, the CIS never attained or claimed statehood: it was an institutional device for managing security relations between the new states during the transition, and for finessing Russia's continuing control over nuclear forces that remained on Ukrainian and other soil.[36]

A similar mechanism could conceivably be established to handle the nuclear and other military issues arising from Scotland's independence. It could provide a means, for example, of organising the control and funding of conventional military assets which had not (yet) been divided between the two new states. Alternatively, the UK could be regarded as still existing for the purposes of managing the nuclear legacy. It is

36. If the CIS had been given statehood, it would in any case have been unlawful under Article I of the NPT for Russia to continue as an NWS since sole control would have been vested in the CIS. So Russia was always going to limit the sovereign status of the CIS.

nevertheless difficult to imagine the international community accepting that this UK or any other confederal institution could retain the UK's former status under the NPT while Scotland and rUK separately sought membership of the UN, EU and other international organisations. The idea that states can pick and choose how they are regarded and may behave has few supporters. More to the point, NPT Parties would surely require that Scotland and rUK, as well as any confederal entity, move quickly to establish their positions under the Treaty, negating the legal point of a confederal solution.

5. Scotland disarms, rUK becomes the sole successor state

Scotland's renunciation of nuclear weapons and rUK's maintenance of its nuclear force appears the most plausible scenario unless international circumstances changed radically. This requires us to consider how Scotland could accede to the NPT as a NNWS, and whether and how rUK could succeed the UK in its position as an acknowledged NWS under the NPT.

Scotland's accession to the NPT as a NNWS

Scotland's accession to the NPT as a non-nuclear weapon state would depend upon satisfaction of five conditions:

i) Scotland would have to gain recognition as a sovereign state. This would naturally follow admission to the United Nations, although recognition can happen without membership of the UN (Switzerland being a notable example of a sovereign state that is outside the UN and a member of the NPT). Until its statehood had been recognised by some means, Scotland would have no right to join the NPT.[37]

ii) Scotland would have to make it clear that it had no direct or indirect operational control over nuclear weapons sited on its territory, and rUK (or the US or any other NWS) would have to ensure that it alone exercised control over nuclear weapons based in Scotland.

iii) Any nuclear warheads or warhead components not forming part of rUK's (or another NWS's) force deployed on Scottish territory

37. Taiwan is an exception to this rule, being a signatory of the NPT even though it is not recognised by the majority of the international community as a sovereign state. But it had already joined the NPT in 1968 before losing its international statehood when the People's Republic of China took its place in the UN and the UN Security Council in the early 1970s.

would need to have been removed from the Scottish Government's control or dismantled. The closure or adaptation to civil use of facilities in Scotland that have provided goods and services to the UK nuclear force (the Chapelcross and Vulcan reactors are the prime examples) might be deemed appropriate but would not be required by the NPT.[38]

iv) The NPT would have to be signed by the Scottish Government, ratified by the Scottish Parliament, and Scotland's instruments of ratification accepted by one of the Treaty's depository governments (currently the Russian, UK and US Governments).[39]

v) As part of Scotland's accession to the NPT, all relevant nuclear facilities and materials would have to be brought under comprehensive International Atomic Energy Agency (IAEA) safeguards. Article III of the NPT gives the IAEA in Vienna primary responsibility for verifying compliance with the Treaty. Membership of the IAEA would have to accompany membership of the NPT. Subsequent to NPT membership, but before the required 'full-scope' safeguards could be applied in Scotland, the IAEA would have to be presented with (and verify) an 'Initial Report' containing a full and detailed account of inventories of uranium and plutonium that were held in Scotland outside the weapons and weapon facilities that remain under rUK's control. Safeguards arrangements for individual facilities could then be negotiated. (Safeguards issues are explored further in Appendix B.)

Although not required by the NPT, an independent Scotland would also be expected to establish its own nuclear export control laws, offices and practices, probably replicating those developed by the UK over decades.[40]

38. The NPT does not prohibit the transfer of weapon-related goods and services from NNWS to NWS (a loophole in Article II that has long been recognised).
39. Russia's recognition as having assumed the USSR's role as NPT depository automatically followed its acceptance as the USSR's successor as NWS under the Treaty.
40. This requirement is not laid down by the NPT. It was, however, enunciated in the Principles and Objectives on Nuclear Non-Proliferation and Disarmament which were agreed by States Parties in May 1995 at the NPT Extension Conference. Scotland would also presumably be pressed to comply with the guidelines of the Nuclear Suppliers' Group which specify the rules under which the UK and most other supplier states have conducted nuclear trade since the mid-1970s.

Export controls are currently administered by the Department of Trade and Industry (DTI) from London in conjunction with other UK government departments and agencies (they are reserved matters under the Scotland Act of 1998).[41]

Acceptance of rUK's status as NWS

When the Soviet Union was dissolved in 1991, the Russian Federation had no automatic legal right to inherit the Soviet Union's status as a NWS.[42] It claimed that right for itself, a claim that was accepted by the other newly formed states of the FSU (under the Alma-Ata Agreement of December 1991) and by the wider community of states. Among the various reasons for conferring this privilege upon Russia, two were uppermost. The first was that Russia held most of the nuclear assets that had been developed and deployed by the USSR, including the entire warhead production infrastructure. Unlike the Ukraine, it could sustain its nuclear arsenal and would not be driven inexorably towards its own disarmament by the huge cost and technical difficulty of acquiring new capabilities. The second reason was that Russia appeared determined to remain a nuclear power: a rejection of its claim to NWS status would have been tantamount to creating a new and formidable nuclear-armed state outside the NPT. This would have been far more damaging to the non-proliferation regime than accepting Russia's claim to succession.

rUK would similarly have no automatic legal right to inherit the UK's standing as an NWS under the NPT. But a claim to that right would probably, as in the Russian example, be accepted. Other governments would be mindful of their wider economic and political interests in maintaining good relations with the rUK, which would remain a major European power. The commitment of the US and EU to continuity would be reinforced if, as currently seems likely, they continued to attach political and strategic value to the existence of a second European nuclear force (besides France's) and to a second nuclear force (besides the US's) assigned to NATO. Other states might, in addition, prefer the UK's successor to remain an NWS so that it could sustain the UK's traditionally constructive diplomatic role within the

41. They include the Foreign and Commonwealth Office, Ministry of Defence, Customs and Excise and intelligence agencies.
42. See Yehuda Blum, *op. cit.*

nuclear club.[43] Last but not least, there would be the same inclination as in the Russian case – subsequently reinforced by India's and Pakistan's emergence as nuclear powers – to avoid forcing rUK to declare itself a nuclear power outside the NPT.

Nevertheless, rUK's position would be unprecedented. This would be the first time that an NWS's nuclear force had been based *entirely* on the territory of a non-nuclear weapon state. One can imagine qualms being expressed about accepting the credentials of such a nuclear power, especially if Scotland's independence raised doubts about rUK's ability to manage and operate the nuclear weaponry safely and predictably. It is hard to gauge international reactions to such an unusual situation, but the response in some capitals to rUK's claim to succeed to the UK's status in the NPT might be more equivocal than in Russia's case as a consequence. This would tend to focus international attention on the nature and tenor of the nuclear settlement between Scotland and rUK. If the settlement was amicable and cooperative, the situation might be accepted without further ado. If it were not, rUK's nuclear standing might well be seen as problematic. Even if it were not deprived of its formal status as a NWS under the NPT, trust in its abilities to function as a reliable nuclear power could be called into question. Rather than see this happen, substantial international pressure would surely be placed on the two governments to settle any differences.

Trident and the secession issue

In this discussion, indeed in all discussions of an independent Scotland's international standing, the questions of secession and of reactions to secession loom large. If Scotland's declaration of independence came to be regarded as an act of secession, and if the international community followed its usual instinct to punish the seceding state, Scotland would find itself out on a limb. This prospect has played a significant part in unionist claims that an independent Scotland would be a poor and isolated Scotland.

43. Even Russia might be wary of contesting rUK's claim if it feared that it could provide critics in Washington with ammunition to question its own claim to succession to bilateral and multilateral security treaties. Its right to succeed the Soviet Union has been challenged by some US analysts in the context of the ABM Treaty. They maintain that the USA is no longer bound by its provisions since the Soviet Union has no rightful legal successor. A rebuttal of this contention is provided by John Rhinelander, *op. cit.*

Bring Trident into the picture, however, and the situation changes. Chapter 5 will show that its relocation to some other part of the UK is not a realistic option in the short and medium terms. Chapter 6 makes it abundantly clear that Trident could not function as a credible, safe and predictable nuclear force if a Scottish government denied it political and administrative support. In consequence, an rUK that wished to sustain the nuclear deterrent would *have* to develop a cooperative relationship with an independent Scotland, and a relationship that enabled Scotland to accede to membership of the military alliances in which the UK nuclear force has a role. This would require an rUK government to lend its active support to Scotland's claims to automatic or near-automatic membership of NATO and, at the same time, of the European Union, the UN and other international organisations. So rUK's dependence on Scotland due to Trident would create a powerful incentive for London to play down the secessionist argument, and to press foreign powers to give equal treatment to Scotland and rUK.

The other side of the coin is that Scotland's insistence on Trident's eviction from the Clyde would remove this incentive. Indeed, it would probably encourage the rUK Government to veer in the opposite direction, insisting in retaliation that Scotland's action *did* entail secession, and that it should be made to suffer all the disadvantages following that judgement. It also follows that a decision by the UK to abandon its nuclear arms (or relocate them if that were possible) prior to independence would make a Scotland seeking independence more rather than less vulnerable to the secessionist charge.

The great irony is therefore that a newly independent Scotland may need Trident to establish a favourable international wind, just as it may need the threat of non-cooperation over Trident to extract political benefits from its location in Scotland. Essentially, those pressing for Scotland's independence have the opportunity (if they have the courage and wisdom to grasp it) to trade Trident's stay in the Clyde for international recognition and membership of the EU and other international organisations. Trident provides a means of preventing Scotland being left out in the cold. By the same token, the unionist claim that Scotland would lose out internationally and thus domestically, if it were ever to seek independence, would be an empty threat so long as the nuclear force remained based on the Clyde.

Chapter Five

Could Trident Be Relocated?

It is possible that agreement could be reached for rUK to continue to base nuclear weapons in Scotland after independence. The implications of such an arrangement are explored in Chapter 6. Yet a prior question for policymakers would be whether alternative bases could be found elsewhere and, if so, how and over what period relocation could take place. The purpose of this chapter is to examine these alternatives in detail.

Three broad observations deserve to be made at the outset. The first is that there would be formidable difficulties involved in building an alternative Trident base in the short term. It took five years (1963–68) to construct the new facilities required for the Polaris programme at Faslane and Coulport, during a period when safety regulations were less restrictive than they are today. It took a further nine years (1984–93) to upgrade these facilities for the additional tasks involved in supporting Trident.[1] Even if cost were no problem and an alternative location could be rapidly identified, it is hard to see new facilities being completed in less than five years. It would probably take much longer.

If Trident were to be removed from Scotland before an alternative permanent base could be completed, it might be possible to use a 'depot ship' (or submarine tender) to supply port services for the displaced submarines. This is the system that the US used to support its own SSBN submarines at Holy Loch during 1960–1992. The most recent US ship used at Holy Loch for this purpose (USS Simon Lake) was able to provide US SSBN's with a wide range of repair and re-supply services, including diving and underwater repair, torpedo overhaul, nuclear repair, fire control repair, resupply of food, fresh water, fuel oil, weapons and

1. The initial application for planning permission was submitted to Dumbarton District Council in May 1984 and the Secretary of State for Scotland gave his approval to the MoD's notice of development in March 1985, subject to a number of requirements. The Explosives Handling Jetty was towed from its construction site at Hunterston to Coulport in April 1992, and was fully commissioned by the end of 1993. Following handover of the ship-lift to the MoD in July, Faslane was formally opened in August 1993.

crane services. It also provided personnel services on a daily basis, including medical (doctors, operating room), shops (including dry cleaning and laundry), soda fountain and barber shops. The submarine tender's mobility enabled it, at short notice, to move to another location in response to strategic requirements. USS *Simon Lake* was decommissioned from service in 1999, having been homeported in Rota, Spain and La Maddelena, Italy as well as at Holy Loch.[2] To our knowledge, it has not yet been scrapped, and it could perhaps (at a cost) be brought back into service in the Royal Navy.

It might also be possible to use a large floating dry dock to carry out those repairs that currently require the use of the fixed ship-lift facility at Faslane. Yet it is likely to be significantly more difficult to find an interim armaments depot to replace Coulport. Because of the particular safety requirements that it would have to meet, such a depot would have to be situated some distance from the main naval base (or depot ship). An ingenious new solution (perhaps involving at-sea replenishment or the use of US or French facilities) might be devised in response to the crisis created by a precipitate departure from Faslane.[3] Yet the technical challenges involved are likely to be considerable, and success would be far from assured. Even if a solution to the armaments depot problem could be found, moreover, the cost of maintaining the submarine force through depot ships – both financially and in terms of demands on personnel – would be difficult to sustain in the long term.

If none of these interim solutions were thought to be workable, it would no longer be possible for Trident to continue its normal operational patrols. In these circumstances, Coulport would presumably be used to unload all in-service warheads as each of the boats returned from patrol, for subsequent transfer (by land) to Aldermaston. Each of the boats would then be laid up, at least temporarily, at another rUK location (perhaps Devonport) until a new base became available.

The precipitate removal of Trident from Scotland would not leave rUK entirely deprived of a capability for using nuclear weapons. Facilities for refurbishing and manufacturing nuclear weapons would still exist at Aldermaston. Given sufficient warning time and investment, it might also be possible to use modified Trident warheads to restore some nuclear

2. Federation of Atomic Scientists, *Nuclear Forces Guide: AS–33 Simon Lake class*, July 2001.
3. The issue of foreign basing in the US or France is discussed later in this chapter.

capability to the RAF's Tornado bombers: a capability that the UK had abandoned in 1998 with the scrapping of the WE–177 free-fall bomb. Yet such a 'belt and braces' RAF nuclear capability could not be introduced (except perhaps in times of national emergency) until the completion of a time-consuming programme of testing and safety improvements. It therefore could not provide continuity in nuclear operations if Faslane were suddenly to become unavailable.[4]

The difficulties involved in rapid relocation would reinforce the argument of rUK negotiators that Scottish independence should not be used to force through changes in the UK's nuclear status without rUK being given sufficient time to provide adequate alternative basing arrangements. The Scottish negotiating team, by contrast, might come under strong domestic pressure to avoid an open-ended commitment that could be seen as undermining aspirations to a nuclear-free Scotland. It might also discern some tactical advantage in leaving the option of expulsion open as a bargaining chip.

The second observation is that the available options for relocation, and the balance of costs and benefits attaching to them, would depend substantially on the timing of independence and how this related to Trident replacement decisions. If the transition to independence occurred late in Trident's operational lifetime (for example, after 2015), and if replacement decisions had been taken in the meantime which foresaw the closure of the Scottish facilities, agreement between Edinburgh and London would be comparatively easy to reach. Indeed, plans for phasing out Faslane and Coulport might have been fully prepared by then, plans with which the Scottish Government might be relatively content to live. By contrast, if independence occurred after a decision had been taken to base Trident's successor system in Scotland, negotiations might be more difficult, and might focus on the possibilities of reversing such a decision. Finally, if a vote for independence had taken place before a replacement decision, it could accelerate the timetable for such a decision, and could force the rUK Government to look much more carefully at non-Scottish sites than it might otherwise have done.

In any event, given the costs involved, relocation is only likely to be tolerable to the government of rUK (or UK) if it forms part of a replacement decision. If one concludes, as we shall, that finding new

4. If precipitate expulsion of Trident were accompanied by a refusal to continue supplying tritium from Chapelcross, rUK would have to find another source of tritium, although there are probably sufficient stocks in hand to last several years.

sites for Trident in rUK or elsewhere would be difficult in any circumstances, two things follow. One is that the London Government would have great problems responding to any demand for Trident's removal if it had not already addressed the replacement issue, just as the Scottish Government would be wary of acceding to any extension of basing rights if definite plans and timeframes for Faslane's and Coulport's future were not forthcoming. The other implication is that the UK Government cannot take for granted, as it did in the 1970s, the long-term availability of basing facilities for an SSBN fleet (in Scotland or elsewhere) when MoD begins considering Trident's replacement in the next decade or so.[5] That being the case, it may be forced to undertake a much more wide-ranging review of its future nuclear policy options than it might otherwise have expected. Those options would have to include delivery systems other than the SLBM, the possibility that the next system might entail greater integration with the French or US deterrents, and indeed the UK's abandonment of its nuclear force. What is commonly referred to as the replacement decision may therefore be more than that: it may more aptly be described as a continuation decision.

The third observation is that opening new nuclear bases in the UK is likely to be qualitatively more difficult than in the past. Today's bases were developments of military sites that had been opened for various purposes during or between the world wars. No planning permission was sought or required for this initial development. As the Crown lost its exemption from planning provisions in the 1970s, the opening of any new sites or the extensive development of old sites now has to be submitted, by MoD or any other governmental organisation, to a local planning inquiry under the Town and Country Planning Act. The Government recently had to jump this hurdle when extending the training grounds on the North Yorkshire moors. It succeeded, but not without stirring up significant public opposition. The opening or radical development of new sites for the operation of nuclear forces – especially of sites required for the storage, loading and unloading of warheads – would be even more problematic.

Under planning guidelines, inquiries are usually confined (unless the Government decides otherwise) to the local implications of altering, constructing and using buildings, roads and other kinds of infrastructure. The policies that lie behind planning applications are not opened to

5. We shall see in Appendix B that many factors, including the cost and feasibility of life extension, will influence the timing of replacement for both the Trident missile and the Vanguard-class submarine.

scrutiny as they are presumed to be matters for the Government and Parliament to decide.[6] On such a controversial issue as nuclear basing, and in a field where protest groups are so active and well informed, any government would have difficulty keeping policy out of the debate if not out of the inquiry. Even if it managed to confine the discussion, the presentation of the safety case would give rise to special problems. The safety implications of civil nuclear installations can and have been subjected to searching examination in public inquiries. But this could not happen with nuclear weapon facilities, especially where warheads are involved, for obvious reasons. The inquiry would be forced to take evidence in secret. That would run counter to accepted practice and would be bound to stoke up controversy.

Matters would be further complicated by the presence in the Public Record Office of the assessment of sites for Polaris that the MoD conducted in the early 1960s (the conclusions of which were discussed in Chapter 1). The MoD would have to explain why the grounds used for rejection in the 1960s no longer applied today. Although technologies and circumstances have changed, this would not be easy.

There is another issue here. Our research into the 1963 MoD assessment of alternative Polaris sites revealed that safety analyses were largely limited to local risks arising from accidental explosions and releases of radioactivity. The exposure of neighbouring populations to an increased risk of nuclear devastation as a result of the bases becoming nuclear targets was not used as an explicit criterion. This methodology appears to have been based on the dual assumptions that (a) deterrence would work; and (b) that if it did not, the entire country would be devastated in a nuclear exchange, with those within range of nuclear bases neither more nor less vulnerable than the general population. A similar 'blind spot' in official criteria was also evident in the Trident decision in the 1980s, when the MoD went to considerable expense to safeguard against the possibility of a 1-in–10,000 years earthquake, but was not willing to acknowledge any increased risk of collateral damage to nearby population centres in the event of a nuclear strike on the Faslane area.

The ability so to confine safety considerations would have been more difficult if the decisions had been opened to public debate (the Government's censorship of the film The War Game in 1965 showed its great

6. There have been exceptions, notably the Windscale Inquiry of 1978 and the Sizewell Inquiry of 1984. In both cases, the Government wished to establish the long-term case for investment in reprocessing (Windscale) and light-water reactors (Sizewell).

reluctance to allow people to understand the realities of nuclear war). Today, it would be hard to prevent the risks of becoming targets entering into the debate about siting in England or Wales, not least if the risk of nuclear devastation had previously been presented by Scotland as a primary reason for rejecting Trident or its successor.[7]

A future government in London, using all the political and administrative power at its disposal, might still be able to gain the site approval that it required to relocate the facilities currently at Faslane and Coulport. It could also, of course, promise local communities many future benefits in terms of employment and economic development. But, given the difficulties involved, it might find itself entering the siting process without a great deal of confidence that it was fully able to control the outcome.

Relocation requirements

In physical terms, the relocation of Trident (or a successor submarine system) would require:

- a Faslane-equivalent facility (with capacity for 3–4 SSBN's and 4–5 SSN's, jetties, ship-lift, stores, staff support facilities etc.);
- a separate Coulport-equivalent facility (with warhead and torpedo stores, explosive handling jetty, capacities for missile removal and storage etc.);
- surrounding infrastructure to enable Trident to operate out of, and support activity at, these facilities (anti-submarine warfare capabilities, secure communications, roads, access to civilian workforce and housing for service personnel, etc.).

It is possible that alternatives to two other facilities in Scotland which currently support the nuclear force would also have to be found. Those

7. Because some potential opponents (for example in the Middle East) may have only small arsenals, a limited nuclear exchange may now be more plausible than in the past. It is also conceivable that the use of the UK Trident force in 'sub-strategic' attacks, for example in order to pre-emptively destroy enemy WMD forces in a crisis, could be matched by an attack designed to destroy part of the UK's own nuclear capability. Because at least one submarine is always on patrol, and more are likely to be at sea in times of crisis, a surprise attack could not hope to destroy the UK's retaliatory capability. By holding the possibility of a direct attack on UK cities in reserve, however, an enemy state might hope to reduce the chances of retaliation against its own cities.

facilities are the Chapelcross reactors (which supply tritium) and the Vulcan research station at Dounreay (where submarine reactor designs are tested). As the Chapelcross reactors are already approaching the end of their lifetimes – closure in 2010 has been mentioned – MoD will have to find another source of tritium come what may. Replacing Vulcan would be expensive but not on the same scale as Faslane and Coulport, and alternative sites could probably be found in England (Harwell would be an obvious candidate).

It should also be recalled that a sizeable part of the infrastructure required to sustain the UK (or rUK) deterrent is already located outside Scotland. It includes Aldermaston (provision of warheads), Northwood and Rugby (submarine communications), King's Bay in the US (missile servicing) and Devonport (submarine refitting and refuelling).

If the Royal Navy were to be removed from Scotland, it might also have to find alternative sites for other linked facilities. Cape Wrath provides a unique site for live naval gunnery exercises that would be very difficult to provide elsewhere. The Navy also uses the BUTEC sound range in the straits near Skye as a 'passive sound range'. The purpose of this facility is to provide a capability to 'noise range' submarines and surface ships, as well as to practise torpedo firing. No comparable facilities exist elsewhere in rUK, and they would not be easy to recreate. They would require a location in territorial waters that combined shelter, deep water and lack of civil traffic. In the absence of such a location in rUK, the Royal Navy would be forced to rely on other facilities (for example those in the Bahamas) for this purpose.

These ancillary problems are significant, and they serve to illustrate the multi-faceted nature of the Royal Navy's current presence in Scotland. Yet the relocation debate would inevitably be focused on finding substitutes for Faslane and Coulport. This will be our concern in the remainder of this chapter.

Site selection criteria

Although their relative weighting might be different, the same five factors identified in the 1963 Polaris studies discussed in Chapter 1 are likely to preoccupy those charged with examining the options for relocating Trident:

i) **Ease of submarine operations.** A new base would have to provide assured, and relatively sheltered, access to the ocean for the 16,000-ton

Trident boats. This would rule out many locations that lack both the depth of water and the shelter needed for Trident to enter and leave with a full load of missiles. It is also desirable that Trident can rapidly reach deep waters, given the importance of avoiding enemy surveillance. Given the decline in Russia's ASW capability and the lack of another hostile power in the Atlantic with the necessary naval capabilities, this requirement might have become less important than in the past, although it would still figure in MoD's calculations.

ii) **Safety**. The sensitive question of populations' exposure to nuclear attack, and the likely future difficulty of avoiding its consideration in public debates, has already been discussed. On the risks of accident and radiation release, the operating bases would have to meet national standards set for both civil and military nuclear facilities. These would, for example, require a ship-lift capable of meeting the stringent requirements for withstanding storms and earthquakes that caused so many difficulties with the Faslane works programme in the 1980s. Safety requirements also dictate that the RNAD be separated from the main operating base by at least a mile. According to the 1963 study of location options, RNAD has to be located at least 4,400 feet from significant areas of housing or population. But increased sensitivity towards risk since the 1960s could require the government to seek locations that significantly exceed this minimum safety distance. Since many of the UK's best port locations (outside Scotland) are close to heavily populated areas, satisfying safety demands would be a tough challenge.

iii) **Logistics**. It would be important to provide all the supporting facilities necessary for a new base, including ease of access for supplies, warheads from Aldermaston, housing and other facilities for service personnel, and access to a civilian workforce. In contrast to the safety factor, this consideration tends to militate against remote locations (this was the main reason why remote Scottish locations were ruled out in 1963). It would also count against island or offshore locations where any of the apparent safety advantages would, in addition, have to be weighed against the costs (in terms of safety and finance) of having to load and unload supplies twice.

iv) **Ownership, development costs and planning permission**. If potential sites were not already owned by the Government, they would have to be bought. This could prove both time-consuming and expensive.

Some sites would require more preparatory work than others, and the time needed to complete planning permission processes and any compulsory purchase would also have to be taken into account.

v) **Overall Cost.** The Government would have a strong incentive to minimise the cost of a new base. Some options could be ruled out on grounds of excessive costs.

A sixth factor would probably weigh heavily on the Government – the political risk at the local, national or even international level of proposing new sites and taking them through the planning process. The sensitivity to political reactions would create particular difficulties for locations in Northern Ireland (terrorism, political instability and objections by the Irish Republic) and, albeit to a lesser extent, in Wales (regional politics).

The possibility of location in Northern Ireland, for example using converted facilities at Harland and Woolf shipyards in **Belfast**, would be highly problematic. In addition to the political and security problems it would pose, an Irish location would pose major logistical problems, with warheads and other supplies having to be transported by road to mainland ports, shipped on secure convoys to Northern Ireland, then unloaded and loaded onto the submarines. We have therefore not examined this option in detail.

Three locations in Wales were considered in the 1963 study. **Fishguard** was not subject to detailed study, perhaps because of its remoteness and lack of existing facilities. The 1963 Working Party described it as 'rather exposed. Just feasible if northern breakwater substantially developed. Considerable dredging required. No site for RNAD jetty'. **Holyhead** was dismissed as 'more exposed than Fishguard. Dredging required. No site for RNAD jetty'.

The most plausible Welsh site would be **Milford Haven Sound** in south-west Wales. It has a deepwater harbour, good access to the Atlantic Ocean and is remote from large population centres. One naval interviewee suggested it would be 'an ideal spot' from a practical point of view. The presence of medium-sized towns (Milford Haven and Pembroke) might also provide a source for some of the several thousand civilian personnel needed for the base, although they would initially lack the variety of skills found in the Clyde, as well as providing possible locations for housing naval personnel within commuting distance of a base. The MoD facility at Pembroke Dock might be a possible location for an operating base.

In 1963, it was estimated that Milford Haven had suitable locations available at the Navy's 70-acre mine depot at Newton Noyes for the base and east of Thorn Point on the south side of the Haven for the RNAD. It was therefore included on the short list of ten sites identified for closer study, only to be rejected because of the risks involved in locating explosives near what was then a major oil storage and transportation port (involving, inter alia, considerable tanker traffic). Texaco and TotalFinaElf still maintain refineries that are supplied through Milford Haven Sound, on the southern and northern sides of the bay respectively. These refineries would have to close if a new submarine base were to be located here. Relocation to Wales might also be fraught with political difficulties, particularly if the success of Scottish nationalism had been accompanied by parallel developments there.

Within England itself, only three sites made it on to the 1963 working party's shortlist of ten: all of them in the south-west of the country.[8] The then naval base at **Portland**, near the town of Weymouth in Dorset, was eventually ruled out because of the lack of a suitable RNAD location. The working party concluded that 'no site can be found for the RNAD on the Isle or on the mainland except well beyond Weymouth, necessitating transport of assembled nuclear weapons through built-up areas. This is unacceptable; and no alternative RNAD site could be provided within one hour's steaming'.[9] It is possible that such constraints might be relaxed in future. Warhead movements to and from Faslane are less frequent than in the past, but customarily involve transport along motorways that pass through the centre of Glasgow. Given the increased effectiveness of the Trident system compared with Polaris, it might be possible to accept an RNAD located some distance away (for example, by a joint arrangement with Falmouth). Yet, even if the RNAD issue could be resolved, a new Portland base would still be put at a disadvantage by other factors, including its exposure to poor weather and distance from deep water.

8. **Barrow-in-Furness** in Cumbria has some obvious advantages as the construction site for the Vanguard-class submarines, and is also relatively remote from major centres of population. It would have to be ruled out, however, because of the need to navigate through mudflats to reach the sea. Even at high tide, Trident boats cannot enter and leave Barrow while fully laden with missiles.
9. *Naval Ballistic Missile Force: Report of Working Party established by SMBA 5268 dated 25 February 1963*, P.O.B./P. (63) 2 (henceforth 'Report of Working Party'), ADM 1/28965, Public Record Office, Kew, p. 8.

Devonport and Falmouth

So we are left with Devonport and Falmouth – the only two sites outside Scotland that were included in the shortlist of six considered by the 1963 working party.

In the absence of a much more detailed technical study, it is impossible for us to come to a definitive conclusion on the costs and benefits of these two sites. A broad idea of the issues that would arise in any reassessment, and the conclusions that might be drawn, can nevertheless be presented.

Location in or near **Devonport** would have a number of clear advantages. It has logistic advantages (shorter lines of supply to Aldermaston and to naval stores) and is under MoD ownership. It already hosts the Royal Navy's largest ship, the 21,000-tonne HMS Ocean, together with fourteen Type 22 and Type 23 frigates, six hydrographic survey ships and seven Trafalgar-class attack submarines. There are an estimated 5,000 ship movements annually, and it is the largest naval base in Western Europe, covering an area of some 622 acres.[10] As a result of the 1993 decision to relocate facilities for major refitting of Trident (including refuelling) at Devonport, the channel to the sea has been widened to allow the larger SSBN boats to enter.

Further shore work would be necessary to accommodate the specific facilities needed for the much larger Trident submarines. But the location of all UK submarines (SSN and SSBN), together with related refit work, at a single location might provide significant advantages compared with building an entirely new base, not least by allowing more efficient use of both naval and civilian personnel, as well as other facilities. As a result of the rundown in the frontline fleet since the end of the Cold

10. 'Nuclear Forces Guide', *Federation of American Scientists*, June 1997. One well-informed interviewee told us that Devonport, or indeed any other SSBN base in the South-West, lacks the favourable geography (e.g., variety of exit points) and ASW infrastructure (e.g., seabed sensors) that have been so important in maintaining the Clyde-based force's detection-free record. While such factors might have left Devonport unacceptably exposed to enemy ASW during the 1980s, the decline in the scale (though not the technical sophistication) of the Russian ASW threat is such that this consideration may now be rather less important. The 1963 study also pointed out that Devonport suffered from the disadvantage of being remote from existing 'sound-ranging' facilities in Scotland, which could not be provided locally. This seems unlikely to be a decisive factor if all other problems could be resolved, not least because it would be a problem that Devonport shared with all possible rUK sites.

War, it has been suggested that the Navy has an over-capacity in its naval base provision.[11] Scottish independence could therefore provide an opportunity for further rationalisation of the Royal Navy's base structure, with additional capital outlays offset, at least partially, by reductions in operating costs.

Yet space at Devonport Naval Base is already at a premium, and the scope for relocating the nine Faslane-based submarines would be further constrained by restrictions (imposed for reasons of safety) on the minimum distances that are maintained between Trident and other ships, as well as the limits on other ships' weapons movements that would be necessary if they were to be stationed near to SSBNs. It is possible, as a consequence, that Devonport's surface ships would have to relocate in order to make room for the additional submarines. Short of building a new base, the only option in these circumstances would be to expand the capacity of the naval base at Portsmouth, where the rest of the surface fleet is already located. Any additional investments that this would require would then add to the already high cost of moving Trident.

Much would also depend on exactly how much new work would have to be done to allow Devonport to be used as Trident's operating base. The most expensive single item in Trident construction costs for Faslane was the massive ship-lift, designed to allow SSBNs to be lifted out of the water for repair and maintenance. Yet a new dry dock is also being constructed at Devonport for use in the Trident refits. If this facility could be adapted for use as part of an operating base, the requirement for a new ship-lift might be postponed or even removed. Such an option might, however, make it more difficult to continue the scheduled Trident refit programme at Devonport without further development of the site. That being the case, relocation would probably require the upgrade of a second Devonport dock into a Trident operating facility (perhaps with a new ship-lift in addition).

Because of the proximity of large areas of housing (Devonport is part of the Plymouth conurbation), the government would also have to overcome safety objections to the use of existing dockyard facilities for the operating base. The traditional association of Plymouth and Devonport with the Royal Navy could make sustained protest from local people less likely than at an alternative site. Even so, the recent controversy in Plymouth over plans for a new raft-based explosives facility as part of

11. 'Privatisation plan for nuclear base', *BBC News Online*, 4 August 2000.

the naval base suggests that local objections to a much bigger development would have to be taken very seriously.

The most serious obstacle to using Devonport as a new Trident base is likely to be the location of the RNAD. Much of the River Tamar's shoreline is densely populated, severely restricting the choices available in the Plymouth area. In 1963, only one location was deemed a possibility: the Wilcove area immediately opposite the dockyard. Even by the safety standards of that time, however, this location was thought to provide only 'marginal explosive safety factor for berths of adequate reactor safety'.[12] Naval quarters in St. Budeaux (on the river's opposite bank), together with the bulk of the Thanckes Oil Fuel Depot and the villages of Wilcove and Cangapool, lie within 4,400 feet of the hypothetical RNAD site. If the safety radius were extended to one and a half miles (to reflect today's reduced public tolerance of risks), large populated areas in the suburbs of Torpoint, Saltash and St Budeaux (as well as the Trident dockyard itself) would also be affected, effectively ruling out Wilcove as a location.[13]

Even if these safety doubts could be allayed, the Wilcove site would have to be purchased and developed by the MoD. The land is adjacent to the National Trust property of Antony House, though we understand that the area itself is mainly owned by the Duchy of Lancaster. The 1963 working party believed that local objections to development in this area would be strong, and would require an extensive process of consultation and eventual compulsory purchase. The agreed design would have to meet, at a minimum, the stringent safety standards required for the Coulport project. Given Wilcove's greater proximity to population centres, the government might feel obliged to tread even more carefully in order to allay local concerns.

An alternative location would be in the **Falmouth area**. The locations proposed there in the 1963 study were judged to have an acceptable safety rating. In most other aspects, however, they compared poorly with Devonport. Exit routes provided poor protection from anti-submarine surveillance, and the proposed berths are exposed to southerly to westerly gales, possibly restricting harbour movements. Extensive work would be required and it would be a very expensive site to develop, with the

12. Report of Working Party, *op. cit.,* p. 6.
13. One of the main criteria used in the 1963 study was that the Polaris operating base and RNAD must be separated by at least 4400 feet. This safe distance may well have increased subsequently, both because of the greater explosive power of Trident missile propellant and increased public sensitivity to risk.

RNAD site (on the west bank of the river near St Mylor) being particularly difficult because of local topography. In addition, the land would have to be purchased, mostly from the National Trust or Duchy of Cornwall which would probably be extremely reluctant – and have no legal right in the National Trust's case – to part with it.[14]

The difficulties involved with the Falmouth site are bound to have increased since 1963. More stringent safety standards would add substantially to the expense involved in constructing new facilities on steep and cliffy locations, as experience with Coulport in the 1980s showed. The National Trust would probably object strongly, with public backing, to the development of its St Just site (part of its impressive investment in preserving Cornwall's coast) into a Trident operating base; and the tourist industry in that part of Cornwall would hardly be likely to welcome nuclear weapons into its midst. Whereas the 1963 study listed only the small settlements of Tregew and Trefugis as falling within the explosive safety distance from the RNAD, 'ribbon' housing development along the road east of Mylor means that many more people could now be affected, including the inhabitants of the village of Mylor Churchtown. The numbers affected might still be small enough not altogether to rule it out as an RNAD location. But the negotiation of compensation for those affected would still add to the costs involved in a Penarrow Point location.

A significant drawback of the Falmouth option, compared with Devonport, is its greater cost, partly a consequence of the need to build two new 'greenfield' sites rather than one, and partly because of the lack of an adequate skill-base. The 1963 working party therefore studied the possibility of combining the two options, locating the operating base in Devonport while building a new RNAD near Falmouth. The study concluded that such an arrangement would 'stretch to an unacceptable degree the requirement for proximity of the operating base and the RNAD'. When this argument was made in 1963, however, the Navy gave high priority to maximising the number of boats at sea at any one time, thereby necessitating the fastest possible turnaround between patrols. In today's different international climate, the Government has made it clear that such a high state of alert is no longer justified. Once account is taken of the reduced need for constant travel to and from the RNAD,

14. The National Trust holds land 'inalienably' – it cannot be sold or mortgaged. However, the land is not protected from compulsory purchase by the Government. Its one extra protection lies in the Trust's special right to petition the House of Commons and submit a proposed compulsory purchase to a vote. (Telephone interview with National Trust legal department, London.)

it is possible that a joint Devonport / Falmouth arrangement could come into play, especially if it were decided that no suitable location for the RNAD existed in the Devonport area. Yet this option still presupposes that it would be possible to expand Devonport's naval base facilities. As suggested above, such an assumption might prove problematic.

Costs of relocation

In assessing the likely cost of constructing new bases for Trident, one possible starting point is the original programme of shore construction at Faslane and Coulport for Trident. The total cost of the shore construction element of the programme came to £1.7 billion at 2000/1 prices (or £1,433 million at 1995/6 prices).[15] In addition to new construction directly related to Trident, relocation would also involve the provision of new facilities for the SSN squadron currently at Faslane, along with the MoD and Marine forces used for force protection. It would also be necessary to provide accommodation for some proportion of displaced personnel.

The use of Devonport (if it were feasible) might be expected to be less expensive, for example, than the development of a completely new base at Falmouth or Milford Haven. Yet even in this case the complications involved, including the possible relocation of surface ships to Portsmouth, would be considerable. Whatever the location of the new submarine base, moreover, major new construction programmes are notoriously unpredictable and prone to cost escalation. The programme to refurbish the Devonport Dockyard to accommodate Trident, for example, suffered a 60% cost increase after the decision to relocate this function from Rosyth.[16]

The cost of relocation would depend crucially on the time available for site preparation and construction. The longer the time available, the more the MoD would be able to seek ways of improving project cost-effectiveness, for example through holding design and construction competitions and assessing other alternatives. The more urgent the timetable, by contrast, the greater the risk of serious mistakes and cost overruns.

---

15. 'Statement on the Defence Estimates 1996', *Seventh Report from the Defence Committee, 1995–1996*, 1996, p. 101. This excludes costs of shore construction at the Rosyth Dockyard, of which £328 million at 1995/96 prices was also included in the Trident programme.
16. 'Royal dockyards sell-off overvalued', *BBC News On-line*, 3 June 1998.

Some factors might tend to reduce cost estimates. Spending on portable items (for example, parts of the explosives handling jetty, which was originally constructed at Hunterston before being towed to Coulport) might not have to be fully replicated at a new location. Furthermore, the experience of running Trident at Faslane/Coulport could also be drawn upon to develop more cost-effective means of operating a new base complex. A new construction programme could also reflect the fact that Trident was now operating at a tempo significantly below the maximum capability for which the force was originally planned in the 1980s. Only 48 warheads are deployed on each boat, well below the plans on which current Coulport designs were based. These operating levels might be reduced still further in future, while allowing some margin for expanding deployments. It might be unnecessary, therefore, to construct a Devonport/Falmouth infrastructure with the same capacity as that at Faslane/Coulport. Reduced warhead numbers might, for example, allow some reduction in the level of investment in a new explosives handling facility. Yet it is doubtful whether many savings could be made through a more pared-down design. In a climate of ever-increasing safety consciousness, which would be particularly marked in this project, it is more likely that a fresh design would be obliged to incorporate additional safety features, further raising costs.

The cost of relocation to another permanent base in the UK therefore seems unlikely to be less than the £2 billion (at today's prices) spent on Trident construction in the 1980s, and likely to be a great deal more. It is hard to conceive of a newly non-nuclear Scotland being willing to finance any part of this cost, which would therefore have to be borne by a country with a somewhat diminished national income, having lost the product of the Scottish economy.

Yet the Scottish Government would also face additional costs, incurred as a result of the closure of naval facilities at Faslane and Coulport. Even if some part of Faslane were retained for use by fishery patrol vessels, most of the area would have to be decontaminated before it could be ready for alternative use. If the base were being closed as a result of a decision in London, the MoD might be expected to meet these costs. In circumstances where the Scottish Government had been the driving force for the base's closure, however, it would almost certainly have to accept responsibility for these costs. Edinburgh would then have to decide whether, and when, a clean-up could be afforded.

For rUK, the costs of relocation could not be justified unless the new facilities had a guaranteed long-term future, probably involving their use by Trident's replacement system. The relocation cost would have to form part of the replacement cost to be at all acceptable. The corollary is that the costs of replacing Trident with a similar system would be significantly inflated if MoD could not count on re-using or upgrading existing facilities at Faslane and Coulport. Come what may, any need to relocate would diminish the attractions of maintaining an equivalent nuclear armament when MoD considered its priorities for investing in defence equipment over the long term.

The foreign basing option

If no alternative base were available in the rest of the UK, yet Scotland still insisted on Trident's removal from its own territory, rUK might be forced to explore more radical options. In this context, one possibility that might be considered would be for the UK Trident force to make use of the well-equipped SSBN bases that already exist in the US or France. In the case of the US, the two navies have a long history of close technical and operational cooperation, as do the respective nuclear establishments. The UK's Vanguard submarines already visit **King's Bay** in Georgia every ten years in order to load and unload unarmed Trident missiles for servicing. An agreement to transfer some of the services provided by Faslane and Coulport to the US would therefore build on a well-established structure of cooperation. Moreover, the US Navy now has excess capacity in warship repair and basing facilities. Since 1990, the number of US SSBNs has fallen from 34 to 18, and it is due to fall further as anticipated cuts in the strategic arsenal are made. As long as the US maintains two SSBN bases, therefore, it may be possible to provide support for the UK submarine force at the King's Bay facility.[17]

The second foreign basing option that the UK might consider is to seek an arrangement whereby Trident would use some of the French SSBN facilities at **Brest** in Brittany. The French submarine force is similar in structure and mission to that of the UK, and the two countries

17. Ten of the US's Ohio-class submarines (carrying the Trident D5 missile) are based at King's Bay, Georgia, using facilities built for the purpose during 1981–90. A further eight Ohio-class submarines (carrying the older Trident C-4 missile) are based at Bangor in Washington state. The long range of the Trident missile (6,500 nautical miles) reduces the need to have two separate Atlantic and Pacific fleets, especially if some increase in warning time of major conflict is assumed. Even so, given the political difficulties involved in base closures, the most likely outcome is still that both bases will remain open.

are the only EU members to operate both SSBNs and SSNs. The French Triomphant class SSBN is almost the same size as the UK's SSBN, displacing 14,300 tons dived, compared with the Vanguard class's 15,900 tons. There could be operational advantages from being based within a short voyage from Devonport on the other side of the Channel. The French option might also have some attraction to those who want to strengthen Anglo-French cooperation in nuclear planning, as part of a wider commitment to EU defence cooperation. It might be combined, for example, with a coordination of replacement programmes and force protection measures.

The distinct design and logistical requirements of UK submarines mean that existing US or French repair infrastructures might be able to provide only a limited level of support for many repair and resupply functions (though access to general supplies, such as electricity, fresh water and food, might be shared). There is little tradition of cooperation between the UK and French submarine forces, in part because of France's absence from NATO's integrated command and from the 1958 US/UK Mutual Defence Agreement. Even the US and UK navies, between whom cooperation is much better developed, have not shared information on reactor design since the 1950s, and have developed very distinct safety cultures. Significant investments in separate UK support systems would therefore be required in order to maintain the Trident fleet from a foreign base.

Until longer-term arrangements could be made, such an arrangement might make use of UK-controlled depot ships and/or floating docks, as discussed at the start of this chapter. In time, it might also involve the creation of distinct docking facilities, built or modified to Royal Navy requirements, but also able to take advantage of the general infrastructure (not least safety clearance and security) of the host base. A large contingent of naval personnel would have to be located in the base. It would presumably also be reliant to a significant extent on a locally employed civilian workforce.

There are precedents for such an arrangement. A large part of the (nuclear-armed) RAF and British Army was based in Germany, and reliant on local base support, during the Cold War. The US Navy was able to maintain a forward operating base for its SSBNs at Holy Loch for more than thirty years. Even so, the technical and organisational challenges involved in such an arrangement should not be underestimated. Perhaps the most difficult operational problem involved in foreign basing would be the location of the RNAD. Although loading and unloading of warheads is relatively infrequent in the normal course of events, facilities for doing so need to be constantly available, for safety reasons, at a location near to the operating base. The establishment of such a facility on foreign soil would always be problematic, not least because of the need to avoid any risk to host-nation forces using the same base area. In addition, a safe method for transporting warheads from Aldermaston would have to be found. Warhead transport across the Channel may be less problematic, and more rapid, than across the Atlantic. Air transport might bring its own risks. Both would require close cooperation between the relevant authorities of the countries concerned.

Basing in the US or France would not necessarily affect the short-term operational independence of rUK's nuclear force: that is, the ability of the rUK Government to order the use of nuclear weapons, even if the US (or France) had not agreed to this action. Provided that separate means of communicating between rUK's command authorities and its Trident missile submarines at sea were maintained, the rUK Prime Minister would remain capable of independently 'pressing the button'.

Even so, reliance on foreign basing would involve a greater degree of medium-term dependence on another state than the long-term 'procurement dependence' on the US that the UK has already accepted.[18] Much would depend on the rUK government's assessment of the risk that some future US or French government might terminate a basing arrangement at short notice, and also on its assessment of whether adequate alternative basing arrangements could be made for such an eventuality. The rUK government would seek assurances on these questions in negotiations with a prospective host government. How far the US or France would feel able to give such assurances, however, is far from clear.

Most of all, such an arrangement could prove problematic in rUK domestic politics. If it were being proposed after a considered comparison of alternative options, there would still be problems in accepting the highly visible logistical dependence on another power that reliance on a foreign base would involve: a dependence that would be shared by none of the other recognised NWS. Even so, it might be accepted as part of a reasonable adjustment to new circumstances (economic and strategic). It would clearly signal that the main role of the UK force was to contribute to wider EU/NATO, rather than national, objectives.

18. For a discussion of the UK's decision to forego 'procurement independence', see Michael Quinlan, *Thinking About Nuclear Weapons*, RUSI Whitehall Paper Series 1997, pp. 75–79.

If the only alternative was the construction of the first new naval base in Britain for a century, moreover, the budgetary attractions of shared basing might appear considerable.

On the other hand, if it were seen to be a forced response to expulsion from Scotland, it could only add to the sense of humiliation that rUK leaders would feel, with potentially costly repercussions for wider rUK/Scotland relations. By its very nature, even more than basing in England and Wales, foreign basing is an option that would be very difficult to discuss in advance of, or even during, independence negotiations. No foreign government would want to be involved in such discussions unless the Government in London took the initiative first. The UK Government, for its part, would not want to discuss this option unless and until the option of continuing basing in Scotland were definitively ruled out.

Other options

In the early 1960s, the Navy considered other radical alternatives for Polaris basing, including a rock shelter base in the Scottish Islands, some East of Suez options, and a depot ship needing no fixed base (on the US Holy Loch model). The rock shelter option would present considerable logistical difficulties, despite its possible attraction from a safety viewpoint. East of Suez options (for example, basing in Singapore) might once have had some rationale when the UK was still a major colonial and naval power in Asia. They appear entirely implausible today. As discussed above, a depot ship might be a more serious alternative, especially as a temporary arrangement while new land bases were being constructed.

The Royal Navy's deepwater dockyards at **Gibraltar** might once have been considered as a possibility. The Trident submarine HMS Vanguard carried out a visit to Gibraltar in November 1998, the first ever port visit by an operational UK Trident submarine. The controversy generated over the Navy's request to carry out minor repairs on HMS Tireless, a nuclear-powered SSN, in 2000, however, suggests that this is not a realistic option.[19]

There may be other alternatives not considered here. Without a detailed feasibility study of all the options, it is hard to come to definitive

---

19. 'HMS Tireless: Repair to Proceed', *Ministry of Defence Press Release*, 15 September 2000.

conclusions. Yet, whatever option appears most favourable, there should be no illusions as to how formidable the task of building a new base complex would be. Faslane is the only naval base to have been built in the UK since 1909–16 (when the dockyard and base at Rosyth were built), and the Faslane/Coulport project was one of the largest construction projects of the 1980s and early 1990s.[20] A comparable project in the early twenty-first century might well involve comparable risks.

Conclusion: the implausibility of relocation

The conclusion we draw from this discussion is that it *might* be possible to relocate Trident, but only at great expense, after lengthy preparation, and at considerable political cost. This would be well understood when the Edinburgh and London governments entered negotiations. Assuming the latter wished to retain an independent nuclear force, therefore, it would be likely to press hard for Trident to remain in Scotland, at least until the viability of an alternative option could be fully guaranteed.

20. Graham Thompson, 'The British Trident Nuclear Programme – full steam ahead', *Armed Forces*, May 1988, p. 230 estimated that the Trident works programme was 'the biggest single project ever undertaken by the Property Services Agency'.

Chapter Six

Keeping rUK's Nuclear Bases in an Independent Scotland

Short of rUK abandoning the nuclear armament, and given the formidable obstacles to relocating Trident discussed in Chapter 5, London's preferred option is likely to be to leave it where it is, as an rUK force based in an independent Scotland. This could be a difficult pill for many Scots to swallow. Besides the history of anti-nuclear feeling, they would have to accept that a newly founded Scottish state which had renounced nuclear weapons under international law would be entitled to *no* control over the nuclear forces that remained on its territory. As we have seen, the Nuclear Non-Proliferation Treaty is emphatic on this point.

Leaving control of the nuclear force in London would thus imply a waiving of sovereignty over the most important military forces on Scottish territory, and a reliance on another government for controlling risks of a particularly acute kind – the risks arising from the practice of nuclear deterrence. This concession would be required at the very moment that a new Scottish Government was striving to express its sovereignty and the rights that went with it. More than this, independence would bring a *lessening* of Scottish political control over the nuclear deterrent, insofar as Scottish politicians and civil servants would no longer be participating in the Government that exercised that control.[1]

Scotland's necessary abstention from operational control over the nuclear armament – control which would remain with an rUK assuming it inherited the UK's legal right to be a nuclear weapon state – seems to us the deepest problem that would confront any Scottish Government which sought to justify Trident's continuation in the Clyde. It would not be the only problem. The new Government would also have to satisfy itself that populations and environments were being adequately protected against accident and radiological damage.

1. While Scotland has been part of the UK, its political representatives have often participated in the groups of senior Ministers who have been involved in the management of international crises and in decisions relating to nuclear weapons.

Yet it is increasingly understood in nationalist circles, whatever their rhetoric, that Trident could not be expelled overnight. Its removal from the Clyde would have to be phased over years. Over how many years is of course a critical question, but even a phase-out implies a continuation, albeit a temporary continuation, of current practices. Some nationalists concede in private that Trident might have to stay rather longer than a few years, possibly even until the end of its anticipated operational life-time, if other essential nationalist goals are to be achieved. They even speculate that Trident could become their most valuable negotiating asset if they could persuade its erstwhile opponents to share their pragmatism. From this perspective, Trident's retention in the Clyde might be traded for, *inter alia*, rUK's acceptance of a fair division of oilfields and other economic resources together with its unequivocal support for Scotland's accession to the EU. On this last matter, it is hard to imagine a Scottish Government being able to rally domestic support for accepting Trident without obtaining an effective guarantee that it would not be left out in the cold in negotiations of membership of the EU and other international bodies.[2] Indeed, support for EU membership seems *the* prerequisite for Scotland's flexibility on nuclear basing.

But it takes two to tango. The Government in London would also have its conditions. Operating Trident out of an independent Scotland would not be the same as operating it out of a Scotland that recognises the ultimate authority of London. There would have to be confidence south of the border that Trident could be operated safely and predictably and without undue interference.

What are the main conditions which Edinburgh and London might attach to Trident's stay in the Clyde? Although much would depend on circumstance, a number can be anticipated. We explore these conditions before considering how Trident's continued basing in Scotland might be formalised by the two governments through agreements and treaties.

Conditions for Scotland's acceptance

In our view, there are five main conditions for an independent Scotland being able to accept the long-term basing of Trident in the Clyde.[3]

2. Although such a decision would be one for EU member states (see Chapter 4), their main interest would be in stability. If rUK were therefore to give its full weight to automatic Scottish membership, the chances of such a bid succeeding would be much enhanced.
3. By 'long term', we mean a period of time greater than that necessary for the

i) **Participation in NATO.** In his book on basing practices under international law, John Woodliffe draws attention to the distinction between 'installations whose rationale is to serve the defence of an alliance of which the host State is a member, and installations whose peacetime purpose is to serve the needs and interests of the user State rather than assist in the defence of the host State'.[4]

While it is commonplace for these rationales to be mixed (the US base at Okinawa providing an example), the second class of installation can only arise in isolation where the host state is subservient to another state. It arose largely during the colonial and immediate post-colonial periods (the US base at Guantanamo in Cuba and the UK sovereign base area at Akrotiri in Cyprus are among the few surviving examples).

It is difficult to imagine that a nuclear base which was regarded as serving *only* rUK's purposes would be tolerated north of the border other than for the time necessary to build an alternative base (and perhaps not even for that long). Commitment to nuclear deterrence would therefore have to be seen to be serving the common security interests of Scotland and rUK, together with the interests of their broader alliance within NATO, and/or whatever EU security institutions were in place at the time of the UK's fragmentation.

In a NATO/EU framework, Trident's presence in Scotland could be justified as a distinctive contribution to European and transatlantic defence in return for which Scotland would gain the protection of other states, including the UK and the US. The positive security guarantee (whereby its members are pledged to regard an attack on any of their fellow-members as an attack on them) that accompanies membership of NATO might appear highly desirable to a state that had a foreign power's nuclear forces deployed on its territory. It also enables minor powers (such as Scotland) to avoid the burden of sustaining unaffordably large defence forces.

A necessary (but not sufficient) condition for Trident's long-term stay in Scotland would therefore be the latter's agreement to adoption of a military approach that emphasised cooperation with other European states through the EU and NATO. The one seems inconceivable without the other. We shall see below that the need to protect the nuclear bases from terrorist and other attack, and to protect their supply chains, would

---

design and construction of alternative facilities in rUK, or for Trident's replacement by another nuclear system.

4. John Woodliffe, *The Peacetime Use of Foreign Military Installations under Modern International Law* (Martinus Nijhoff Publishers: Dordrecht, 1992), p. 31.

also tend to drive Scotland and rUK into close military and intelligence cooperation.

ii) **Continued acceptance of nuclear deterrence.** The security advantages associated with Trident would also have to be mutual. The rUK's commitment to maintaining nuclear deterrence, and thus Trident, would have to be seen to be a result of considered and shared security needs. If London's desire to hang on to Trident was perceived to stem largely from inertia and an obsession with prestige, it would be hard – unless there were other overwhelming advantages to Scotland – for the new Scottish Government to mount a sufficient case domestically for granting rUK long-term rights to operate its nuclear force out of Scottish territory. The willingness to allow rUK to use the nuclear bases would therefore be influenced by the presence or absence of foreign threats of great seriousness, and on the strength of support in Scotland for nuclear deterrence as the most effective protection against those threats. It would also be influenced by the credibility of the traditional argument that nuclear disarmament must be pursued by nuclear weapon states multilaterally or not at all (not a straightforward argument for a Scottish Government proposing its own unilateral disarmament).

There is, however, a catch here. While evidence of military necessity might affect the credibility of the case for nuclear deterrence in Scotland, protest movements tend to gather strength in periods of international tension, precisely the time when (for others) deterrence has greatest utility. If Trident in Faslane were seen simply as a relic which Scotland had to suffer because the English could not afford to shift it, or if at the other extreme Trident were on the front line in some future politico-military confrontation, the politics of nuclear weapons could become very difficult in Scotland. The issue might be most manageable if Trident had some utility but not too much utility.

UK governments have had no great liking for taking the argument for the nuclear deterrent into the public domain. Although the current UK Government has shown more openness on these matters than any of its predecessors, it has made little effort to argue the case for Trident (either in Scotland or elsewhere), leaving its opponents with a comparatively free run. Its silence stems partly from the complexities of judgements about deterrence, partly from a calculation that this is not an issue with serious electoral consequences, and partly (in the case of Scotland) from its instinctive desire to preserve the pre-eminence of London in the security field and to sustain the essential unity of security discourses in the UK: what is good and a sufficient argument for the UK is good and sufficient for Scotland as a part of it, even under devolution.

Just for the rUK Government or its allies to argue the pitch for Trident's retention in the Clyde would not be enough. To have a chance, the case for anything other than a short stay would have to be supported in Scotland by the Scottish Government. If that Government were formed by the SNP, this would entail a reversal of current policy. The Labour Party showed in the early 1990s that such a U-turn on nuclear disarmament is not out of the question. But it could be especially dangerous to the SNP, and for the cohesion of a new Scottish Government, if such a policy shift had not been signalled and prepared before the elections and referenda leading to independence.

iii) **Consultation on nuclear use, strategy and alert status.** Under the NPT, an independent Scotland would not be entitled to any control over the nuclear weapons in its midst. That is no different from the situations that Germany and a number of other European states have lived with for decades.[5] Within NATO, member states participate in the Nuclear Planning Group (NPG) which meets regularly in Brussels to discuss broad policy issues, and Scotland could expect to be fully represented in this group. NPG doctrine also provides for host states – currently including Belgium, Greece, Germany, Italy, Netherlands and Turkey, as well as the UK – to have special arrangements for consultation in relation to the US nuclear forces based on their territory. Within this generally accepted norm, a Scottish Government could also insist on the establishment of special mechanisms for consultation with the Government in London. For example, Scottish military and civilian officials could be attached to the relevant directorates of the MoD in London.

Although providing some opportunity for addressing issues connected

5. For discussion of US foreign nuclear bases, see Robert Norris, William Arkin and William Burr, 'Where they were', *Bulletin of Atomic Scientists*, 55:6, November/December 1999, pp. 26–35. For a history of UK nuclear bases overseas, see Richard Moore, 'Where Her Majesty's Weapons were', *Bulletin of Atomic Scientists*, 57:1, January/February 2001. Some of the US nuclear weapons that remain in Western Europe are assigned to 'dual key' arrangements, in which US warheads would be released for use by the air forces of (non-nuclear) European NATO member states in times of war. This arrangement is deemed to be compatible with the NPT in peacetime, while ensuring close involvement in nuclear operational planning by the NNWSs concerned. Even if Scotland were interested in some such arrangement, it is hard to see how it could work for a submarine force.

to the deployment and usage of nuclear weapons, these consultation mechanisms might be insufficient to allay the anxieties that accompany the absence of control. What other steps could be taken to reassure Scotland that its exposure to nuclear risks as a consequence of the policies and actions of its larger neighbour would be minimised? One option would be to adopt an arrangement similar to that still in force between the US and the UK, and last updated at the height of the controversy over the planned deployment of US Cruise missiles at Greenham Common in England. According to the key statement made by then Prime Minister Margaret Thatcher at the time:

> The existing understandings between the UK and the US governing the use by the US of nuclear weapons and bases in this country have been jointly reviewed in the light of the planned deployment of Cruise missiles. We are satisfied that they are effective. The arrangements will apply to US Cruise missiles based in the UK, whether on or off bases. The effect of the understandings and the arrangements for implementing them is that no nuclear weapons would be fired or launched from British territory without the agreement of the British Prime Minister.[6]

The precise nature of these 'arrangements', which continue to apply to US nuclear weapons based in the UK today, have not been made public. At a minimum, one can assume that they involve the maintenance of secure communication facilities (a military 'hotline') between and within the two Governments, together with the maintenance of sufficient UK capability for processing the necessary information for timely consideration by political leaders. Although there is no physical means by which the UK can exercise a veto over a US nuclear strike, therefore, the joint understanding that no launch from British territory can take place without the Prime Minister's agreement implies that procedures and infrastructure must be in place that allow the UK to make its views on a proposed launch known in a timely and informed manner.

A similar undertaking given by rUK to Scotland would have an important political and symbolic value, and the principle of parity between their relationship and the previous US/UK agreement would be a difficult one for the rUK Government to reject. If implemented, this would imply an rUK pledge not to fire Trident missiles from Scottish

6. Written Answer by the Prime Minister, *House of Commons Debates*, 12 May 1983, col. 433.

territorial waters without prior agreement: the same as the arrangements covering the US's basing of Polaris in the Holy Loch from 1960.

Yet Trident missiles are much more likely to be launched while submarines are on patrol than when they are in territorial waters, not least because the Government would not want to leave submarines as 'sitting ducks' in Faslane in the event of a serious crisis. A Scottish Government might therefore insist on a more meaningful pledge, for example by insisting on prior consultation before any rUK use of Trident's nuclear weapons.

In order to make such a pledge meaningful, the new Scottish Government would need to establish procedures and infrastructure that could support such consultation in a timely, informed and secure fashion. This might include secure means of communications between the two Governments and within the Scottish Government and a technical capacity to understand and analyse intelligence data and targeting information, together with sufficient foreign policy expertise in the Scottish civil service to make sense of the wider context of perceived threats. An independent Scotland could not develop such capabilities by itself. But it could draw on rUK technical assistance, and insist on institutionalised arrangements for data exchange, as part of a prior consultation agreement.

There might be objections to such an arrangement if it were felt that it was significantly stronger than those available to other non-nuclear weapon states in NATO, such as Belgium and the Netherlands. Yet Scotland and rUK might counter that their circumstances could not be compared with those elsewhere in NATO, and therefore their arrangements would have to be *sui generis*. In particular, they could argue, nuclear consultation arrangements would have to reflect the unique character of the (evolving) political relationship between two Governments and armed forces that had previously been integrated, and that would remain highly interdependent.

Perhaps even more important than arrangements for consultation prior to use would be an agreement to give Scotland a meaningful say in decisions over Trident deployment and doctrine. For example, Scotland could press for regular updates on the operational readiness of Trident submarines to fire their missiles, and on the circumstances in which that readiness could be increased. In the 1998 Strategic Defence Review, the Labour Government announced that 'only one Trident submarine is on deterrent patrol at any one time', that 'the submarines are routinely at a 'notice to fire' measured in days rather than the few minutes quick reaction alert sustained throughout the Cold War', and that 'their missiles are de-targeted'.[7] These commitments might be clarified and elaborated in order to provide further assurances that the Trident force would be operated as a weapon of last resort and only in a manner that minimised the threat to bases and population centres in Scotland. Where consultation on alert status is concerned, a precedent was set after US forces in Europe were put on the highest alert during the Yom Kippur war in 1973 without consulting allied governments. The US responded to their objections by pledging to consult any NATO ally before issuing an alert to US forces on its territory. The UK Government also announced that it expected to be kept informed about the state of readiness of US forces stationed in the UK.[8] A Scottish Government could insist on the same treatment.

Scotland could also insist on its right to be consulted over questions of rUK nuclear doctrine and policy, including areas such as threat assessment, targeting policy and warhead requirements. This would give Scotland's leaders a significant, if in reality always limited, opportunity to exert influence over rUK nuclear weapons policy and might be acceptable to rUK provided that Scotland did not gain any veto rights. Like the 'dual key' arrangements between the US and several non-nuclear NATO member states, however, such agreements would also be seen as implicating Scotland in the nuclear business, with all the moral dilemmas that this involves. A 'Scottish eye on the button' might therefore have the effect of undermining, rather than reinforcing, support for Trident basing.

One way in which the Scottish Government might respond to related concerns that it was being exploited in such arrangements could be to insist on major changes in UK nuclear policy. Scotland could argue, for example, for rUK's adoption of a no-first-use strategy. The subject of much international controversy in recent years, such a strategy would be based on a commitment never to be the first to launch a nuclear attack, a pledge which might (in some circumstances) be thought to lessen the likelihood of pre-emptive or accidental nuclear war. Whether rUK would be prepared to make such a commitment, and whether its actions would carry legitimacy if NATO refused to abandon its current policy, is very doubtful. Any change in NATO policy would have to

7. *The Strategic Defence Review: Supporting Essays* (London: The Stationery Office, 1998), p. 5–2. For further discussion of these commitments, see Malcolm Chalmers, 'Bombs Away? Britain and Nuclear Weapons under New Labour', *Security Dialogue*, 30, 1, March 1999, pp. 61–74.
8. John Woodliffe, *op. cit.*, pp. 161–162.

come primarily from the United States, its dominant nuclear power. Hitherto, the US has shown no interest in adopting no-first-use, and it is unlikely to be influenced in this regard by a small and newly emergent state like Scotland.

iv) **Scottish oversight of health, safety and environmental regulation.** There would have to be confidence in Scotland that the regulation of nuclear sites was handled competently, and that the regulators were accountable to the Scottish Government and Parliament. As noted in Chapter 3 and Appendix A, all regulation of health, safety and environmental impact at the naval bases in Scotland is presently conducted by organisations that answer to the Government in London. The Captain Naval Nuclear Regulatory Panel, which oversees submarine reactor safety, and the Strategic Systems Integrated Project Team, which oversees weapon safety, are based in Bristol and report to the Ministry of Defence in Whitehall. The Health and Safety Executive (HSE) and its Nuclear Installation Inspectorate answer to the Department for Transport, Local Government and the Regions and have their main offices in Bootle in Lancashire. Only the Scottish Environmental Protection Agency, which regulates radioactive emissions, answers to Ministers in the Scottish Executive.

This concentration of regulatory responsibility in London has good reason. It eases problems of co-ordination and allows for any interdepartmental issues to be addressed through the Cabinet and Cabinet Office. However, substantial responsibility would have to pass to Edinburgh if Scotland gained its independence. But the required regulatory expertise could not be grown in Scotland overnight, and there would be significant activities and matériel at Faslane and Coulport that could *not* be opened to Scottish regulation for security and legal reasons, including the Nuclear Non-Proliferation Treaty's prohibition on non-nuclear weapon states having access to nuclear weapon information. This again points in the direction of co-operation: the effective and politically untroubled regulation of nuclear bases in Scotland would require extensive co-operation between Scotland's and rUK's regulatory bodies and governmental institutions. How that co-operation would work, and where the boundaries of responsibility would be drawn, would have to be negotiated during any transitional period. The regulatory rights and responsibilities of a third party – the United States – would also have to be addressed, given the US's key role in supporting the Trident system.

v) **Securing other benefits from Trident's stay**. The possibility that Trident's continued basing in Scotland might be 'traded' for various economic and political benefits has already been mentioned. The argument can be turned around. A newly independent Scotland would be unlikely to be flexible on Trident if rUK were inflexible on other matters. For example, an insistence that Scotland was seceding from the United Kingdom, with all that this would imply for rights to membership of the EU and other treaties and organisations (see Chapter 4), would hardly encourage a Scottish Government to look kindly on demands that Trident should remain at Faslane and Coulport. Likewise, Scotland could not be expected to provide a home for an asset as important (so it is claimed) to European security, yet potentially so dangerous to its own security, if the European Union – and NATO – turned down a Scottish request for membership.

There would nevertheless be obvious dangers to Scotland-rUK relations, and to their chances of negotiating a robust settlement, if there were too strong a linkage between nuclear and other issues when they came to negotiation. What would be required for success would be a negotiating atmosphere in which both sides understood the need for concessions and accepted that the objective was to establish a co-operative relationship rather than pander to nationalism and selfish and narrow concepts of interest.

Conditions for rUK's acceptance

For the Government in London, one question would be uppermost when it considered its attitude towards keeping Trident in Scotland for a sustained period after independence: whether it would still be able to operate the nuclear force and its associated facilities safely, effectively and without interference. Confidence would depend on three factors in particular – the Scottish Government's unequivocal political support for the basing arrangements, satisfaction that safety measures would not be compromised, and co-operation in military and paramilitary protection of the base, the nuclear force and their supply chains.

i) **Scottish political support**. No state could contemplate basing its nuclear force, and especially its only nuclear delivery system, in another state whose government was not prepared to provide the support and services necessary for the equipment and facilities to operate in a predictable manner. An important element of that support, entailing military cooperation, is considered in some detail below. Here we shall highlight one other vital element: the willingness of a Scottish Government to use the capacities of the Scottish state to protect the bases and their employees against peaceful or not so peaceful protest. Could rUK count on the Scottish police and state apparatus to provide an effective outer guard of the nuclear installations? More than that, could it have confidence, given the history of antagonism towards nuclear weapons in both the SNP and the Scottish Labour Party, that a Scottish Government would avoid providing tacit or overt support for protestors? In recent times, the protest movement against Trident has gained potency from the backing that it has gained from the nationalist community and from some venerable Scottish institutions (including the Moderator of the General Assembly of the Church of Scotland who joined a protest march at Faslane in March 2001). Its potency would be magnified several times over if a Scottish state itself became an agent of protest, or if it was reluctant to sanction the police actions that would be needed to maintain the bases' security.

In entering negotiations after independence, one can easily envisage a Scottish Government being torn between *raison d'état*, which would push it towards making concessions to rUK in the interests of recognition and other stately purposes, and the desire to avoid setting itself in any way against the democratic right to free expression. It might therefore feel bound to secure an explicit democratic mandate for the extension of basing, through the Scottish Parliament, before it could confidently enter such an agreement with rUK. The result of such a vote might depend on how public opinion evolved during the period of negotiation following a referendum in favour of independence.

From London's point of view, concerns about the Scottish state's ability and will to provide the necessary political protection for Trident would probably encourage it to formalise the arrangements in binding treaties and agreements, thereby committing Scottish governments of whichever hue to honour their undertakings (these treaties and agreements are discussed below). Those concerns would discourage adoption of the informal agreements that have characterised the basing arrangements with the United States (also see below).

ii) **Maintenance of high safety standards**. Ensuring safety at the nuclear bases would have paramount importance for rUK as much as for Scotland. However, conflicts of interest could arise from demands for greater transparency and accountability and for the primary regulation of safety to be carried out from Scotland, set against the jealous guarding of safety responsibilities by organisations south of the Border. Suffice it to say that both sides would have to be satisfied that the optimisation of safety had precedence over other ambitions.

iii) **Protection and supply**. The UK nuclear force does not operate in isolation from the rest of the security services. It depends on several additional capabilities for protection and logistical support. This deserves some elaboration.

First, a key role in the defence of Trident submarines is played by the Royal Navy's nuclear hunter-killer submarines (the SSNs). They are used to guard the Trident boats against attack by enemy ships and submarines, including while they are stationary when launching their missiles. Their superiority in this role stems above all from their invisibility. As of 2000, the UK had 12 SSNs in service, including five Swiftsure-class boats based at Faslane, three of which are due to be replaced by new Astute-class submarines.[9]

Second, capabilities are needed to protect the routes through which Trident submarines transit from Faslane to the ocean. Current multi-purpose capabilities, that would be available for this role if necessary, include shore and seabed-based sensors, five minehunters and four patrol craft operating out of Faslane. In addition, three squadrons of Nimrod maritime patrol aircraft are based at RAF Kinloss on Scotland's north-east coast, aircraft which can be deployed to RAF Machrihanish at the entry to the Firth of Clyde if necessary. The Royal Navy also deploys anti-submarine helicopters at Prestwick on the Ayrshire coast, although these are due to be relocated to Culrose in Cornwall during 2002.

Third, the west coast of Scotland is the location for several other facilities linked to the presence of submarines at Faslane. The British Underwater Test and Evaluation centre (BUTEC), which has its headquarters at Kyle of Lochalsh, monitors submarine noise trials, and the Ministry of Defence has submarine berths at Campbeltown, Loch Long,

9. Seven of the SSNs, belonging to the newer Trafalgar class, are based at Devonport. Current plans provide for two of the Swiftsure boats at Faslane (*Splendid* and *Spartan*) to be decommissioned in 2003 and 2006. As a result of a decision made in the Strategic Defence Review, the total SSN force is due to fall eventually to ten boats, with the three older Swiftsure boats being replaced by Astute-class submarines between 2006 and 2010. See 'The Strategic Defence Review', *Eighth Report from the Defence Committee*, September 1998, p. xcii. Plans are now well advanced to build the new facilities at Faslane necessary to accommodate the larger Astute-class submarines.

Loch Goil, Loch Striven, Loch Ewe, Rothesay Bay and the Isle of Skye which can be used in the event of major conflict. Cape Wrath is used for practising live firing with conventional munitions, both by the Royal Navy and other NATO navies. No alternative facility is available in northern Europe, and relocation to England or Wales is unlikely to be feasible.

Fourth, military, police and intelligence forces are used to protect Faslane, Coulport and adjoining sea areas from infiltration and attack. A security unit of the Royal Marines is deployed at Faslane to protect high-security areas from land and sea assault. Police are also active in base defence, both military and police forces being equipped with high-speed guard boats and inflatables and having diving units in the area. The 1998 Strategic Defence Review also announced that five infantry batallions are assigned to contribute to the nuclear force's defence if necessary.

Fifth, various forces are needed to transport warheads and related supplies by road between Aldermaston in England and the storage facilities at Coulport, and to provide protection en route. Warhead convoys are tracked on a regular basis by peace campaigners such as Nukewatch, and there is the ever-present possibility that they will be disrupted by direct action.[10] The Ministry of Defence has to work closely with local police forces along the several hundred mile-long route in order to protect the convoys. Precautionary measures are also needed to protect them against possible attack or hijack by terrorists, requiring the rapid deployment of mobile special forces in the event of emergency.

Trident as a force for military integration?

It is therefore evident that support for the UK's nuclear deterrent consists of much more than the Trident boats with their associated infrastructure. A significant part of the rest of the Royal Navy, and elements of the other two services, also need to be ready to protect it if circumstances demand. In addition, the operation of Trident does not rely just on the Faslane and Coulport bases with their defined boundaries. It requires

10. For example, on 21 June, 2001 a group of protestors stopped a Coulport-bound nuclear weapons convoy on the Stirling/Dumbarton road, just outside Stirling, by getting underneath the vehicles. Protestors estimate that the convoy was held up for between 20 and 30 minutes. Eleven people were arrested by local police and held overnight. 'Activists stop nuclear convoy outside Stirling', *Trident Ploughshares Press Briefing*, 21 June 2001.

access to and usage of a wider geographical terrain, including the Clyde estuary, and a larger set of facilities.

If Scotland and rUK moved towards the creation of entirely separate conventional forces, therefore, the problems involved in protecting and re-supplying a Trident base in Scotland might be insuperable. The rUK might be reluctant to rely on newly formed Scottish security forces to protect Trident operations given their uncertain quality and dedication (at least initially). The new Scottish Government, for its part, might find it difficult to accept the permanent basing of rUK conventional forces, including Marines, aircraft and minesweepers, in and around the Clyde. The role of intelligence services might be another bone of contention. These strains could quite quickly undermine the acceptability of basing Trident in Scotland, pushing both governments to seek alternatives.

It seems inescapable, therefore, that the rUK nuclear force would not be able to operate in Scotland without deep military co-operation and co-ordination between the two countries. A decision to leave Trident in Scotland would thus have many implications for the shape and deployment of Scotland's and rUK's conventional forces, just as decisions on those forces would affect the manner in which Trident could be operated. Like it or not, there would be a strong interconnection between the conventional and nuclear force 'settlements', especially regarding maritime forces, which would have be negotiated. Equally, the need for close cooperation would encourage both sides to consider whether some conventional forces should continue to be operated on an integrated basis, partly with the protection of Trident in mind.

Cooperation would be particularly important in personnel policy, both in relation to Trident and more broadly. Perhaps as many as 40% of Faslane-based naval personnel identify themselves as Scottish, as do most locally recruited civilian personnel. It is highly probable, moreover, that residence would be the main criterion for citizenship in an independent Scotland. Although the Scottish Government would not have political control over Trident, many of its citizens would therefore be involved in Trident operations at every level. As a consequence, rUK would be dependent for the operation of its nuclear force on service personnel a substantial proportion of whom had another nationality.[11] Such an arrangement could only work if defence relations between Scotland and

11. The presence of Irish citizens in the UK armed forces (and, at times, in Royal Navy submarines) provides a precedent in this regard. Dual citizenship might also be a possibility, depending on the arrangements reached on this question between Scotland and rUK.

rUK were so close that military personnel were not seen to be facing divided loyalties, and if there were agreement in Scotland and between Scotland and rUK on how secrets would be protected (Scotland's adoption of an equivalent of the current Official Secrets Act could be tricky in Scottish politics).

Because of this inevitable dependence on Scottish personnel, Trident basing in Scotland would help to protect Scottish personnel from the loyalty pledges and expulsions that have accompanied the break-up of armed forces in collapsing states (most prominently in the former Soviet Union in the early 1990s). If recent recruitment difficulties persisted, moreover, rUK would not only want to retain its existing Scottish personnel. It might also want to be able to seek new recruits from Scotland, not least for the naval forces based at Faslane.

If rUK armed forces remained open to Scottish citizens, this might have considerable benefits for Scotland. It would reduce pressure on the new Government to establish new conventional forces of its own primarily as a means of creating defence-related employment.[12] At the same time, it would avoid the waste and disruption that would be the inevitable result of seeking to subdivide organisations that are designed to operate on an integrated all-Union basis. No doubt, an independent Scotland would still want some independent armed forces of its own, fulfilling necessary ceremonial and quasi-policing roles (such as fishery protection and back-up to emergency services). It might also choose to build up selected areas of specialist contribution to international capabilities. In general, an independent Scotland would have the option of taking an incremental approach to building defence forces, establishing them only when a need was clearly identified. It might seek to emulate the developed military capabilities (and relatively high defence budgets) of countries such as Norway and Sweden. But it would also have the choice of arguing that its main contribution to common defence was its agreement to allow Trident to stay at Faslane. It might then use the combination of Trident basing and close alliance with rUK to maintain defence spending at a level nearer to that of Denmark (which spends 1.5% of its GDP on defence), Ireland (which spends 0.9% of GDP on defence, but is not in NATO), or even Iceland (which has no armed forces but is a NATO member).

Such a package could bring major savings if compared with the

12. This has been the predominant thrust of proposals for defence policy by SNP spokespersons. See, for example, Jack Hawthorn, *Some Thoughts on an Independent Scottish Defence Force*, Scottish Centre for War Studies Occasional Paper 1, University of Glasgow, 1997.

traditional SNP option of moving rapidly towards a repatriation of Scottish-based elements of the UK armed forces – including all the Scottish regiments – to national control. This latter option might appeal to nationalist sentiment, and might be forced upon Scotland in response to a decision to expel Trident. It would be strongly opposed by many Scots in the armed forces, who would lose the opportunities available in the larger forces of the UK. It might also provide a poor return on investment in whichever military capabilities were acquired.

In the longer term, the viability of a settlement that involved Trident basing and low defence spending would depend on whether Scotland was content with a limited self-defence capacity. Many nationalists would baulk at the continuing dependence on rUK that such an approach might imply. Others inside and outside the nationalist camp will reject arguments that independence could be managed without significant disruption to the country's armed forces. If independence did take place, however, the financial benefits could shift opinion in favour of a co-operative approach.

Vulcan at Dounreay

Before moving on, we should not overlook the Ministry of Defence's Vulcan submarine reactor test facility at Dounreay on the northern edge of the Scottish mainland (Vulcan is managed and operated on MoD's behalf by Rolls-Royce which has manufactured all of the UK's submarine reactors). We noted in Chapter 4 (see also Appendix C) the likely pressures to close the Vulcan facilities in the event of Scotland's independence, not least because of the difficulties that Vulcan might pose for international safeguards.

Like Faslane, Dounreay has been an emotive issue in Scottish politics. There have long been accusations that activities carried out there pose unacceptable risks to public safety and the environment, and that Dounreay provides yet another example of the UK foisting dangerous works on Scotland. The problems have arisen from the site's civil rather than its military activities, the latter having attracted surprisingly little comment in Scotland. Dounreay was the primary location of the research and development programme on fast breeder reactors and reprocessing technology that the UK Atomic Energy Authority (UKAEA) carried out for over thirty years. Two substantial research reactors and their associated reprocessing plants were built and operated on the site. After rising costs and safety concerns (not least arising from the dumping of plutonium wastes in a borehole), the facilities were closed down in the mid-1990s. No civil research facilities are now operating at Dounreay and the UK Government is committed to a massive decommissioning and waste removal operation which is expected to last for sixty years.

It is currently estimated that it will cost £4bn to restore the civil parts of Dounreay to a greenfield site. How these costs might be borne and by whom in the event of Scotland's independence would doubtless be a contentious issue between Edinburgh and London. We simply point out that Scotland's consent to Trident's stay in the Clyde, and to Vulcan's continuing operation, might provide Scotland with the leverage to load most of the costs at Dounreay on to rUK. One option might even be to offer the whole Dounreay site (civil and military) to rUK on a long-term lease, subject to Scottish political and regulatory oversight.

Treaty and basing arrangements

How might Trident's stay in Scotland be formalised through treaty and agreement between the governments of Scotland and rUK?

Perhaps controversially, we discard two options at the outset. The first is that the arrangements should *not* be formalised – that the bases should be opened, operated and closed according to informal *ad hoc* processes. This was the approach adopted towards basing by the UK and US governments when US bases, including Holy Loch, were established in the UK in the 1940s, 1950s and 1960s. Although the stationing of Polaris at Holy Loch was justified in terms of the North Atlantic Treaty's commitment to joint defence, although Holy Loch bases functioned in conformity with the practices set out in the NATO Status of Forces Agreement 1951, and although US personnel were subject to the provisions of the Visiting Forces Act 1952, the US presence at Holy Loch was not licensed through any specific basing agreement. The same applied to Fylingdales, Mildenhall and other US installations in the UK.

This was and remains highly unusual. It arose out of the UK's great dependence on the US during and after World War II, and out of the 'special relationship' that the two states sought to establish at the time. It is also worth noting that the UK Parliament and courts have played no part in the sanctioning of these basing arrangements. As Woodliffe writes:

> ... the admission of foreign armed forces to the UK in peacetime is a matter for administrative decision alone. This is a facet of the

> executive's pre-eminent role as regards both the organisation and command of the armed forces and foreign policy, the conduct of which embraces the conclusion of treaties and declarations of peace and war. These matters remain largely within the domain of the royal prerogative, the exercise of which is largely outside the control or supervision of Parliament and the courts.[13]

Such informality might be politically feasible and advantageous to both parties if there were agreement in the independence settlement on an early removal of Trident from Faslane, or if the UK Government had already committed itself and instituted plans to phase out the nuclear bases. But we cannot envisage it being the preferred option if rUK's nuclear force were to be stationed there over a longer period (say beyond five years). It would create too much unpredictability. Nor can we easily envisage a Scottish Parliament being prepared to allow the Executive in Edinburgh freedom to decide basing policy without consultation and consent.

The second option which we discard involves rUK retaining ownership of and sovereignty over the land on which the Faslane and Coulport bases are situated and, if considered essential to security, retaining sovereignty over areas adjoining the bases and their sea approaches. The creation of sovereign base areas was the solution adopted when the Irish Free State seceded from the United Kingdom in 1921. The Anglo-Irish Treaty of that year sanctioned the retention of three British naval bases in Ireland together with associated defensive facilities, an agreement which remained in place until annulled by mutual consent in April 1938. More recently, it was the solution adopted when Cyprus gained independence in 1960. In the Treaty of Establishment between the UK, Greece, Turkey and Cyprus, the UK retained sovereignty over two areas on the island of Cyprus (Akrotiri and Dhekelia) which became Sovereign Base Areas.

In both the Irish and Cypriot cases, sovereignty over areas containing military assets (and intelligence assets in Cyprus) was retained by a dominant power in the process of granting independence to a former colonial territory. Times have changed. Cyprus was the last instance in which sovereignty was retained for this purpose anywhere in the world, all subsequent basing agreements having involved leases. In any case, a newly independent Scotland would be unlikely to accept that a sizeable chunk of territory, especially territory so close to Glasgow (and to Loch

13. John Woodliffe, *op. cit.*, p. 42.

Lomond), should remain under London's sovereign control. Nor is it likely that the Scottish Parliament and, for that matter, the rUK Parliament would be prepared to derogate all responsibility for the basing decisions to the executives in Edinburgh and London.

We therefore assume that any long-term arrangements for keeping Trident in the Clyde would have to be formalised by the Scottish and rUK governments. And we assume that those arrangements would involve the leasing of Scottish sovereign territory in conformity with the now standard international practice. In our view, the continued deployment of Trident in Scotland would have to rest upon:

- a political understanding between Scotland and rUK;
- a framework treaty on nuclear weapons between Scotland and rUK;
- a military base agreement covering Faslane and Coulport.

We assume that civil nuclear issues, such as the supply of fuel for Scotland's nuclear power reactors and the distribution of liabilities associated with them, would be covered in separate agreements.[14]

One can imagine the **political understanding** entailing a joint statement of the fundamental principles and norms which would guide relations between the two new states. Besides expressing their commitment to uphold certain human values and political and economic processes (liberal democracy etc.), the statement would emphasise the co-operative nature of relations between the two states and peoples. It would aim to set aside whatever differences or animosities had arisen in the lead-up to the UK's fragmentation. The co-operation would entail *inter alia* a commitment to respect and support for each other's objectives in regard to the European Union, NATO and other international entities, and to pursue common goals together and with other states through these organisations. And the co-operation would extend into the military field through a commitment to act in alliance with one another and with other states, especially in the European and transatlantic contexts.

The **framework treaty on nuclear weapons** would establish the principles and norms governing the stationing of rUK's nuclear weapons on Scottish territory. It could have one of two purposes, depending on whether Trident's stay in Scotland was short-term (essentially a phase-out treaty) or long-term albeit with opportunity for periodic review

14. Those liabilities could include the costs of decommissioning and of storing and otherwise dealing with the Scottish-origin separated plutonium and radioactive wastes that are stored at Sellafield.

(essentially a continuation treaty). We can envisage either treaty having provisions drawn from the following list:

- mutual recognition of Scotland's and rUK's status as non-nuclear and nuclear weapon states respectively under the NPT;
- commitment by both states to honour the former UK's arms control and non-proliferation undertakings, including those made under the NPT, the Comprehensive Nuclear Test-Ban Treaty, Chemical Weapons Convention, Biological and Toxin Weapons Convention, Missile Technology Control Regime and any subsequent treaties and agreements;
- commitment by both states to pursue global nuclear disarmament and to honour the undertakings made by UK governments under the NPT Principles and Objectives of 1995, the NPT Final Document of 2000, and any subsequent international agreements pertaining to nuclear disarmament;
- provision by rUK of positive and negative security guarantees to Scotland (such guarantees would be automatic if Scotland and rUK were both NATO members);
- acknowledgement that rUK's nuclear deterrent would be assigned to NATO or whichever is the pertinent European alliance;
- commitment by rUK that the nuclear forces would be kept at the lowest alert consistent with effective deterrence, and that nuclear missiles would not be fired within Scottish territorial waters without Scottish consent;
- acknowledgement of Scotland's sovereign jurisdiction over the territories on which the nuclear bases were situated;
- principles governing the use of approach waters to nuclear bases;
- provision by Scotland of guarantees to protect the nuclear bases and their supply routes from terrorist and other attack, in co-operation where appropriate with rUK's security forces;
- principles governing transport of nuclear warheads and other matériel to and from the nuclear bases, and governing the co-operation between Scotland's and rUK's police, security forces and intelligence agencies in managing that transport;
- procedures for consultation between the Scottish and rUK governments on all matters other than the detailed operation of, and

command and control over, the nuclear armament. Those matters would include alert status, nuclear strategy and safety and environmental protection.

A *phase-out* treaty, if it existed, would include additional provisions on:

- the timescale over which the nuclear force's removal from Scotland would be phased;
- the management and financing of decommissioning, site recovery and waste disposal.

The *continuation* treaty would include additional provisions on:

- the procedures for periodic review by the governments of Scotland and rUK;
- procedures for consultation and decision-making on weapon replacement.

Turning to the **military base agreement**, the precise juridical nature of military bases in modern international practice has been the subject of considerable debate among legal experts.[15] Do rights exist independent of the host state's (i.e. Scotland's) consent? If so, has the host state effectively ceded sovereignty? The answer to both questions appears to be 'No', but with various qualifications.

Woodliffe comments on the changing connotations attached to the term 'lease' in basing practices. In colonial times, leases were 'barely distinguishable from an outright cession or annexation of territory and were couched in a form that was legal in only a symbolic sense ... modern leases of military bases partake of a wholly different character; the term lease today describes a grant by one state to another of 'a right of exclusive use over a part of a territory' in respect of which the grantor state maintains sovereignty while 'conceding enjoyment of the liberties of the territorial sovereignty''.[16] He goes on to summarise Rousseau's argument that:

> the grant [of basing rights] does not involve the exercise by the beneficiary state of territorial sovereignty as such, but rather the use of certain logistic facilities for a limited time. This meshes in with the second characteristic, namely, the absence of any division of

15. The arguments are rehearsed in John Woodliffe, *op. cit.*, Chapter 7.
16. *Ibid.*, pp. 114–115. Woodliffe is here quoting from I. Brownlie, *Principles of Public International Law*, 4th edition 1990, p. 110.

territorial competence between the two states; instead the sending state simply has various powers pertaining to the operation of its defence forces on territory that remains subject to the sovereignty of the host state.[17]

Assuming that Faslane and Coulport would become part of the sovereign territory of Scotland after independence, the purpose of a basing agreement would be to define the rights, duties, privileges and powers of the respective parties, acting in compliance with the framework treaty discussed above. There are several models for such an agreement, involving US, UK and other states' bases in various parts of the world, and NATO drew up its own Status of Forces model agreement (NATO-SOFA) in 1951.

An agreement between Scotland and rUK would probably have to encompass, amongst other things:

- identification of the sites, installations and facilities covered by the agreement, their precise locations, and the purposes to which they would be put;
- admission to the sites and movement between them by rUK military personnel and by personnel acting for regulatory bodies;[18]
- access to installations and facilities, including access through adjoining waters, and including access across road networks and through ports and airfields;[19]
- rights and powers of the sending state (i.e. rUK) within the bases, including rights and powers to develop facilities and communications, to deepen harbours, and (for example) to 'construct, instal, maintain and employ in any facility or area any type of installation, weapon, substance, device, vessel or vehicle on or under the ground, in the air or on or under the water that may be requisite or appropriate';[20]

---

17. *Ibid.*, p. 122 summarising C. Rousseau, *Droit International Public*, vol. 3, p. 8.
18. Article III. 1 of the NATO-SOFA of 1951 provides members of visiting armed forces with exemptions 'from passport and visa regulations and immigration inspection on entering or leaving the territory of a receiving State ... and from the regulations of the receiving State on the registration and control of aliens' subject to compliance with 'the formalities established by the receiving State relating to entry and departure of a force or the members thereof'.
19. The 1947 US–Phillipines Agreement granted the US 'all the rights, power and authority within the limits of territorial waters and airspace adjacent to or in the vicinity of the bases which are necessary to provide access to them ...'.
20. This language comes from the US–Japan Security Agreement.

- rights and powers of the sending state outside the bases, including overflight, manoeuvres and guaranteed provision of services and utilities, including electricity;[21]
- emergency arrangements involving police, ambulance and fire services, and responsibility for the protection of the bases, their facilities and weaponry;
- the scope and division of criminal jurisdiction arising from actions by rUK personnel, and the settlement of civil claims;
- arbitration procedures in the event of disagreement.

Financial aspects

Negotiations might be particularly tough on the financial aspects of the military base agreement. Under a leasing arrangement, the new owners of Faslane and Coulport, i.e. the Government of Scotland, could ask for the payment of rental by rUK. Scotland might seek a rent that reflected the considerable past investment in the base, which it could be argued represented Scotland's main claim to a proportional share of the MoD's large asset base (to which Scottish taxpayers had contributed over many years). The asset's uniqueness would also strengthen its ability to claim a high figure. It could point to the money that rUK could save, and the risks it could avoid, by not having to build an alternative facility elsewhere. On this basis, an annual rent of the order of £100 million per annum might not be unreasonable.[22]

An agreement whereby rUK paid rent for the use of Faslane and Coulport might well prove politically controversial in both countries, not least in the charged atmosphere of independence negotiations. Yet it might have political advantages for governments in both countries. In the short term, it could help persuade Scottish public opinion that its new government had struck a good bargain on Trident, thus easing the pressure for precipitate expulsion, with all the destabilising consequences that this might bring. In the medium to long term, moreover, it would provide a measurable incentive for rUK to relocate its force if this proved to be practical and cost-effective.

21. The ship-lift at Faslane requires particularly large supplies of electricity.
22. The UK Ministry of Defence's current move to 'resource accounting' is designed to ensure, *inter alia*, that managers take explicit account of asset depreciation costs in their budgets. It is possible that this could provide a useful starting point for the rental negotiations.

A new Scottish Government could increase this latter incentive further, if it wished, by insisting on regular rental reviews (say at five-year intervals) and by making clear that rents would rise in real terms over time. While avoiding the confrontation that the imposition of artificial deadlines would involve, such a policy would still make clear that Scotland's tolerance for an rUK nuclear base on its soil would progressively decline over time. Not least, it would have the distinct advantage of making a contribution to filling the considerable revenue gap which an independent Scotland might face.

These discussions would be situated within a more general negotiation over the principles that should underpin the division of UK government assets and liabilities between Scotland and the rUK. The rules applied to the division of defence-related assets would be shaped by these wider considerations. Yet they would also have to take into account particular features of military assets and liabilities, reaching specific agreements where necessary.[23]

The peaceful division of assets and liabilities between successor states historically involves some combination of two basic principles: division by geographical location, and division on the basis of population proportionality. Where physical assets and liabilities relate directly to the provision of local services in one of the successor states, are located in that state, and are immobile, the principle of geographical location is normally used. Where assets and liabilities relate to union-wide activities, have no fixed location and/or a location outside the union, and can readily be moved, they would normally be divided initially on a proportional basis. Examples of the latter would include financial assets (such as foreign exchange reserves), financial liabilities (such as the national debt), and government property overseas.

Yet there is a third category of government assets and liabilities that does not fall clearly into one or other of these categories. They are assets and liabilities that have a geographical location but are related to union-wide services. In these cases, either location or proportionality could be used to divide assets and/or employees between successor states. Often a combination of the two principles, negotiated between the states concerned, is used. Military assets can fall into this third category, as the experience of recent state break-ups (for example in the Soviet Union and Czechoslovakia) shows.

---

23. For further discussion, see for example Allan Macartney, *The Transition to Independence*, Scottish Centre for Economic and Social Research, 1996, pp. 25–26.

There is likely to be a strong presumption, which we accept, that each of the two successor states to the UK would inherit all military land situated on its own territory. In the absence of an agreement to the contrary, this is the 'default option' in international law. As well as being entitled to charge rent for Faslane and Coulport, therefore, Scotland would also be entitled to do so for any other bases that rUK chose to maintain on its territory.

The principles for the division of military equipment between successor states need not be the same as those governing land and buildings. Although the military equipment of the Soviet Union and Czechoslovakia was divided mainly according to location, the Irish Free State inherited none of the military equipment of the UK in 1921. Moreover, as a practical matter, a strictly geographical division would leave both countries with distinctly unbalanced forces unrelated to their own post-breakup requirements.

Yet Scotland would have a strong case for arguing in favour of dividing military equipment according to the principle that both Scotland and rUK should be entitled to a share equivalent to their respective share in the total UK population. This need not mean that every individual asset would be subdivided according to the ratio 91:9. In return for giving up its notional share in some assets (especially in regard to lumpy assets like aircraft carriers), Scotland could be entitled to a more than proportional share in others, or alternatively to some other form of compensation.

This principle might be particularly applicable to the UK's nuclear forces. In the event of Scottish independence, both governments would be likely to agree that the entire Trident nuclear force – including missiles and SSBN's, as well as the entire warhead infrastructure – should be immediately transferred to rUK ownership. It would also be in the mutual interests of both countries for the SSN fleet to be inherited by rUK, since Scotland would have neither the military requirement nor the economic resources to support it. In compensation for surrendering its 9% share of nuclear assets, Scotland could then claim entitlement to assets of equivalent value or direct financial compensation. Alternatively, compensation might take some other form, either in the military sphere or in some other, perhaps unrelated, area. Given a constructive approach from both parties, agreements on compensation should be possible. But it would take time. The potential for deadlock, in the fraught period that might follow an independence referendum, cannot be excluded.

Conclusion

Our discussion suggests that, whatever current attitudes, the continued basing of Trident in an independent Scotland cannot be ruled out. Indeed, Trident's stay could provide an opportunity to forge a co-operative relationship between Scotland and rUK in the military and other domains. It could act as a symbol and practical manifestation of that relationship, and of the essential pragmatism of both states.

But the obstacles to this outcome should not be underestimated. A distinguished observer of Scottish history and politics remarked to us that Trident's stay in an independent Scotland could only result from the exercise of statesmanship of a high order in both Edinburgh and London. We are also struck by the bureaucratic skill and energy that would be needed to engineer this solution to everyone's satisfaction. Unless there had been a sea-change in attitudes in the meantime, it would require a big shift in the preferences of a large slice of the political establishment in Scotland, the Edinburgh Government's willingness to take political risks and to commit the Scottish state to the protection of another country's nuclear force (including protecting it against its own citizens' objections), and the London Government's trust that Scotland would provide security for that force. It would require a Scottish state to accept some weakening of its sovereign powers at its inception (even if some of its political influence, especially in foreign negotiation, might be strengthened in compensation) and a preparedness to tolerate the absence of Scottish control over the firecracker in its midst. Not least, it would require the quelling of nationalist passions in both countries when one would expect them to be most aroused.

Chapter Seven

The Disarmament Option

The previous chapter assumed that a successor state of the United Kingdom would try to maintain the nuclear deterrent. We now turn to the situation in which rUK, or the UK, decided to eliminate its nuclear arms.

This is not the place to assess the *likelihood* that the UK or a successor state will decide to abandon its nuclear arms over the next ten, twenty or thirty years. Suffice it to say that prospects for global nuclear disarmament waxed in the early and mid-1990s only to wane later in the decade. As we write in mid-2001, the outlook has seldom been so depressing: arms control is in trouble, partly but not entirely because of shifts in US policy, and there are worrying signs that the competitive arms racing and power balancing that characterised the Cold War period are returning to the international scene. This said, the commitment to reduce nuclear arsenals and constrain nuclear proliferation remains powerfully institutionalised, and America's unilateralist mood may prove temporary. However destabilising the US missile defence proposals may be in the short run, moreover they are forcing the nuclear powers to submit their deterrence policies to serious examination for the first time since the end of the Cold War.

Even in the absence of wider international agreement, circumstances could arise in which the UK – already the most disarmament-oriented of the nuclear powers – decided that it no longer needed to maintain an independent nuclear force. The factors which might precipitate such a change of heart cannot be predicted. Yet they could include traumatic events (accidents or conflicts), escalating costs (perhaps as a result of replacement needs), or radical domestic political change, as well as more systemic factors (reduced threats, substantial progress in arms control, evolving relationships with the US and European allies). UK nuclear disarmament seems improbable over the next two decades, especially if multilateral disarmament is not being pursued. But it is possible, even without the Scottish question.

Could Scottish independence be the precipitating factor for UK nuclear disarmament?

Given Trident's dependence on its Clyde bases, some disarmament advocates speculate that the UK could be compelled to relinquish its nuclear force through Scotland's independence. As we argue elsewhere in this volume, however, the price of trying to force disarmament upon a reluctant London Government could be massive. It is certainly possible that London would refrain from retaliation against an attempted expulsion of Trident, not least if disagreement over Trident risked escalating into a conflict that would seriously damage its domestic and international interests. A Scottish Government might also try to claim the moral high ground by citing the injunctions to pursue nuclear disarmament in the Non-Proliferation Treaty, recently strengthened in the Final Document of the 2000 Review Conference (see Chapter 4). If it did decide to make an absolute commitment to Trident expulsion, however, a Scottish government would weaken its bargaining position; and the UK's allies abroad would probably have little sympathy for what would doubtless be seen as an ill-advised effort to denuclearise a recognised NWS and NATO partner against the wishes of its government. By expelling Trident, a newly independent Scotland would risk exclusion from the EU for some significant period of time, with all the damage that this could inflict on its economic and political prospects.

Yet the emergence of the Scottish question may still make the UK's nuclear disarmament more likely under certain conditions. It is unlikely to be the decisive factor if there is a strong political consensus in favour of continuance, especially if the international environment remains inhospitable. If the wider debate were to be more divided, however, the Scottish dimension might tip the balance, for example by increasing the risks and difficulties involved in major investments in Trident's replacement.

A 'Scottish effect' could be seen under devolution, with it becoming increasingly difficult to press ahead with new nuclear developments in Scotland without some form of Scottish consent. A similar phenomenon might also take place if Scotland became independent. Although some form of basing deal seems the most likely outcome of post-referendum talks, over time the rUK Government could find that such an arrangement was simply not workable. In these circumstances, it could attempt to find an alternative basing solution. But it could also, especially if the wisdom of maintaining the deterrent was already under question, decide that enough was enough.

For disarmers, therefore, an indirect approach to the Scottish question might be more likely to bear fruit than an attempt to use independence as a means of forcing UK nuclear disarmament. The existence of the distinct Scottish polity that has been created by devolution, or even the separate state that independence would involve, would not in themselves make Trident basing impossible. If popular resentment over Trident's presence in Scotland continued to grow, however, the UK could find it increasingly difficult to rely on the Scottish institutions for support.

Implementing nuclear disarmament

What would the UK's nuclear disarmament entail in technical terms, and would it have any significant implications for relations between London and Edinburgh, whether it happened when Scotland had devolved governance or after independence? Our answer to this question need not be lengthy because the issues are comparatively straightforward and amenable to solution, because legal aspects of disarmament have already been addressed in Chapter 4, and because the issue that would probably be the trickiest to resolve – the division of economic costs and liabilities – is largely beyond the scope of this chapter.

For the UK as for any other nuclear power, nuclear disarmament would have to begin with a reorientation of military strategy and a restructuring of the relevant armed forces. Again, this is not a subject that can be tackled here except to stress that disarmament cannot be switched on overnight: it would have to be preceded by a substantial overhaul of defence and foreign policy, and it would involve major changes for the Navy and its career structure, equipment and installations. As the Army and RAF have no surviving nuclear role, they would only be affected insofar as they provide protection for the Navy's nuclear force.

Much has been learned about the implementation of disarmament from the experiences with the former Soviet Union, South Africa and Iraq in the 1990s. There are three main processes: the legal renunciation of nuclear weapons and its verification; the decommissioning of weapons and facilities; and the disposition of weapon materials.[1]

1. In the former Soviet Union, special measures had also to be taken to secure nuclear sites against theft or diversion of weapon material, and to protect and store weapons prior to dismantling them. The need arose from the political and social instabilities that accompanied the collapse of Communism and the weakening of central authority.

Legal renunciation and its verification

The legal steps entailed in renouncing nuclear weapons and in verifying renunciations through international safeguards are examined in Chapter 4 and Appendix C. The basic issues would be the same if the UK in its current form was the state that was disarming, or if Scotland and rUK were together disarming after independence (assuming that rUK was accepted as the UK's successor state). All nuclear materials and facilities in whichever state would have to be submitted to full IAEA safeguards so that the international community could verify that they were not being re-used in nuclear weapons. The main questions would be how to nullify the UK's (or rUK's) standing as a nuclear weapon state under Article IX of the NPT; how to draw up 'Initial Reports' of inventories of plutonium and enriched uranium, the fissile materials used in nuclear weapons, that would be sufficiently comprehensive to satisfy the IAEA; and how to deal with the safeguarding of nuclear materials if they continued to be used in nuclear hunter-killer submarines and submarine test reactors (see Appendix C). Nullifying nuclear weapon status could be achieved through full-scope safeguards and a formal statement of renunciation; the Initial Reports would require a thorough reconstruction of the history of fissile material acquisition to demonstrate the inventory's completeness; and methods would have to be established internationally to deal with the hitherto unprecedented withdrawal of materials from safeguards that would be required if nuclear submarines were to remain in service in conventional roles. Although there would be plenty for bureaucrats and international lawyers to chew over, all of these questions seem open to solution.

Decommissioning

The nuclear force would have to be taken out of operation and its warheads dismantled in a verifiable way. Unless refitted with conventional warheads, the missiles would presumably be taken to the United States to be dismantled.[2] The submarines could either be taken apart or adapted for use with conventional weapons, depending on circumstance. The decommissioning of submarine reactors has long been a troublesome issue for the Ministry of Defence. We are not in a position to tell

2. This usually entails removing the solid fuels through chemical dissolution, and mechanically dismantling or crushing the rocket motors and missile casings.

whether the decommissioning of the Vanguard/Trident reactors would be easier or more difficult than the decommissioning of reactors on Polaris and the hunter-killer submarines.

Dismantling the warheads would have to take place at Aldermaston and Burghfield as there is no equivalent capability in Scotland or elsewhere in the UK. The techniques are tried and tested: the disassembly and reassembly of warheads have been practised for many years in order to ensure reliability and gain economies through refurbishment. The novel task would be to establish techniques enabling the outside world to verify that the warheads had indeed been dismantled. Through a pioneering study carried out by Aldermaston and published in 2000, the first steps have already been taken in the UK to identify how this might be achieved by the nuclear weapon states.[3]

Although expensive, decommissioning the facilities could be phased over years or even decades. Unless there were a pressing need to use sites for other purposes, it would not have to be carried out immediately. Radioactive contamination at the naval bases is likely to be much less than contamination at sites where fissile materials were produced and warheads fabricated. The bases at Faslane and Coulport are essentially storage rather than processing sites, although contamination could be more of a problem at Rosyth where submarine reactors were serviced, refuelled and dismantled over a long period. Across the UK, the main problems of radioactive contamination have arisen from activities at Sellafield, Dounreay and Aldermaston. To our knowledge, nearly all of the releases of radiation at Dounreay came from civil rather than from military activities.

Most of the physical activity associated with weapon decommissioning would therefore have to take place in England where the bulk of the contamination arising from the UK's long involvement with nuclear weaponry has also occurred. If disarmament took place after independence had been declared, rUK would no doubt be asking Scotland to carry its fair share of the financial burden arising from the decommissioning programme. We leave it to others to determine what might constitute a fair share, and how these matters might be settled.

---

3. *Confidence, Security and Verification*, Atomic Weapons Establishment, Aldermaston, 2000. On the regulation and verification of disarmament, see also *Dismantling the Bomb and Managing the Nuclear Materials*, Office of Technology Assessment, US Congress, September 1993; and Steve Fetter, *Verifying Nuclear Disarmament*, Occasional Paper 29, Henry L. Stimson Center, Washington, DC, October 1996.

Material disposition and waste disposal

The plutonium and uranium used in nuclear weapons is 'weapon-grade', indicating that it has a high concentration of the isotopes that can be readily fissioned.[4] In order to provide confidence that the materials will not be stolen or used again in weapon programmes, the Russian and US governments have agreed that the form of the materials taken from dismantled weapons should be changed to render them militarily useless. 'Excess' highly enriched uranium is being diluted to low enriched uranium for use in power reactors, and 'excess' plutonium will either be burned in reactors or blended with nuclear wastes.

The 'disposition' programmes launched in consequence have been controversial and will take decades to complete, so great are the quantities of material.[5] The total inventory of plutonium currently assigned to the UK nuclear weapon programme is only 3.5 tonnes, compared to over two hundred tonnes that were produced for the US and Soviet programmes. Disposition would therefore be a much lesser undertaking for the UK but for the fact that another enormous inventory of plutonium (now exceeding 60 tonnes and approaching 100 tonnes in the coming decade) has built up at Sellafield due to civil reprocessing, including the reprocessing of spent fuels from power reactors in Scotland. While priority would no doubt have to be given to the disposition of weapon-grade material, any future difficulties will arise primarily from civil rather than military legacies in these regards. Currently, the UK Government has no disposition policy for civil or military material.[6]

The waste management and disposal problems are similarly driven by

4. Uranium found in nature contains 0.7% and 99.3% of the isotopes uranium–235 and uranium–238 respectively (together with traces of uranium–234). In weapon-grade uranium, the proportion of the fissile isotope uranium–235 is raised above 90% through enrichment. Weapon-grade plutonium typically contains 93% of the fissile isotope plutonium–239.
5. See Office of Technology Assessment, *op. cit.*; *Managing and Disposition of Excess Weapons Plutonium* (National Academy of Science: Washington, DC, 1994); *Disposing of Weapons-Grade Plutonium*, CSIS Panel Report, Washington, DC, March 1998; and David Albright, Frans Berkhout and William Walker, *Plutonium and Highly Enriched Uranium: World Inventories, Capabilities and Policies* (Oxford University Press: Oxford, 1997), Chapter 15.
6. An impressive analysis of the civil disposition problems and options has been provided by Fred Barker and Mike Sadnicki, *The Disposition of Civil Plutonium in the UK*, April 2001. Funded by the John D. and Catherine T. MacArthur Foundation, the study has been published privately by the authors. Copies may be sought by contacting them at fbarker@gn.apc.org and sadnicki@aol.com.

the civil fuel-cycle. Following the collapse in 1997 of the public inquiry into constructing an underground laboratory at Longlands Farm near Sellafield for testing the disposal of intermediate-level wastes, there are now no sites under development or consideration for the disposal of high-level or intermediate-level wastes. Despite government pronouncements to the contrary, long-term storage is becoming the only realistic option. On the military side, this means that submarine spent fuels, and the radioactive parts of decommissioned submarine reactors, will probably end up being stored indefinitely at secure sites above ground (Sellafield has hitherto acted as the main repository).

In conclusion, no study has yet been carried out on how exactly the UK's disarmament might be carried out. Technically it does not seem difficult. It would not be cheap, but nor would it be unduly expensive – who would pay for what would probably be the main stumbling block. Where international law and non-proliferation are concerned, the safeguarding of materials in the fuel-cycles of surviving submarines and test reactors would be a matter for concern, but the problem has been recognised for many years and solutions could surely be found. Compared to the difficulties encountered in the former Soviet Union, the UK's or rUK's disarmament seems simple and relatively risk-free in technical terms. The number of weapons would be much smaller, and the resources available for dealing with them much larger; the infrastructure has been reasonably well maintained; the UK has a well-established international 'safeguards culture' due especially to its obligations under the Euratom Treaty; and the societies would not be undergoing transformations from Communism to some form of capitalism, with all that has entailed, and do not suffer the high levels of corruption and criminality that have bedevilled Russia and other post-Soviet states. Indeed, of all the nuclear weapon states, the UK or its successor state would probably have the greatest ease in disarming itself.

Chapter Eight

Conclusions

When this study began, we never imagined writing a book. Some articles, perhaps a report, but not a book. The subject's breadth, complexity and fascination came as a surprise to us. It kept growing before our eyes as we dug into the issues and spoke to more and more people. So our first message is this: if the politics of the UK nuclear deterrent's location in Scotland seem simple, they are not simple, and there are few simple solutions around.

Our purpose has not been to predict. There is no way of knowing whether Scottish nationalism will wax or wane, whether the processes of devolution will strengthen or weaken the Union, and whether political change in the UK will be affected in one direction or another by changes occurring in the European Union and beyond. Nor can we know whether nuclear weapons will retain their value for political and military strategists in the coming international environment, whether UK strategists in particular will continue to regard investment in nuclear weaponry as a sensible way to use scarce public resources, and whether NATO and the transatlantic relationship will survive and in what form. We cannot foretell these contextual changes, nor the manner in which they – and events associated with them – will interact with the circumstances created by Trident's basing in the Clyde.

So why write the book? A reader of an earlier draft suggested that we were 'sending a rocket into the sky', and this does convey our intention rather well. We wish to alert people inside and outside government, inside and outside the UK, to a set of problems and predicaments that deserve attention, to illuminate them as best we can, and to encourage everyone to think through their implications for public and party policy and for governmental practice. It may turn out that we have created a mountain out of a molehill. But the consequences of getting the politics of this issue wrong could be momentous. It is therefore only prudent to assume that there is indeed a mountain out there to be climbed, and that it should be scaled if only to make its terrain familiar and thus manageable.

What, then, are the main conclusions of the study? Seven 'facts' about the nuclear situation in the UK need highlighting at the outset.

1. The UK is a nuclear weapon state under international law. For fifty years, nuclear deterrence has been a central feature of its security policy. The UK nuclear force is made available to NATO and has been developed in close cooperation with the United States.

2. Following its restructuring in the 1990s, the UK nuclear force today comprises just four Vanguard submarines and their Trident missiles, and only the Royal Navy retains a nuclear role. As the submarines are based at Faslane and Coulport on the Clyde, the UK deterrent now operates entirely out of Scotland. No UK nuclear weapons are deployed in England.

3. Polaris and Trident nuclear forces were based on the Clyde largely due to its favourable geography. Relocating the Trident bases outside Scotland would be politically very difficult, extremely costly and require many years of preparation. There would also be severe difficulties in the short and medium terms in replacing Trident with a strategic deterrent force that was not submarine-based.

4. Constitutional change in the UK in the late 1990s led to the establishment of devolved government in Scotland, and to the reopening of the Scottish Parliament and creation of the Scottish Executive. The Scottish Parliament and Executive have no rights or responsibilities in regard to the formulation and execution of nuclear policy which is 'reserved' to the UK Government in London.

5. Ensuring the safety and security of nuclear weapons, installations and supply chains requires exceptional administrative measures and capacities that extend into the civil domain. Trident cannot operate without close cooperation between governmental authorities in Scotland and England.

6. The Scottish political elite and public opinion are, by and large, more sceptical about the political and military utility of nuclear weapons than their English counterparts. A significant anti-nuclear movement exists in Scotland driven by moral objection, concerns about safety, and nationalist claims that nuclear weapons have been foisted on Scotland.

7. The Scottish National Party is the main opposition party in the Scottish Parliament. Its objective is to gain independence for Scotland. Its longstanding policy has been to remove Trident from an independent Scotland, and to bring Scotland into the Nuclear Non-Proliferation Treaty as a non-nuclear weapon state.

A tension is therefore created by the concentration of nuclear weapon deployment in a sceptical Scotland that, despite gaining greater political autonomy, has no say over a nuclear policy which remains determined in London. This tension is not sufficiently alleviated by Scottish MPs' participation in the Government and Parliament of the UK, nor by the Memorandum of Understanding and Concordats through which the Scottish Executive has voluntarily committed itself to help implement the policies set by London. Furthermore, even the *possibility* that Scotland could become independent during Trident's lifetime may now have to be taken into account by nuclear decision-makers.

What are the implications for nuclear policy and politics under devolution or if Scotland has gained independence? Let us take each in turn.

Devolution

If the devolution settlement remains stable, it is likely that the political institutions in Edinburgh and London will continue to work closely and successfully together to ensure that Trident's deployment in Scotland is safe and secure. There are three circumstances in which the nuclear force could nevertheless become politically vulnerable:

- if there were a serious accident or 'incident' in the Clyde involving nuclear weapons or bases;
- if the complexions of the Scottish and UK Parliaments changed (especially if the SNP became the largest party in Edinburgh and/or the Conservative Party regained office in Westminster) so that their unity of purpose became harder to sustain on nuclear as on other reserved matters;
- if the Scottish Parliament exerted itself on issues (such as emergency planning) that are not clearly reserved to London, if the Parliament's powers were extended into fields (such as health and safety) having significant implications for the nuclear force's operation, and/or if judicial decisions on 'devolution issues' began seriously to impinge on MoD's ability to execute its nuclear policies.

The prospect of Trident's future replacement also raises tricky questions for the relationship between the two Parliaments. The current system's lifetime will depend on various technical, military and economic judgements. Decisions on replacement will probably have to be taken at some time between 2010 and 2015. Whereas previous decisions on

Polaris and Trident were taken by the UK government without any specific Scottish consent, procedures would probably have to be found next time round for establishing the legitimacy in Scotland of replacement decisions that again involved basing nuclear weapons on the Clyde. Although much would depend on circumstances at the time (including the complexion of the UK Government), the replacement decision might have to be affirmed in *both* the Westminster and Scottish Parliaments after appropriate scrutiny and debate.

Hitherto, the nuclear relationship between the UK Government and the Scottish political institutions has been entirely administrative. To have lasting stability, it needs to become more political and policy-infused. In Chapter 3 we posed some questions that the UK Government and Ministry of Defence would be wise to ask themselves. How can an effective dialogue be established with the Scottish Parliament and Executive on nuclear policy, insofar as it has particular implications for Scotland? How can a 'culture of international security' be nurtured in Scotland? How can the UK Government best establish confidence in Scotland in the safety of its nuclear forces and facilities? Should Parliamentary Committees in Westminster and/or Edinburgh be positively encouraged to conduct investigations into such matters?

It has been assumed in the discussion so far that the UK will remain committed to sustaining its nuclear deterrent. Yet it is possible that a UK government will decide to abandon its nuclear arms in the next ten or twenty years, whether due to the MoD's judgement that resources are better invested in other military assets, to multilateral agreements to achieve global nuclear disarmament, or to other factors (including uncertainties about Scotland). If it so decided, the main issues requiring joint attention would concern the decommissioning and clean-up of nuclear facilities, and the storage and disposal of nuclear wastes. The sharing of costs and choice of storage and disposal sites would probably be controversial, but it should be negotiable.

Internationally, implementing the UK's nuclear disarmament would require a number of novel but not insuperable problems to be addressed: how to nullify the UK's formal recognition as a nuclear weapon state in Article IX of the NPT; how to verify that all warheads had been dismantled; how to bring all nuclear materials and facilities under IAEA and Euratom safeguards; and potentially trickiest of all, how to enable the UK to continue operating its conventionally-armed nuclear submarines without creating unacceptable difficulties for the non-proliferation regime.

Independence

Most people assume that, if independence were to take place, it would be preceded by a referendum, the result of which would then be accepted as a decisive mandate by the Governments in Edinburgh and London. In this scenario, the Governments of Scotland and the rest of the UK (rUK) would then have to negotiate settlements which would decide their future economic, political and military relations. The nuclear settlement would be high on their agenda.

Our starting observation is that Scotland could not impose nuclear disarmament on rUK. In the event of independence, Scotland's paramount foreign policy interest would lie in gaining international recognition and membership of the European Union and other international organisations, and in securing its economic relationship with rUK (e.g. on the division of North Sea assets and of pension funds). Scotland would enter negotiations with a comparatively weak hand, being much the smaller partner, and having probably (in the eyes of foreign governments) perpetrated an act of secession. rUK's cooperation would be essential to advance Scotland's case for entry to the European Union, and to reach a settlement on economic and other issues.

At the same time, rUK could not impose Trident on an independent Scotland. Trident could not operate safely, securely and reliably without the extensive cooperation of the new Scottish state and of organisations under its jurisdiction. The areas around the nuclear bases would have to be protected, as would their supply routes; police, fire and medical services would be required, together with reliable supplies of electricity and other utilities; and the bases' operation depends on the free movement of service personnel and skilled labour into and out of the surrounding region. Even if it were politically acceptable in rUK and abroad, which is very unlikely, military occupation of the areas around Faslane and Coulport, including their sea and loch approaches, would be impractical and unsustainable.

This being the situation, the two Governments would be pressed into cooperation either to dismantle the nuclear force, or to establish the conditions under which Trident's stay in the Clyde could be extended over the medium and long terms.

The first of these options (dismantling Trident) would be palatable to an independent Scotland, but probably unpalatable to rUK unless decisions had already been taken in London to phase out the nuclear deterrent. Its implementation would be no different from the implementation of disarmament by the UK, except insofar as two states would now be involved and they would have to agree on the division of decommissioning and disposal costs.

The second option (extending Trident's stay) would be the reverse – palatable to rUK but probably unpalatable to Scotland. However, it is politically implausible that a Scottish Government could achieve its international objectives while expelling Trident against rUK's will. It is equally implausible that rUK could deny Scotland its support in achieving those objectives if it depended on Scotland's cooperation to operate Trident.

Providing rUK was accepted by foreign powers as the UK's successor state in the NPT (likely but not automatic), the NPT's rules would allow it to base nuclear weapons on the territory of a non-nuclear weapon state, in this case Scotland. The NPT's rules, together with the particular nature of submarines, would also prevent a Scottish Government from having any control over those weapons.

Even so, we reject as politically unworkable and anachronistic the solution of creating sovereign base areas under rUK's jurisdiction around the nuclear sites (only in Cuba and Cyprus do such base areas survive, although this was also the arrangement used for the UK's naval bases in Ireland between 1921 and 1938). The standard international practice is now for the host state to lease the land on which bases are situated. To provide confidence in both capitals that commitments would be fulfilled, the nuclear basing arrangements would, in our view, need to be accompanied by three levels of agreement between the Scottish and rUK Governments (both would have to belong to NATO for the arrangements to work):

- a political understanding entailing a joint statement of the fundamental principles and norms which would guide security relations between the two new states;
- a framework treaty on nuclear weapons which would establish the principles, norms and rules governing the stationing of rUK's nuclear weapons on Scottish territory, including their protection and safety regulation;
- a military base agreement which would establish how precisely the bases would be operated (questions of access, criminal jurisdiction, land use etc.).

Three ironies

We cannot resist ending with three ironies about the situation we have been discussing.

The first is that Trident would become a valuable asset to nationalists if and when independence is realised – an asset not to be grabbed and used militarily but to be traded for political goods of great worth to a Scottish state striving to establish its international position. How to justify their political expediency and drop their moral objections would, of course, be the challenge that nationalist leaders would face within their own ranks. But the Labour Party showed in the early 1990s how a dogged opposition to nuclear weapons can evaporate if wider political objectives are at stake. It follows that, if Trident were indeed tradable for international recognition and economic favours, the nuclear deterrent could be as secure in an independent Scotland as in a devolved Scotland, if independence resulted in the new Scottish state's unambiguous long-term commitment to support Trident.

The second irony is a variant of the first. From London's perspective, Trident's deployment in Scotland is one of the factors that makes the Union still worthwhile. In this respect, Trident shelters rather than threatens the Union, and London's reliance on Scotland's acceptance of the nuclear *status quo* might encourage it to concede yet more privileges and resources to Edinburgh were the threat from Scottish nationalism to persist. But Trident is also politically useful to the nationalists as a symbol of southern domination, and it would become more than useful as a guarantee of foreign attention and entry to international organisations in the event of independence coming about. So if everyone is honest, there is a certain unity of political commitment to continuity despite the often noisy displays of disunity.

Beyond a certain point, however, the *status quo* could become insupportable from the standpoint of either London or Edinburgh. There might come a stage where even Trident no longer justified, in London's eyes, the price that was being paid for holding the Union together; and/or where the problems of running Trident in Scotland, in the MoD's and the Royal Navy's eyes, were becoming more than they could stand. Trident could then begin to be regarded as expendable in Whitehall, provoking a serious examination of alternatives, including the deterrent's abandonment. And for politicians in Scotland of all hues, the more that devolution threw up questions about Trident's operation and management, and the more problematic the broad relations between Edinburgh and London become, the more they might be driven by public and party opinion to harden their public stances on the deterrent. Given these circumstances, the balance of opinion in both places could switch from tolerating the nuclear *status quo* to ending it.

The final irony concerns the general situation that arises when states fragment (we return to it in the Postscript). The presence of nuclear weapons, the most threatening of all human creations, can make it *more* rather than *less* likely that peaceful relations will be established between the emerging states and that there will be smooth transitions to international statehood. This applied in the Soviet Union in the early 1990s, and it would apply in the UK. The reasons are that nuclear weapons raise the international stakes, guarantee the attention of foreign powers whose great concern is that the newcomers should settle their differences, and provide the weaker of the emerging states with invaluable bargaining cards. The provisos are that the weaker states must be prepared to cede their nuclear assets once their objectives have been gained, and that fragmentation must not be accompanied by collapses of internal political authority. In the UK, there need be no concern on either count.

Our final remark is for an international audience. The UK's political fragmentation has received hardly any attention from scholars and policy-makers abroad, and when the possibility is raised it tends to be given little credence. Like everyone else, we have no idea whether, how and when it might happen. But that it *could* happen, and happen in the next ten or twenty years, is widely acknowledged within the UK even if a rather low probability is still attached to it by most observers.

Even if this nuclear weapon state should break apart, following a Scottish declaration of independence, the outcome should not be regarded as necessarily threatening to regional or global security. Of course it would have many implications, some of considerable significance. But it would not be an event on anything like the scale or severity of the collapse of the Soviet Union. Given a modicum of good fortune and sensible leadership on all sides, it would probably be managed in a peaceful and responsible fashion.

Postscript: Nuclear Weapons in Fragmenting States

One of the least questioned assumptions during the Cold War was that the nuclear armed states were stable entities. Responsibility for the development and deployment of nuclear weapons, and for their political and military usage, would remain vested in states which held permanent sway over defined territories and which had strong governmental systems. The errors of this assumption were revealed by the break-up of the Soviet Union in the early 1990s. Our study has concerned another nuclear state whose fragmentation *could* occur in years ahead. Other nuclear powers whose internal unity is sometimes called into question are China, India and Pakistan, and some of the states that have been actively pursuing military nuclear programmes (notably Iraq and North Korea) could also be prone to collapse. One could even include Israel as a state possessing nuclear weapons that is undergoing a kind of fragmentation as Palestinians seek more political autonomy. So the nuclear states where there appears to be *no* risk of fragmentation (France and the US) are in a minority, not a majority.

Are there any lessons that can briefly be drawn by comparing our case with its Soviet precursor and the imaginary situations that might arise in these other contexts? Six observations seem appropriate.

1. Each fragmentation of a nuclear power will be *sui generis* and will have to be dealt with in its own idiosyncratic way. What lends our case its uniqueness is that the entire nuclear force is based in the part of the country (Scotland) that aspires to become a non-nuclear weapon state, and that there would be severe difficulties in relocation or replacement. In the Soviet Union, the majority of nuclear weapons were deployed in the Russian heartland, the submarine force operated only out of bases on Russian territory, and bombers could easily be withdrawn from airfields in the Ukraine and elsewhere. The UK's break-up would give rise to the unusual situation in which a nuclear weapon state had its nuclear force located solely on the territory of a non-nuclear weapon state, albeit on the territory of a neighbouring ally; and in which the close co-operation of that neighbour would be

required for the safe and credible operation of the deterrent. There are other important sources of uniqueness, among them the distinctive history of the United Kingdom and the peculiar nature of its polity, and the UK's membership of the European Union and NATO.

2. The physical scale, nature, quality and distribution of physical assets matter. The former Soviet Union had a massive and hugely varied arsenal of weapons deployed across a wide area, whilst the UK has just one delivery system with fewer than two hundred warheads based in one place. Much of the Soviet infrastructure was in poor repair and weakly regulated, whereas the UK infrastructure is comparatively robust and has benefited from years of investment to increase its safety and security. What both have in common is the concentration of warhead development and production capabilities within the dominant political region – in the nuclear cities in Russia, and at Aldermaston and Burghfield (and formerly Sellafield) in England. This conjunction of the locations of political power and technological capability effectively determines the choice of successor state. If the core technological capabilities were otherwise distributed, outcomes would be different and possibly more complex.

3. The 'maturity' of political and economic institutions within and across the fragmenting state also matters. Democracy has deep roots in Scotland as in other parts of the UK, the rule of law is well established, economic performance is strong if uneven, and the UK sits in a region of comparative peace and stability. Although much would be changed by the UK's break-up, there would (one trusts) be more social and institutional continuity than discontinuity if it happened. The wrenching transformations experienced by the Soviet Union and all its parts, transformations which gave rise to particular security risks (such as the leakage of nuclear matériel to other states or non-state actors), are not in prospect for the UK. Of all the future candidates for fragmentation among the nuclear powers, the UK may be considered to present the fewest problems from this perspective.

4. The framework of international law has great importance in providing clarity and predictability in these circumstances, as well as a starting point for the construction of international responses. There would be much greater uncertainty and thus insecurity without the NPT framework and its associated safeguards system. The NPT is therefore important to the management of dramatic change within state struc-

tures, as it is to the management of relations between states. Even when nuclear-armed states are not NPT members (as is the case with India, Israel and Pakistan), the NPT provides a set of norms and procedures against which behaviour might be judged. This said, much of a legal nature still depends on *political* choice, especially where the laws of succession are concerned. We have seen that succession to the EU and NATO, or to the status of nuclear weapon state, or to permanent membership of the UN Security Council, is not automatic. They are essentially in the gift of the international community, and particularly its great powers. This is appropriate as it provides the international community with the means of excluding new states if they do not respect the common interest, just as it provides emergent states with a powerful incentive to conform with that interest.

5. What happens when a nuclear armed state collapses? This is the question usually posed by scholars and policy-makers. However, the case of the UK shows that there is an intermediate condition between state unity and state collapse – that in which powers are devolved to regions which have their own identities, agendas and practices. Those powers need not extend to powers over defence and foreign policy to have relevance to the safe and effective management of nuclear weapon forces and capabilities. The UK is an unusual state in that it is neither a unitary state in the French tradition, nor a federal state in the German or US tradition: it has sometimes been referred to as a 'union state' containing a set of distinct and often restive polities that have retained sufficient common interests and purposes to live together within the state that is the UK. Despite the centralisation of power in London, the safety and credibility of the nuclear deterrent therefore depends upon co-operation across the internal boundaries of the union state. This is not unique to the UK. The political make-ups of the Russian Federation and India show, for instance, some of the same characteristics. It is an aspect of 'nuclear governance' that deserves more scholarly attention.

6. The collapse of the nuclear-armed Soviet Union was often discussed in apocalyptic terms back in the early 1990s. In retrospect, the presence of nuclear weapons seems to have helped rather than hindered the establishment of stable relations among the new states. It forced co-operation on them, encouraged the weak and strong amongst them to cut deals that might otherwise have been unattainable, and enticed the United States and other external powers into an engagement with

the new states that was ultimately constructive. Nuclear weapons are great concentrators of political attention. The same would apply in the UK, probably with beneficial effect. One should nevertheless beware of turning this into a general rule. There are circumstances in which the presence of nuclear weapons and capabilities in fragmenting states would be very dangerous, and in which the international community's ability to shape outcomes might be quite limited. Perhaps the greatest risk would come from a state that suffered a collapse of authority at all levels, enabling non-state actors to vie for control of its nuclear assets.

Appendix A

Safety and Environmental Regulation at HM Naval Base Clyde

Submarine reactors

Activities relating to submarine reactors (design, operation, dismantling etc) are regulated by the Captain Naval Nuclear Regulatory Panel (CNNRP) which is based in Abbey Wood, Bristol. CNNRP 'authorises' sites involved in the Nuclear Propulsion Programme to conduct nuclear work in compliance with 36 Authorisation Conditions. In Scotland, this covers reactor activities at Faslane, Coulport, Rosyth and MoD's site at Vulcan/Dounreay. CNNRP's regulatory practices mirror those adopted by the Nuclear Installations Inspectorate (NII) in the civil domain. NII is a division of the Health and Safety Executive (HSE) which answers to the Department of Transport, Local Government and the Regions (DTLR).

The Nuclear Propulsion Integrated Project Team (NP-IPT) at Abbey Wood effectively owns the submarine reactor safety case. This interfaces with the respective site safety cases when the submarine is alongside. The Commanding Officer is responsible for submarine and reactor safety at all times, directly to Flag Officer Submarines at sea and to the Site Authorisee when alongside. Flag Officer Submarines has arrangements to ensure that the submarine's staff are suitably qualified and experienced. Whenever a reactor stops being a complete reactor, regulatory responsibility passes to NII. Thus all refuelling operations at Rosyth and Devonport are regulated by NII rather than CNNRP.

The NII also has the ability to regulate nuclear reactor activities under the Ionising Radiation Regulations and a special MoD/HSE Agreement. The NII have a Site Inspector appointed for HM Naval Base Clyde, who regularly visits the site. The NII have the powers to call for Special Hazard Assessments of any activity, but in practice they place their confidence in the robustness of regulation carried out by CNNRP.

Nuclear weapons (warheads and missiles)

The *current* approach is as follows. The Strategic Systems Integrated Project Team (StratSys IPT) at Abbey Wood effectively owns the warheads allocated to Trident. The Director of HM Naval Base Clyde operates the weapons on the Team's behalf. StratSys IPT holds the safety case and has responsibility for the safety of weapons throughout their lives. In effect, Naval Base Clyde is audited by a StratSys IPT-sponsored 'proficiency inspection' to ensure that rules and procedures are being correctly applied, and that materials, equipment and facilities are in satisfactory condition.

A similar auditing approach is followed by the US Government in regard to the Trident missiles which it supplies. American inspectors regularly visit Coulport to conduct joint US/UK proficiency inspections. The StratSys IPT equivalent in the US is the Strategic Systems Programs (SSP) office which has representatives in the UK.

If all goes according to plan, a different approach will be adopted by MoD to warhead regulation from 2002 onwards. Following the recommendations of an internal MoD study, an independent internal regulator will be set up to mirror the approach that is applied to submarine reactors. StratSys IPT and the Director HM Naval Base Clyde will both be 'authorised' to carry out activities relating to nuclear weapons. Responsibility for nuclear warheads will, in effect, be transferred to the Director of HM Naval Base Clyde when they are under his control, with StratSys IPT retaining responsibility for the weapon through its life. The new regulatory body will probably be responsible to the MoD Centre but is likely to be co-located with CNNRP at Abbey Wood.

The American approach to missile safety regulation will be unchanged.

The HSE (NII) also has the ability to regulate nuclear weapon activities under the Ionising Radiation Regulations and the MoD/HSE Agreement. They have another Site Inspector appointed for HMNB Clyde for Weapons activities who, like his reactor counterpart, regularly visits the site.

Explosives safety

MoD is at present exempt from the various UK explosives Acts. However, it has set up an internal regime that mirrors that exercised by the HSE in civil industry. Conventional explosives safety is locally regulated by the Defence Logistic Organisation's Inspector of Explosives (IE-DLO) who licenses facilities for the storage of, and conduct of operations involving, explosive material.

Site emissions

The discharge of radioactive material from nuclear sites is regulated by the Scottish Environment Protection Agency (SEPA) which answers to Scottish Ministers. The discharge and exposure criteria are identical to those applied in the civil field. As MoD is exempt from the Radioactive Substances Act of 1993 (RSA93), there is no statutory requirement to honour its procedures. In practice, however, MoD behaves 'as if' it were subject to the Act, and discharges are agreed with SEPA rather than being formally authorised in accordance with RSA93. One consequence is that changes to discharge agreements are now put out to full public consultation as if there were no Crown exemption to RSA93.

Health and safety

Faslane and Coulport are both regulated under the Health and Safety at Work Act, 1974. This applies to the health and safety of both naval and civil staff, although the Act ceases to apply when boats are at sea. The regulation is mainly carried out by the HSE Field Operations Division. The Hazardous Installations Directorate's Offshore Division also inspects diving operations.

Partly for security reasons, HSE Field Operations Division inspectors largely confine themselves to site facilities and operations rather than the vessels at the two sites. An MOD-HSE agreement determines what inspectors can and cannot see. Two specially approved NII inspectors (one covering submarines reactors, the other weapons) have powers to assess operations against the Health and Safety at Work Act and are more involved in waterfront activities.

After devolution, a Scottish Director of HSE was appointed, answering to the Secretary of State for Scotland. He has formal responsibility for HSE Field Operations Division (but not NII) regulatory activities at Faslane and Coulport, although reports are normally submitted directly to HSE's offices in central England.

Security

The Director HM Naval Base Clyde is responsible for ensuring adequate security arrangements are in place at its sites. The Defence Logistics Organisation (based at Ensleigh, Bath) provides external scrutiny of these arrangements by inspection and exercise.

Emergency planning

Under new UK regulations dating from 1999, Argyll and Bute Council, the local authority in the area encompassing Coulport and Faslane, has responsibility for coordinating the preparation of the offsite safety plan and for managing consultations with the public. These Radiation Emergency Preparedness and Public Information regulations have been introduced in response to a European Union Directive. The regulations give the Council direct responsibility for ensuring that the public who are affected by a radiation emergency receive information which is both timely and appropriate. The resulting Offsite Emergency Plan for Naval Base Clyde will, when completed, replace the previous Clyde Area Public Safety Scheme. The Plan relates to emergency responses by the fire service, police, hospital and other services (civil and military) to the offsite effects of accidents at HM Naval Base Clyde and at the current Z berths at Loch Goil, Loch Striven and Rothesay Bay where nuclear submarines may be tied up. Henceforth, emergency exercises will also be multi-agency-led rather than MoD-led. Emergency planning and exercising within HM Naval Base Clyde is MoD's responsibility.

There are no active civil defence plans (i.e. evacuation and other plans in the event of an actual or threatened attack with nuclear weapons) for Faslane and the surrounding area.

Local liaison

A Local Liaison Committee meets annually. It has been established mainly because of the requirement to co-ordinate, manage and liaise with local emergency services (police, ambulance, fire etc). Its remit is being broadened to provide a forum for discussion of more general health, safety and environmental issues. The Committee's membership comprises representatives of HM Naval Base Clyde, the emergency services, Argyll and Bute Council and other local bodies.

There is no formal liaison with the Scottish Parliament, Executive or other Scottish bodies on safety issues, although the Scottish Executive has some involvement in Nuclear Accident Response Exercises. We are told that efforts are being made to increase informal dialogue.

Appendix B

Timetables for Trident Replacement

During the next two decades, the UK Government will have to decide whether, and if so how, to replace Trident. Many factors will need to be taken into account, including the security environment, changes in technology and military strategy, US (and perhaps French) technological preferences, the UK's weapon design and production capabilities, developments in arms control, and the competition for the MoD's resources. This time round, the Scottish question is bound to be one of those factors. Even the *possibility* of Scottish independence will affect the options open to the UK Government and could tip the balance against replacement altogether. The possible timetable for Trident replacement is therefore of direct relevance to the debate on nuclear weapons and Scotland.

The experience of Polaris replacement provides a useful starting point for a discussion of likely timetables for replacement of Trident missiles and Vanguard-class submarines. The first Polaris submarine became operational in 1968. Yet less than a decade after this, in 1976–77, a Chatham House Study Group under Ian Smart, acting in parallel with studies being pursued within government, estimated that 'the planning assumption must be that the existing British force will cease to constitute a reliable deterrent at a date which, for technical reasons, is likely to occur in about 1993'.[1] Initial political decisions on the parameters of Polaris replacement were taken in 1979–80, shortly after these initial studies.

The government was obliged to invest in substantial new mid-life investments for Polaris almost immediately after it had entered service. In 1972, the then Conservative Government launched the Chevaline programme to replace the missile front-end, a massive commitment that eventually cost around £4 billion (at today's prices) through the late

1. Ian Smart, *The Future of the British Nuclear Deterrent: Technical, Economic and Strategic Issues* (London: Royal Institute of International Affairs, 1977), p. 4. See also Ian Smart, 'British foreign policy to 1985: beyond Polaris', *International Affairs*, vol. 53, no. 4, October 1977.

1970s and early 1980s.[2] As a result of US test firings in the late 1970s, a further programme (costing £1.1 billion at today's prices) had to be carried out to replace the UK's Polaris missile engines. This involved the re-opening of Lockheed production lines and re-employment of retired personnel, a reflection of the problems involved in a UK-only programme.[3] Finally, by the late 1980s, 20 years after they entered service, growing problems were also being encountered with the Polaris submarine hulls, problems that were making it increasingly difficult, and expensive, to maintain even one boat continuously on patrol. In all three cases, the costs of maintaining the force in operation were substantially increased by the need for uniquely UK programmes.

Table B.1. Polaris and Trident submarine replacement timetables compared

	Polaris (25-year lifetime)	Trident (30-year lifetime)
Commissioning of submarines	1967–1969	1994–2000
Detailed public studies of replacement	1976–1977 (RIIA)	c. 2009–2011
Replacement decisions taken	**1979–1982**	**c. 2011–2014**
Decommissioning of submarines	1992–1996	c. 2024–2030
Commissioning of replacement submarines	1994–2000	c. 2026–2033

Current MoD expectations are that both the Trident missile and the Vanguard-class submarine can remain in service for significantly longer than their predecessors: at least 30 years in both cases, compared with the 25-year average lifetime (from first patrol) of the four Polaris submarines. The operating costs of the force, and the risk of major technical failure or obsolescence in key components, may tend to increase with time. But improvements in systems design may make modular upgrade – especially in relation to software – easier to implement without requiring the major engineering works that might endanger the overall integrity

2. 'Ministry of Defence: Chevaline Improvement to the Polaris Missile system', *Ninth Report from the Committee of Public Accounts, 1981/82* (HMSO: London, March 1982). The Ministry of Defence estimated the cost of the programme to be £530 million at Autumn 1972 prices, equivalent to £4,115 million at 2000/2001 prices.
3. Polaris re-motoring cost £600 million at 1985 prices. E. R. Hooton, 'The United Kingdom Trident Programme', *Military Technology*, January 1986, p. 16. At 2000/2001 prices, this is equivalent to £1,080 million.

and safety of the submarine design. Moreover, it is argued, the UK's Trident force is now operating in a more benign international environment than the one for which it was originally purchased. Requirements for both force size and operational readiness, as a consequence, are significantly less than in the 1980s. It also seems less likely than in the Cold War that missiles and warheads will need major upgrades in response to predicted new threats (as was the case with both Chevaline and Trident).[4] Provided that the UK's security situation does not deteriorate significantly, future decision-makers may therefore be more willing to take risks with the projected capabilities and reliability of the force than were their predecessors in the 1970s and 1980s. Both factors could increase the lifetime of the force, possibly by a significant period of time.

The UK's increased dependence on the US for Trident D5 missile servicing and technical upgrades should help to avoid some of the problems faced with Polaris. If technical problems arise with the D5 missiles that require major overhaul, the UK will share the costs with the US. Moreover, because of the unique nature of the UK's access to D5 missile stocks and servicing, it will have assured access to missiles as long as the US Navy's programme lasts. Current estimates suggest that the US can retain D5 missiles in service for at least 30 years, with 'anti-obsolescence' programmes under way at King's Bay designed to determine whether it is possible to extend this further. Since the US was continuing to buy new D5 missiles in 2001 (for retrofitting onto older Ohio-class submarines), large stocks will probably remain available – for both the US and UK – until around 2025 or even later.[5]

The UK's first Vanguard-class submarine (which entered service in 1994) is also expected to have a lifetime of around 30 years. If this is the case, its retirement would begin around 2024, with replacement of the entire Vanguard fleet completed by around 2030. This estimate is subject to a considerable margin of error (in both directions), given uncertainties about technical performance and judgements of acceptable levels of risk. The consequences of an illustrative 30-year submarine lifetime timetable in the case of Trident are shown in Table B.1.

MoD may assume for planning purposes a lead-time of around 12–15 years from initial replacement decision through design and production

4. The prospect of potentially hostile states acquiring effective ballistic missile defences, for example, seems very distant.
5. Congressional Budget Office, *Rethinking the Trident Force*, July 1993, p. 10; Rear Admiral Irwin, in 'Progress of the Trident programme', *Eighth Report from House of Commons Defence Committee, 1994/95*, July 1995, p. 16.

to entry into service of replacement submarines and weapons systems. This implies that decisions on replacement may have to be made by around 2011–2014, and that detailed study of available options might begin in or around 2010.

While this seems a reasonable central estimate at this stage, a number of factors (the Scottish factor aside) could accelerate the timing of replacement.

First, the timetable for the UK's missile (and thus submarine) replacement will be influenced by the US's own timetable for Trident replacement. The US Trident programme started before that of the UK, and it is therefore possible that the US will want to adopt a successor system at an earlier date. It is true that the UK continued to operate Polaris for several years after its withdrawal from US service, albeit with rapidly increasing difficulty. Given its greater dependence on servicing in the US, however, a similar policy would be highly problematic in the case of Trident.

The prospects for a US Trident missile replacement may be one of the issues raised in the US's 2001 Defence Review. There is already some Congressional discussion of plans for developing a system that would replace Trident and the Minuteman III land-based strategic missile. Such discussion is likely to intensify as Trident procurement comes to an end in the US. Both industrialists and politicians are likely to argue that US capabilities for offensive missile design and production will be compromised without the development of new programmes. Even if Trident missiles remain technically sound, therefore, there may be growing pressure for a replacement programme to begin.

Second, Trident's lifetime will depend on the future of the four Vanguard-class boats. Recent problems with the UK's SSN fleet have not inspired confidence in Devonport's ability to return nuclear-powered submarines rapidly to service when faults are discovered. As of July 2000, only one of the seven modern Trafalgar-class SSN's was operational (the rest were being refitted or on trials).[6] Although the Vanguard submarines were not affected by this problem, the possibility of major faults developing – as in any complex system – may increase over time. It therefore cannot be assumed that the Trident submarines will outlive the average

6. Macer Hall, 'Six of seven killer subs unfit for service', *Sunday Telegraph*, 27 August 2000. The single SSN submarine in service was the minimum necessary to provide protection to the Trident SSBN on patrol.

25-year lifetime of their Polaris predecessors (the first of the Trident submarines will have been in service for 25 years in 2019.)

Third, the prospective lifetime of the UK's warheads is also hard to predict, but will be closely related to Aldermaston's ability to maintain the safety and effectiveness of warheads without explosive testing. With the end of the Cold War and of explosive testing (by the UK at least), it is possible that AWE could find it more difficult to attract new high-calibre staff, either for maintenance or design functions, without a replacement programme.

Fourth, further evolution of the UK nuclear relationship with France, in the context of deeper European defence cooperation, might conceivably lead to greater co-operation between the two countries on upgrade and replacement programmes for their strategic forces. New military systems and technologies now being developed for the US are bound to reflect its considerable economic resources and strategic ambitions, and thus may not always be suited to the more modest requirements, and resources, of the two European nuclear powers. Although access to US technologies will remain very important for the UK, greater UK/French co-ordination of development and replacement programmes might prove increasingly attractive.

In the face of these uncertainties, together with the long lead-times involved in most likely replacement programmes, the UK Government may find itself impelled to make some outline decisions on whether and how to replace Trident by about 2010. The same reasoning applies to the US – and France – in relation to their SLBM forces. Even before this date, each country could be faced with demands for significant investment in mid-life upgrades of one or more force components.

Appendix C

The UK, Scotland and International Safeguards

The purposes of international nuclear safeguards are to ensure, mainly by applying the techniques of material accountancy and site inspection, that nuclear materials in civilian usage are not diverted into the military sector and that states are not running clandestine weapon programmes.[1] Safeguards were developed primarily as a device for verifying that non-nuclear weapon states were honouring their renunciations of nuclear arms. Because military nuclear activity has always involved great secrecy, military facilities and materials in the NWS have seldom been accessible to international safeguards.

International safeguarding in the UK has nevertheless become quite extensive over the past 30 years. This Appendix explains its background and scope together with the safeguards implications of Scotland's independence.

Euratom and IAEA safeguards

The UK is in fact subject to *two* international safeguards 'systems' due to its membership of the Euratom Treaty and of the NPT. The purpose and scope of these systems differ in important respects, notwithstanding the efforts made by the International Atomic Energy Agency (IAEA), and Euratom to coordinate their approaches and avoid duplication.

Euratom safeguards were instituted by the Euratom Treaty of 1957. Its Chapter VII requires the Euratom Safeguards Directorate, which is

1. The NPT verification system is focused on the fissile materials plutonium and enriched uranium due to their usage in nuclear warhead and their unique physical and nuclear properties. For discussion of nuclear safeguards, see David Fischer and Paul Szasz, *Safeguarding the Atom* (Taylor & Francis: London, 1985) and of plutonium, uranium and safeguards, see David Albright, Frans Berkhout and William Walker, *Plutonium and Highly Enriched Uranium: World Inventories, Policies and Capabilities* (Oxford University Press: Oxford, 1997), Chapters 14 and 15.

based in Luxembourg and is part of the European Commission, to ensure that nuclear materials 'are not diverted from their intended uses as declared by the users'. Euratom safeguards were designed (a) to give confidence to external suppliers of uranium and other matériel that their products would not be used for military purposes and (b) to enable a free market in nuclear materials (which are formally owned by Euratom) to be established within the European Communities without facilitating the manufacture of nuclear weapons.

All materials that are declared as serving civil purposes must therefore be placed under Euratom safeguards in *all* EU member states, including the NWS member states (France and the UK). However, only peaceful uses are affected as Article 84 of the Euratom Treaty states that 'safeguards may not extend to materials intended to meet defence requirements'. This same Article has been cited when France and the UK have invoked rights to withdraw materials from Euratom safeguards. Indeed, any Euratom member state has rights to re-designate civil materials as being needed for military purposes. Euratom safeguards are not underpinned by non-proliferation undertakings which have to come from NPT membership and other commitments.

NPT safeguards are implemented by the IAEA (regional safeguards systems such as Euratom are not recognised by the Treaty). IAEA safeguards are designed to verify that materials used by non-nuclear weapon states for civil purposes (the only purposes allowed them by the NPT) are not diverted into undeclared programmes. Article III.1 of the NPT calls for comprehensive safeguards to be applied by the IAEA in all NNWS Parties to the Treaty.[2] A model safeguards agreement was drawn up in 1971 which is customarily referred to as INFCIRC/153.[3] An agreement broadly based on this document (INFCIRC/193) was approved in 1973 by NNWS members of Euratom, the IAEA and Euratom itself. This agreement coordinated relations between the IAEA and Euratom safeguards systems to render them more compatible and avoid unnecessary duplication of safeguarding activities within the European Union.[4]

2. 'Full-scope safeguards' mean that all relevant materials on a given territory are placed under safeguards.
3. INFCIRC is short for information circular and follows its pronunciation.
4. Such coordination has been taken a step further by the 'New Partnership Approach' between the IAEA and Euratom which has been developing since the early 1990s. See James Larrimore, 'Directions for improving IAEA safeguards cost effectiveness: wider application of procedures developed for the New Partnership Approach', *International Nuclear Materials Management*, July 1997.

Unlike the Euratom Treaty, the NPT does not require nuclear weapon state Parties, the UK included, to place any of their nuclear materials or facilities under safeguards. Many states argued that this exemption was unfair and discriminatory during the NPT's negotiation. To assuage their concerns, the UK, US and Soviet Governments offered in 1967 to submit peaceful nuclear activities to international safeguards on a voluntary basis. As a result, they and France (which did not join the NPT until 1992) concluded 'voluntary offer' agreements with the Agency in the second half of the 1970s. The UK voluntary offer agreement was the first to be concluded in September 1976.[5]

These agreements are voluntary in two respects. The NWS voluntarily specify the facilities (on a 'facilities list') which may be submitted to IAEA safeguards; and the IAEA chooses which of those facilities will be 'designated' for inspection.[6] The IAEA may withdraw this designation just as the NWS may withdraw facilities and thus materials from safeguards.

IAEA safeguards were reformed in the mid-1990s after the IAEA's failure to detect Iraq's nuclear weapon programme. Through the Additional Protocol INFCIRC/540 to the NPT safeguards document INFCIRC/153, the IAEA acquired new powers in 1997 which, if states allow the Protocol to be implemented, will help it to detect clandestine weapon programmes. Although focused on NNWS Parties to the Treaty, the NWS separately announced that the Additional Protocol could be applied on their territories albeit with marked disparities in scope – the UK conceding the most comprehensive and China the least comprehensive coverage.

During the 1990s, it was also accepted that the IAEA would increasingly take on the task of verifying that materials removed from weapon programmes would not be re-used for military purposes. In the Principles and Objectives agreed at the 1995 NPT Extension Conference, the NWS acknowledged that 'nuclear fissile materials transferred from military use to peaceful nuclear activities should, as soon as practicable, be placed under IAEA safeguards'. Russia and the USA are currently negotiating a trilateral agreement with the IAEA which will establish the rules and procedures

5. The UK voluntary offer agreement carries the IAEA information circular (INFCIRC) number 263. China also concluded a voluntary offer agreement with the IAEA after joining the NPT in 1992.
6. Although this is formally the approach, a rather different practice has developed for the UK. Sites which may be considered for safeguards are identified to the IAEA. The UK will accept the IAEA's designation of facilities on those sites providing they are not being used for defence purposes.

governing the IAEA's verification of their former weapon materials. In addition, the IAEA is expected to be given the task of verifying the Fissile Material Cutoff Treaty (FMCT) if and when it is negotiated.[7]

International safeguards coverage in the UK

The principal nuclear sites in the UK, and the current application of international safeguards at them, are detailed in Tables C.1 and C.2. It is evident that the bulk of safeguarding in the UK is carried out by the Euratom Safeguards Directorate consequent upon the Euratom Treaty. The IAEA currently inspects only two facilities in the UK – the plutonium stores at Sellafield and the enrichment plants at Capenhurst – despite many sites being included in the UK's Facilities List and thus available for inspection by the IAEA.[8] This would have to change if the UK or any of its constituent parts became (or came to be regarded) as non-nuclear weapon states under the NPT. A similar table for Germany or Japan or South Africa would show that *all* of their nuclear facilities and materials are routinely inspected by the IAEA.

Table C.1. International safeguards status at nuclear sites where fissile materials are present in Scotland, January 2001

Sites/facilities	Euratom safeguards	IAEA safeguards [a]
Faslane & Coulport		
Nuclear warheads and submarine reactors	No	No
Rosyth		
Nuclear submarine fuelling and de-commissioning	No	No

7. The FMCT would establish a worldwide ban on the production of fissile materials for weapons purposes. Its negotiation was requested by the UN General Assembly in 1993 but has been obstructed for complex political reasons despite repeated calls for the negotiations to begin.
8. The plutonium stores at Sellafield are designated for inspection by the IAEA because plutonium from non-nuclear weapon states (notably Japan and Switzerland) that do not belong to Euratom are held there. The centrifuge plants at Capenhurst are also routinely inspected because the UK was Party to the Hexapartite Safeguards Project which established safeguards practices for such facilities.

Sites/facilities	Euratom safeguards	IAEA safeguards [a]
Dounreay [b]		
Vulcan naval research facility and associated HEU stores	No	No
Civil facilities and materials	Yes	Not designated
Chapelcross [c]		
Reactors	No	No
Tritium extraction plant	Not applicable	Not applicable
Uranium stores	Yes	Not designated
Power reactor sites		
Torness and Hunterston AGRs	Yes	Not designated

Table C.2. International safeguards status at nuclear sites where fissile materials are present in the UK outside Scotland, January 2001

Sites/facilities	Euratom safeguards	IAEA safeguards [a]
Aldermaston and Burghfield		
Warhead manufacture, servicing and disassembly; plutonium and HEU stores	No	No
Derby		
Submarine fuel fabrication, uranium processing and HEU store	No	No
Devonport		
Submarine refuelling	No	No
Springfields		
Fuels for Chapelcross [c]	No	No
Fuel fabrication plants	Yes	Not designated
Sellafield		
Submarine spent fuel stores	No	No
B205 reprocessing plant	Yes	Not designated
THORP reprocessing plant	Yes	Not designated
Plutonium stores [d]	Yes	Designated
Calder Hall reactors	Yes	Not designated
Capenhurst		
Enrichment plants [d]	Yes	Designated
Depleted uranium stores	Yes (except defence-related material)	Not designated

Sites/facilities	Euratom safeguards	IAEA safeguards [a]
Harwell		
Research activities and fuel stores	Yes	Not designated
Defence-related material samples	No	No
Winfrith		
Nuclear material stores	Yes	Not designated
Power reactor sites		
Magnox, AGR, LWR	Yes	Not designated

Notes to Tables C.1 and C.2:

[a] IAEA safeguards are applied in the UK under the voluntary offer agreement INF-CIRC/263 (which is trilateral between the UK, IAEA and Euratom). The IAEA 'designates' materials and facilities that it wishes to inspect from the Facilities List provided by the UK Government. Facilities that are listed as 'designated' or 'not designated' in these Tables are on the Facilities List and are thus open to IAEA inspection. 'Not applicable' indicates that facilities or materials (notably tritium, which is not a fissile material) are outside the current scope of IAEA safeguards. 'No' indicates that facilities are being kept outside international safeguards.

[b] The Prototype Fast Reactor and its associated reprocessing plant (both closed but not yet decommissioned) at Dounreay were designated between 1978 and 1982.

[c] Because tritium is being produced in Chapelcross for military purposes, Chapelcross is being held outside safeguards, as are uranium fuels fabricated at Springfields for the Chapelcross reactors. Tritium is produced by irradiating lithium targets, other reactor channels being used, as normal, to irradiate uranium to raise heat for electricity generation. Irradiated uranium from Chapelcross is brought under international safeguards when it is delivered to Sellafield for reprocessing. The irradiated lithium targets are processed at Chapelcross.

[d] The centrifuge enrichment plants at Capenhurst are routinely inspected by the IAEA because the UK was party to the Hexapartite Safeguards Project (now defunct) which established safeguards practices for such facilities.

Tables C. 1 and C. 2 show that the most significant military and civil nuclear production sites are in England. Prominent among them are Aldermaston and Burghfield (warhead production), Sellafield (reprocessing plus plutonium and waste storage), Capenhurst (uranium enrichment) and Springfields and Derby (fuel fabrication). Following the closure of the Dounreay civil research facilities in the 1990s, uranium and plutonium are no longer processed anywhere in Scotland. Plutonium is still produced when uranium fuels are irradiated in power reactors at Chapelcross, Hunterston and Torness, but the plutonium-bearing spent fuels are either stored on site or transferred to Sellafield for reprocessing. This plutonium is not used in nuclear weapons.

There are four sites in Scotland where nuclear materials are involved in military activities which have hitherto kept them (or parts of them) outside safeguards:

- *Coulport* and *Faslane*, where fissile materials are present in warheads and submarine fuels;
- *Rosyth*, where operational submarines are refuelled and retired submarines are decommissioned. All refuelling will be transferred to Devonport in England when new facilities are completed there in 2002. Fissile materials unloaded at Rosyth from retired submarine reactors are taken to Sellafield for storage;[9]
- *Dounreay*, where the two land-based naval reactor prototypes (Vulcan NRTE) are located. Placed in the far north of Scotland for reasons of public safety, naval reactors are run at power at this facility to test new reactor and system designs. All current UK submarine reactors are fuelled with highly enriched uranium, quantities of which are used and stored on the Dounreay site. Submarine reactor and fuel manufacture takes place at Derby in England. As Design Authority for Naval Nuclear Plant, Rolls-Royce has operated Vulcan for the Ministry of Defence since 1960.
- *Chapelcross*, where tritium for UK warheads is produced. Whereas most of the Chapelcross reactor cores are fuelled with uranium and irradiated to supply electricity to the grid, a proportion is given over to the production of tritium through the irradiation of lithium targets. Chapelcross's sister reactors at Calder Hall (Sellafield) are not involved in tritium production and have been fully safeguarded since 1998. Although safeguards could be applied at Chapelcross, MOD has hitherto resisted them on the grounds that the quantities of tritium produced for the UK's nuclear warheads might be calculated from information supplied to safeguards agencies.

---

9. The Scottish Environment Protection Agency report for 2000 states that 'there were no consignments of solid radioactive waste from the Rosyth Royal Dockyard since January 1999 following a general embargo placed by BNFL on MoD(N) waste. This was because carbon–14 was detected in solid radioactive waste from Devonport Dockyard at much higher levels than previously assumed ... Consignment of waste to Drigg will not resume until BNFL are satisfied that past consignments of waste have been adequately reassessed ...'. Presumably this applies to low-level waste and not to submarine reactor spent fuels. See *Radioactivity in Food and the Environment, 1999*, Food Standards Agency and SEPA, September 2000, p. 106.

In the event of Scotland becoming an independent state and an NNWS Party to the NPT, the Chapelcross reactors would have to be brought under full IAEA safeguards if they were still operating and involved in the storage or processing of nuclear materials (whoever operated them, the reactors would in all likelihood come under Scottish jurisdiction). Coulport and Faslane would remain outside safeguards if nuclear weapons belonging to and controlled by a foreign NWS Party were sited there. If the weapons were removed and the military facilities decommissioned, any fissile material remaining on the sites would have to be safeguarded.

Applying safeguards at the Chapelcross facility would be technically and procedurally straightforward. Euratom already safeguards the sister reactors at Calder Hall, and safeguards could be applied at Chapelcross even if tritium production continued there.[10] The situation at the submarine research facilities at Dounreay would be more complex (see below).

Turning to rUK, the reach of safeguards need not change *if* it retained the UK's status as NWS under the NPT and succeeded to its voluntary offer safeguards agreement with the IAEA. Should rUK (or the UK before it) choose to disarm, the task of placing the entire nuclear infrastructure under international safeguards would be a more formidable undertaking. Given that most facilities at the main fuel processing sites (Sellafield, Capenhurst and Springfields) are already safeguarded, the task would be concentrated on Aldermaston and Burghfield. The weapon manufacturing facilities at those sites would presumably have to be dismantled and the components and materials from disassembled warheads reduced to a form in which they could be opened to international verification. Governments and safeguards agencies would not, however, be starting from scratch: the verification of such activities has received considerable attention in the past few years in the IAEA, US, Russia and the UK itself.[11]

Overall, the application of safeguards seems manageable for both Scotland and rUK. There are, however, a couple of important snags that need attention: the transition (if it occurred) to membership of the treaties that determine and the institutions that implement safeguards; and the safeguarding of submarine reactor fuels.

---

10. This already happens at a power reactor in Canada which produces tritium for civil purposes.
11. In preparation for the FMCT's negotiation, various studies have been carried out to help determine how it could be verified that production facilities were no longer supplying materials for weapons purposes. The US, Russia and the IAEA have also been negotiating a trilateral agreement whereby excess materials from dismantled warheads will be submitted to verification by the IAEA.

Euratom and IAEA membership

Any state joining the European Union accedes to the Euratom Treaty and accepts obligations to have Euratom safeguards applied on its territory. An independent Scotland's submission to Euratom safeguards would therefore go hand-in-hand with its membership of the EU. By the same token, Euratom safeguards would no longer apply in Scotland if it failed to gain EU membership or if membership took several years to negotiate after independence.

EU membership would therefore be important in maintaining the continuity of safeguards in Scotland (Table C.1 shows that *only* Euratom currently safeguards facilities in Scotland). Euratom safeguards would become still more important if there were any obstacles to Scotland joining the NPT and thus opening itself to mandatory IAEA safeguards. EU membership would also remove a bureaucratic responsibility from the Scottish state. Countries outside Euratom are required by law to establish a centralised State System of Accounting and Control (SSAC) through which safeguards information routinely passes to the IAEA.[12] For EU member states, Euratom provides that service – it formally constitutes the national accounting system for all EU non-nuclear weapon states and relays safeguards information to the IAEA on their behalfs. All matters pertaining to safeguards (accounting information, inspection activities and so on) are thus handled bilaterally between site operators and the Euratom Safeguards Directorate with no intervention by national governments. If Scotland did not quickly gain EU membership, it would therefore be obliged to establish its own SSAC and satisfy the IAEA's Board of Governors that the SSAC was fit to perform its tasks (one assumes that arrangements could be made for Euratom safeguards to continue during any transitional period). This would entail establishing a safeguards office in the appropriate department in the Scottish Government.

Two steps would have to be taken in regard to the IAEA. Firstly, an independent Scotland would need to gain membership of the Agency (and rUK would have to secure its succession to the UK's membership). The procedure, laid down in the IAEA Statute, is that a state's application for membership is transmitted to the IAEA Board of Governors after

12. The requirement is defined in the NPT model safeguards document INFCIRC/153.

receipt by the IAEA Secretariat.[13] The Board then makes a recommendation to the IAEA General Conference (held every September) which has the formal powers of decision.[14] IAEA membership is not linked to membership of the NPT or any other treaty. Providing Scotland had already gained recognition as an independent state, providing it was not in significant dispute with rUK, and providing it committed itself to honour the IAEA Statute (and pay its dues to the Agency), we cannot anticipate any difficulty in joining the IAEA. Membership might, however, take a year or more to secure – it could not be instant.

The next step would follow Scotland's accession to the NPT. Article III.4 of the NPT states that:

> Non-nuclear weapon States Party to the Treaty shall conclude agreements with the International Atomic Energy Agency ... Negotiation of such agreements shall commence within 180 days from the original entry into force of this Treaty. For States depositing their instruments of ratification or accession after the 180 day period, negotiation of such agreements shall commence not later than the date of such deposit. Such agreements shall enter into force not later than eighteen months after the date of initiation of negotiations.

The model document that guides the negotiation of such agreements are INFCIRC/153, taken together with INFCIRC/540 which encompasses the reforms agreed in 1997. The version of INFCIRC/153 applied in the EU is INFCIRC/193 which is trilateral between the IAEA, Euratom and the state in question. If Scotland's membership of the European Union (and thus Euratom) were secured and it acceded to the NPT, the Scottish Government would therefore negotiate its safeguards arrangements with the

13. Article IV. B of the IAEA Statute states that '[new] members of the Agency shall be those states, whether or not Members of the United Nations or of any of the specialized agencies, which deposit an instrument of acceptance of this Statute after their membership has been approved by the General Conference upon the recommendation of the Board of Governors. In recommending and approving a State for membership, the Board of Governors and the General Conference shall determine that the State is able and willing to carry out the obligations of membership in the Agency ...'. The Board of Governors comprises appointees of IAEA member states.
14. The UK has a quasi-permanent membership of the Board of Governors (the Governor being a senior DTI official) following its status as one of the 'nine members most advanced in the technology of atomic energy'. Whereas rUK would probably still qualify for such membership, Scotland would not – it would have to join the list of states eligible for rotating membership.

IAEA in accordance with INFCIRC/193 and INFCIRC/540.[15] If it were not accepted into the EU, INFCIRC/153 would provide the relevant model.

Once a safeguards agreement with the IAEA had entered into force, Scotland would have to submit its Initial Report to the IAEA giving details of 'all nuclear material which is to be subject to safeguards under the Agreement'. Both INFCIRC/153 and INFCIRC/193 require the Initial Report to be sent to the Agency 'within thirty days of the last day of the calendar month in which this agreement enters into force' (in practice, this 30-day period is often exceeded). Completion of the Initial Report would require considerable co-operation between the Scottish and rUK Governments: it would depend upon Edinburgh's acquisition from London and from site operators of full details of material inventories in Scotland and satisfaction that other materials (including those contained in wastes) had not gone unrecorded. The UK's voluntary offer agreement with the IAEA has not hitherto required the UK to present such full details of material inventories to the IAEA.[16]

Any loss of continuity in safeguards would be cause for international concern, more because of the precedent it might set than because of worries that a Scottish government might divert material to military usage. It could also be problematic for an independent Scotland's electricity industry. If international safeguards were not applied, fuel for Scotland's nuclear power stations could no longer be imported under current international trade rules.[17] As the designs of fuel elements used in Magnox and AGR power stations are unique to the UK, and as they are manufactured only at the Springfield site in England, rUK would in effect be a monopoly supplier of nuclear fuel to power reactors in Scotland. In the negotiations between London and Edinburgh on nuclear and other issues, Scotland's dependence on rUK in this regard would give London another potential political lever, much as Russia was able to exploit its monopoly on fuel supplies to Ukrainian reactors during the negotiations between Moscow and Kiev in 1993–94.

---

15. Scotland would also have to sign and ratify INFCIRC/540 (the Additional Protocol) which has the character of an international treaty.
16. We are informed by the UKAEA that a fully detailed inventory of fissile materials at its Dounreay site has now been assembled, including the materials in the notorious waste shaft. We cannot tell whether an equivalent inventory can be drawn up for the Vulcan NRTE at Dounreay.
17. The application of full-scope safeguards in non-nuclear weapon states has been accepted by most suppliers as a condition of trade under the Nuclear Suppliers Guidelines since 1992.

Safeguarding submarine reactor fuels

The NPT is focused on nuclear weapons and other explosive devices. Its safeguards system (managed by the IAEA) is designed 'with a view to preventing diversion [by non-nuclear weapon State Parties] of nuclear materials from peaceful uses to nuclear weapons or other nuclear explosive devices'.[18] The NPT exempts nuclear weapon states from safeguarding *any* nuclear materials and facilities, including the materials in weapons and submarine reactors sited on the territories of non-nuclear weapon states.[19] It would thus be legitimate for rUK to base its nuclear weapons on the territory of a non-nuclear Scotland without any requirement to submit the materials contained therein to international safeguards.

A particular set of complications arises for fissile materials involved in non-explosive military activities, notably in power reactors used to propel submarines.[20] The NPT does not prohibit such activities even when they are happening in, and under the control of, non-nuclear weapon states. Removing materials for such activities also cannot be defined strictly as 'diversion' in the Article III sense of the term as they are not being removed for nuclear weapon purposes. Yet it has long been recognised that such usage poses significant problems for the non-proliferation regime as it entails NNWS holding materials outside safeguards, albeit temporarily, and because naval reactors are fuelled with weapon-grade uranium which can be used directly in nuclear weapons. On the other hand, the NNWS have been reluctant to waive their rights to deploy such submarines, and states operating nuclear submarines have often contested the idea that safeguards could be applied anywhere in the fuel supply chains. There would always be concerns that other states

18. Article III.1.
19. These exemptions are made legal by limiting the Article III safeguards obligations to non-nuclear weapon states, and by allowing (in Article I) NWS to transfer nuclear weapons *under their control* to non-nuclear weapon states. As noted earlier, the NWS have voluntarily submitted some facilities and materials to IAEA safeguards.
20. For discussions of the safeguards problems associated with naval reactors, see Tariq Rauf and Maria-France Desjardins, 'Opening Pandora's Box? Nuclear Powered Submarines and the Spread of Nuclear Weapons', *Aurora Paper 8*, Canadian Centre for Arms Control and Disarmament, Ottawa, 1988; Ben Sanders and John Simpson, 'Nuclear Submarines and Non-Proliferation: Cause for Concern', *PPNN Occasional Paper Two*, Centre for International Policy Studies, University of Southampton, July 1988; and Norman Dombey, David Fischer and William Walker, 'Becoming a non-nuclear weapon state: Britain, the NPT and safeguards', *International Affairs*, vol. 63, no. 2, Spring 1987.

might gain knowledge about the operation of submarine fleets from safeguards information.

Two types of nuclear submarine might be based in an independent Scotland. One is the Trident submarine or any successor carrying nuclear-armed ballistic or Cruise missiles. The other is the conventionally armed nuclear-powered submarine (SSN), twelve of which are currently operated by the UK (five are currently based at Faslane). While Scotland could not own or operate the former, it could conceivably claim a share of the latter fleet if and when military assets were divided between the new states. However, Scotland could neither justify militarily its possession of SSNs, nor has it the capabilities needed to support their operation. This possibility can therefore be discounted.

So long as they were operated by an rUK which had gained recognition as an NWS, these submarines would probably pose no issues for international safeguards if based in Scotland since they would be operated by a state which is entitled to keep relevant supplies of nuclear matériel (warheads and reactor fuels) outside safeguards. Furthermore, all routine fuelling of nuclear submarines will soon be carried out at Devonport in England.[21] If, however, the UK (or rUK after Scotland's independence) chose to abandon its nuclear arms, the problem could return with a vengeance if it chose (as it probably would) to continue operating a fleet of SSNs.

The prospect that a non-nuclear weapon state might operate naval reactors was foreseen when NPT safeguards were designed in the early 1970s. Some reconciliation with non-proliferation norms was sought in Article 14 of INFCIRC/153. It requires *inter alia* the State to confirm that its use of material in non-proscribed activities will not conflict with its non-proliferation undertakings; that materials used in such activities will not be used for any explosive purposes; and that the IAEA and the State 'shall make an arrangement so that, only while the nuclear material is in such an activity, the safeguards ... will not apply ... [They] shall again apply as soon as the nuclear material is reintroduced into a peaceful nuclear activity'.[22]

Whilst INFCIRC/153 thereby provides a framework for dealing with the fuelling of nuclear submarines, establishing and implementing detailed

21. Unlike power reactors which are usually refuelled annually, modern submarine reactors are designed to operate for long periods (a decade or more) without refuelling. There is therefore less need to return to base for refuelling than in the past.
22. INFCIRC/153, Article 14 (b).

procedures would be far from straightforward. There has still been no precedent forcing the IAEA to develop clear rules and procedures. Brazil and Canada briefly toyed with proposals to acquire nuclear-powered submarines, only to abandon them. Where would safeguarding begin, end and begin again in the fuel supply chain? Could techniques be applied which would allow the submarines' owners to protect sensitive information about fuel design?

Given the potentially serious costs to the non-proliferation regime, the international community has long discouraged any attempts by an NNWS to acquire and maintain nuclear-powered submarines (Brazil and Canada dropped their plans partly in response to intense international pressures and threats that technology would be denied them). The same would doubtless apply in our case. However, operating such submarines is perfectly legal: no state could deny a disarmed UK or rUK the right to deploy them and to remove materials temporarily from safeguards. If the UK or rUK insisted on continuing to deploy nuclear-powered submarines, the IAEA would have no option but to develop detailed arrangements with the state in question.

Safeguarding the Vulcan test reactors at Dounreay

The submarine test reactors at Dounreay would pose similar difficulties. In their case, the problems would arise even if rUK remained a nuclear weapon state with wide exemptions from IAEA safeguards. In that event, these military reactors would then be situated in a non-nuclear weapon state, Scotland, and under its jurisdiction (the option of declaring Dounreay a sovereign base area under rUK jurisdiction can be ruled out for the same reasons that are discussed for Faslane and Coulport in Chapter 6). As the reactors serve non-explosive purposes, submitting their fuels to international safeguards would not be mandatory under the NPT for either Scotland or rUK (they could even be operated under Scottish control). The obligation to apply safeguards would be called into further question if, as now happens, the reactor fuels were fabricated at Derby in England and thus in a nuclear weapon state which had no requirement to apply safeguards. There would then be no question of the materials returning to safeguarded 'peaceful uses' in Scotland, the non-nuclear weapon state. Once encased in fuel elements, there would in any case be no opportunity to establish accurate inventories of the fissile materials contained therein.

Having said this, the same grave concerns for the non-proliferation regime would doubtless be expressed. Whatever the special circumstances, there would remain a strong international preference for the Vulcan reactors' closure. There is a precedent. The Soviet Union ran two submarine training reactors at the Paldiski Training Reactor Facility in Estonia. After Estonia's independence, the fuel was removed and shipped to Russia in August and September 1994 and the reactors were transferred to Estonian control in September 1995. The reactors have been closed down and are being decommissioned.[23] In that case, however, Russia had other reactors on its own teritory to which the research and training activities could be transferred.

23. We are grateful to Christina Chuen, Center for Nonproliferation Studies, Monterey Institute for International Studies, for this information.

Index